THE ASSOCIATIONAL COUNTER-REVOLUTION

THE SPREAD OF RESTRICTIVE CIVIL SOCIETY LAWS IN THE WORLD'S STRONGEST DEMOCRATIC STATES

by

Chrystie Flournoy Swiney
JD, MA, MPhil

Series in Law

VERNON PRESS

In the Americas:
Vernon Press
1000 N West Street, Suite 1200,
Wilmington, Delaware 19801
United States

In the rest of the world:
Vernon Press
C/Sancti Espiritu 17,
Malaga, 29006
Spain

Series in Law

Library of Congress Control Number: 2021950198

ISBN: 978-1-64889-455-8

Also available: 978-1-64889-182-3 [Hardback]; 978-1-64889-416-9 [PDF, E-Book]

This book is dedicated to Gabe, whose endless patience, unconditional love, and bottomless support made this project possible. Thank you.

TABLE OF CONTENTS

LIST OF FIGURES

CHAPTER 1:

INTRODUCTION

The steady concentration of power in the hands of states that began in 1648 with the Peace of Westphalia is over ...[1]

Jessica Mathews, *Power Shift, in* Foreign Affairs (1997)

Why, and to what extent, are the world's strongest democratic states adopting legislation restricting the ability of Civil Society Organizations (CSOs) to operate autonomously from government control?[2] This book seeks to explore, document, and explain this perplexing global phenomenon.

Civil society, an amorphous term defined in numerous ways, is primarily composed of organizations established voluntarily by coalitions of individuals to advance certain shared interests or to address common concerns, which can include virtually anything with the exception of profit-making.[3] Civil society organizations (CSOs), the so-called *third sector* wedged between the state and the market, include advocacy organizations, student groups, cultural and sports clubs, social movements, community associations, philanthropic foundations, religious organizations, professional associations, labor unions, chambers of commerce, and informal voluntary groups, among others. They include Human Rights Watch, Doctors without Borders, Parent-Teacher Associations, and community babysitting clubs, in addition to the Ku Klux Klan, the Alt-Right, and the United Aryan Front.[4] They can operate entirely domestically or venture across state borders to perform their work, in which

---

[1] Jessica T. Mathews, *Power Shift*, 76 FOREIGN AFF. 50–66 (1997).

[2] Civil Society Organizations (CSOs) and Non-Governmental Organizations (NGOs) are often used synonymously or interchangeably. However, CSO is a broader, umbrella term, while NGO is more specific: the latter is just one type among many different types of CSOs. The research presented in this manuscript intends to focus on this broader category of not-for-profit groups that lie outside both the government and corporate sectors; as such the Author has chosen to use the broader term CSO and not NGO.

[3] *See* U.S. DEP'T OF STATE, NON-GOVERNMENTAL ORGANIZATIONS (NGOs) IN THE UNITED STATES (2017); JONAS WOLFF & ANNIKA E. POPPE, FROM CLOSING SPACE TO CONTESTED SPACES: RE-ASSESSING CURRENT CONFLICTS OVER INTERNATIONAL CIVIL SOCIETY SUPPORT 5 (2015). *See generally* NIALL FERGUSON, THE GREAT DEGENERATION: HOW INSTITUTIONS DECAY AND ECONOMIES DIE (Allen Lane ed., 2012).

[4] *See* Thomas Carothers, *Civil Society: Think Again*, FOREIGN POL'Y, 18, 19–20 (2000).

case they are referred to as international or transnational CSOs.[5] Perhaps the only thing that unites this disparate array of organizations is what they are not: they are *non-governmental* and *not-for-profit*.[6] Though their work often overlaps with the state and the market, and their collaboration with both sectors is typical, their autonomy from both spheres, particularly the state, is what makes CSOs distinct.[7]

Yet, in an increasing number of countries around the globe, representing all regime types, in all regions, with all levels of economic and military strength, civil society's autonomy from the state is being slowly chipped, and in some cases, entirely stripped, away.[8] While this erosion of civil society's autonomy is accomplished in a variety of ways, many of which are illegal and extralegal in nature, including assaults, murders, stigmatization campaigns, and bureaucratic harassment, an increasingly popular tool used by government actors, particularly those in democratic states, is the law. Through the passage of new legal restrictions

---

[5] Domestic CSOs are CSOs that are headquartered in a single nation, where they also perform all of their activities and work. International and transnational CSOs are synonymous and refer to CSOs that despite being headquartered in a certain nation, have offices and perform activities in other nations throughout the globe. *See* Kelly Anne Krawczyk, *International NGOs, Transnational Civil Society, and Global Public Policy: Opportunities and Obstacles in the Twenty-First Century, in* THE OXFORD HANDBOOK OF GLOBAL POLICY AND ADMINISTRATION (Diane Stone & Kim Moloney eds., 2019).

[6] *See* Audie Klotz, *Transnational Activism and Global Transformations: The Anti-Apartheid and Abolitionist Experiences*, 8 EUR. J. INT'L REL. 49, 50 (2002); BRINGING TRANSNATIONAL RELATIONS BACK IN: NON-STATE ACTORS, DOMESTIC STRUCTURES AND INTERNATIONAL INSTITUTIONS 3 (Thomas Risse-Kappen ed., 1995).

[7] *See generally* EDUARDO SZAZI, NGOS: LEGITIMATE SUBJECTS OF INTERNATIONAL LAW (2012); INT'L CTR. FOR NOT-FOR-PROFIT LAW & WORLD MOVEMENT FOR DEMOCRACY SECRETARIAT AT THE NAT'L ENDOWMENT FOR DEMOCRACY, DEFENDING CIVIL SOCIETY REPORT n.1 (2012).

[8] *See* GODFREY MUSILA, FREEDOM UNDER THREAT: THE SPREAD OF ANTI-NGO MEASURES IN AFRICA 9 (2019); ANDREW CUNNINGHAM & STEVE TIBBET, INT'L COUNCIL OF VOLUNTARY AGENCIES: SCOPING STUDY ON CIVIL SOCIETY SPACE HUMANITARIAN ACTION 1 (2018); Kendra Dupuy et al., *Do Donors Reduce Bilateral Aid to Countries With Restrictive NGO Laws? A Panel Study, 1993–2012*, 47 NONPROFIT & VOLUNTARY SECTOR Q. 89–106, at 100 (2018) [hereinafter Dupuy et al., *Panel Study*]; Kendra Dupuy et al., *Hands off my Regime! Governments' Restrictions on Foreign Aid to Non-Governmental Organizations in Poor and Middle-Income Countries*, 84 WORLD DEV. 299–311, at 306 (2016) [hereinafter Dupuy et al., *Hands off my Regime!*]; Kendra E. Dupuy et al., *Who Survived? Ethiopia's Regulatory Crackdown on Foreign-Funded NGOs*, 22 REV. INT'L POL. ECON. 419–56 (2014) [hereinafter Dupuy et al., *Who Survived?*]; Douglas Rutzen, *Aid Barriers and the Rise of Philanthropic Protectionism*, 17 INT'L J. NOT-FOR-PROFIT L. 1, 6 (2015); THOMAS CAROTHERS & SASKIA BRECHENMACHER, CLOSING SPACE: DEMOCRACY AND HUMAN RIGHTS SUPPORT UNDER FIRE 1 (Carnegie Endowment for Int'l Peace, 2014).

on the ability of CSOs to form, operate, access funding, and assemble, what are referred to throughout this book as *restrictive CSO laws,* national-level governmental actors are gaining greater control over the non-governmental, not-for-profit sector. Not only are such laws appearing in countries where they might be expected – Azerbaijan, Burundi, China, Egypt, Ethiopia, Russia, Zimbabwe, and countries throughout the Middle East.[9] More curiously, they are appearing in democratic states too, including strong, fully consolidated democratic states that have historically supported a vibrant and independent civil society sector. Over the course of the past two decades, restrictive CSO laws have appeared in Canada, India, New Zealand, Spain, Israel, Hungary, Poland, Australia, the UK, and the United States, to name just a few.[10]

Restrictive CSO laws, which are perhaps unsurprising in authoritarian-leaning states, are puzzling in the context of democratic ones, which have historically been the primary funders and champions of an independent civil society.[11] Democracies, by definition, are polities created by and for the citizens that comprise them.[12] To ensure that the people rather than a single party or individual leader control their nation's destiny, democratic states — typically by constitutional design — grant their citizens the rights to freedom of

---

[9] *See* INT'L CTR. FOR NOT-FOR-PROFIT LAW, CIVIC FREEDOM MONITOR (2019), http://www.icnl.org/research/monitor/index.html [https://perma.cc/5MM3-LREW], for reports on these countries which detail the legal frameworks for civil society.

[10] *See* Chrystie F. Swiney, *Undemocratic Civil Society Laws are Appearing in Democracies,* OPENGLOBALRIGHTS (Mar. 28, 2019), https://www.openglobalrights.org/undemocratic-civil-society-laws-are-appearing-in-democracies-too/ [https://perma.cc/EH95-E3X3]; Chrystie F. Swiney, *Laws are Chipping Away at Democracy Around the World,* THE CONVERSATION (Apr. 2, 2019), https://theconversation.com/laws-are-chipping-away-at-democracy-around-the-world-113089 [https://perma.cc/RW9Y-TJA6]. Poland adopted a restrictive CSO law in October 2017 and Hungary adopted one in June 2017. Though both could be characterized as *unconsolidating* in recent years, both are characterized as "full" democracies according to the Polity IV project, a highly-respected and frequently cited database relied on by many political scientists. Both countries have received the highest score (a 10) on Polity's scale since 1990 (for Hungary) and 2003 (Poland), which means that qualify as the highest form of democracy, a "full" democracy.

[11] *See, e.g.,* STAFF OF S. COMM. ON FOREIGN RELATIONS, 109TH CONG., REP. ON NONGOVERNMENTAL ORGANIZATIONS AND DEMOCRACY PROMOTION: GIVING VOICE TO THE PEOPLE 73 (Comm. Print 2006).

[12] *See* HARVARD UNIV., DEFINING DEMOCRACY, https://sites.hks.harvard.edu/fs/pnorris/Acrobat/Democracy1.pdf [https://perma.cc/6BVK-PLX7]. There are of course many different measures and definitions of democracy, which can alter depending on the particular type of democracy that one is speaking of: constitutional democracy, liberal democracy, representative democracy, etc.

expression, association and assembly, all of which are inherent to the right to form into voluntary, non-governmental groups.[13] This ability of individuals to form independent groups on the basis of shared concerns or interests is essential for the establishment and maintenance of any democracy. Non-governmental groups are critical to holding elected leaders to account and ensuring that the voices and opinions of the people, especially the marginalized and destitute, are heard.[14] Individuals acting on their own are powerless in the face of the modern nation-state, which holds the monopoly on force and unmatched access to resources.[15] Without the ability for individuals to coalesce together, to unite their voices and resources, a democratic state can slowly morph into an authoritarian one where the people's will is neglected.[16] In short, the independence of civil society matters because democracy matters, and an independent civil society sector is essential to the functioning of any genuine democracy.[17] The two – democracy and an independent civil society – go hand-in-hand.

The right for CSOs to form and operate free from unwarranted government restrictions is rooted in the freedom of association, a fundamental human right enshrined in a variety of international and regional legal instruments, including Article 20 of the *Universal Declaration of Human Rights*, Article 22 of *the International Covenant on Civil and Political Rights* (ICCPR), Article 24 of *The Arab Charter on Human Rights*, Article 10 of the *African Charter on Human and Peoples' Rights*, Article 16 of the *American Convention on Human Rights*, and Article 11 of the *European Convention on Human rights*, among others.[18]

---

[13] UNHR, OFFICE OF THE HIGH COMMISSIONER, FREEDOM OF PEACEFUL ASSEMBLY AND ASSOCIATION.

[14] *See* EMILY VON SYDOW, CIVIL SOCIETY AND DEMOCRACY: THE CITIZEN'S SHORTCUT TO THE EU 4 (European Economic and Social Committee, 2013) (arguing that "civil society ... is an essential pillar of democracy.").

[15] *See generally* MAX WEBER, WEBER'S RATIONALISM AND MODERN SOCIETY (Tony Waters & Dagmar Waters eds., 2015).

[16] This was one of the many claims made by French historian Alexis d' Tocqueville after conducting a study on why democracy in the United States took root and developed so robustly. His conclusion: a strong commitment to free association. His findings and observations are contained in his renowned book, DEMOCRACY IN AMERICA (1835); Open Society and ICNL, *Defending Civil Society*, 2nd Ed. (June 2012), available at https://move democracy.org/wp-content/uploads/2017/09/English-Defending-Civil-Society-Report-2nd-Edition.pdf.

[17] MAINA KIAI, UN HUMAN RIGHTS COUNCIL REPORT OF THE SPECIAL RAPPORTEUR ON THE RIGHTS TO FREEDOM OF PEACEFUL ASSEMBLY AND ASSOCIATION (A/HRC/20/27, 2012).

[18] This right is also recognized in various International Labor Organization conventions, as well as the founding charters and constitutions of nations around the world, such as

According to the ICCPR, a foundational international human rights treaty ratified by 167 countries around the world,

> Everyone shall have the right to freedom of association with others …
> No restrictions may be placed on the exercise of this right other than
> those which are prescribed by law and which are necessary in a
> democratic society in the interests of national security or public safety,
> public order (*ordre public*), the protection of public health or morals or
> the protection of the rights and freedoms of others.[19]

Under international human rights law, any legal restriction placed on the freedom to associate – which would include any restrictive CSO law – is presumptively impermissible.[20] While certain restrictions on CSOs are permissible under international human rights laws, as further discussed in Chapter 5, such restrictions must be narrowly tailored and subject to a strict three-party test, which ensures that they are lawful, necessary and proportionate.[21] Regardless, permissible restrictions on the freedom of association are considered exceptions requirements on the autonomy of CSOs are considered exceptions to the general rule that CSOs should be free from government control are narrowly tailored and subject to strict requirements.[22]

To satisfy international human rights law and for civil society to play its democracy-maintaining role, it is essential that CSOs remain genuinely *independent* from the state; this is key. Saudi Arabia, North Korea, and Eritrea, which are among the world's most authoritarian countries, all claim to have civil society sectors.[23] This might be true, but their civil societies have no

---

Art. 2 of the Canadian Charter of Rights and Freedoms which identifies the right to association as a "fundamental freedom".

[19] International Covenant on Civil and Political Rights (ICCPR) (Dec. 16, 1966). For the full text of the ICCPR go to http://www.cirp.org/library/ethics/UN-covenant/ [https://perma.cc/SL8 M-ZE98]. For information about the ICCPR go to: http://cil.nus.edu.sg/1966/1966-international-covenant-on-civil-and-political-rights-iccpr/.

[20] Sidiropoulos v. Greece, 4 Eur. Ct. H.R. 500 at 40 (1998).

[21] Report of the Special Rapporteur on the rights to freedom of peaceful assembly and of association, Maina Kiai, UN Human Rights Council, May 2012 (A/HRC/20/27), at 51–76, available at https://undocs.org/A/HRC/20/27.

[22] International Standards on the Rights to Freedom of Peaceful Assembly and of Association, UN Office of the High Commissioner, available at https://www.ohchr.org/EN/Issues/AssemblyAssociation/Pages/InternationalStandards.aspx.

[23] *See* Gavin Haines, *Mapped: The World's Most (and Least) Free Countries*, THE TELEGRAPH (Jan. 23, 2018), https://www.telegraph.co.uk/travel/news/the-worlds-most-authoritarian-destinations/.

independence from the state apparatus, making such a claim devoid of meaning. Where CSOs are under the control of the government, they become mere appendages or mouthpieces of the state's agenda, undermining their ability to hold governments to account or offer alternative perspectives.[24] Without legal guarantees and enforceable protections securely in place protecting their independence, CSOs can easily succumb to co-optation, manipulation, or all-out eradication by the state; as has happened in a variety of non-democratic settings in recent years, such as the Democratic Republic of the Congo, Ethiopia, and in parts of China.[25]

Though less restrictive than their counterparts in non-democratic countries, the accelerating appearance of restrictions imposed on CSOs, including the passage of restrictive CSO laws, in historically strong democratic states and in a relatively short period of time, is a perplexing and growing concern among civil society activists, democracy observers, and a small, but growing number of political scientists.[26] Strangely, this phenomenon which implicates classic international relations theories and concepts, including balance of power and national sovereignty, as well as democratic theory, state-civil society relations, and international human rights, has largely eluded political scientists, and even more so, legal scholars. This book is an attempt to rectify these gaps in the existing political science and legal scholarship on an interdisciplinary

---

[24] Both the International Center for Not-for-Profit Law and CIVICUS track civil society related developments in virtually all countries around the world. Individual reports for each country, between the two of them, can be accessed. These reports can confirm the lack of civil society or the lack of independence pertaining to the civil society sectors in these countries. This is less true of Ethiopia than the other countries cited.

[25] *See Democratic Republic of Congo*, HUMAN RIGHTS WATCH (July 2019), https://www.hrw.org/africa/democratic-republic-congo [https://perma.cc/KR7A-GHSN; Carolyn Hsu et al., *The State of NGOs in China Today*, BROOKINGS (Dec. 15, 2016), https://www.brookings.edu/blog/up-front/2016/12/15/the-state-of-ngos-in-china-today/ [https://perma.cc/X9JV-EHBJ]; Paul Kariuki, *Citizens and Civil Society Must Fight to Protect our Democracy*, DAILY MAIL & THE GUARDIAN (Aug. 5, 2019), https://mg.co.za/article/2019-08-05-00-citizens-and-civil-society-must-fight-to-protect-our-democracy [https://perma.cc/4AC2-827J].

[26] *See generally* ANTHONY J. DEMATTEE, COVENANTS CONSTITUTIONS, AND DISTINCT LAW TYPES: INVESTIGATING GOVERNMENT'S RESTRICTIONS ON CSOs USING AN INSTITUTIONAL APPROACH (2019); Suparna Chaudhry, The Assault on Democracy Assistance: Explaining State Repression of NGOs (Dec. 2016) (unpublished Ph.D. dissertation, Yale University); Dupuy et al., *Panel Study*.

phenomenon with profound consequences for the state of democracy around the world.[27]

KEY ARGUMENT & METHODOLOGY

This book argues that the world's strongest democratic states, like so many of the world's states, are restricting the autonomy of their civil society sectors through the passage of restrictive CSO laws because they feel that their national sovereignty is increasingly under threat by the rise of non-state actors, including CSOs. This perception gradually emerged during CSOs' so-called 'golden age' in the 1990s, when their numbers, popularity (primarily among the world's democratic states), and funding soared, and when they became increasingly involved in both national and international politics. Individual CSOs coalesced with other CSOs, oftentimes across state borders, to form large-scale transnational advocacy networks (TANs), and together they acquired new tools and strategies, such as the "boomerang," to advance their agendas.[28] By the turn of the new century, CSOs' ability to successfully inject themselves into the center of the political arena, whether domestic or international, had reached such levels that states began to fear that their place in the international order was under threat. States began pushing back, attempting to re-balance the scales of global and national power in their decisive favor. This was done in a variety of ways, including through the passage of laws that lessen the autonomy, the most critical aspect, of CSOs.

Methodologically, this book utilizes various methods drawn from both legal and political science scholarship to defend the argument advanced above. In order to document the phenomenon being examined herein, the associational counter-revolution, cross-national legislative mining, or the attempt to look for similar types of laws spanning multiple national contexts, was used in conjunction with comparative legal analysis. International human rights law,

---

[27] This phenomenon – the stripping away of the autonomy and independence of civil society organizations in democratic states – has applications that are not only legal in nature. In addition, to be negatively impacted by the passage of restrictive laws, CSOs suffer from harassment by governmental actors, intimidation and stigmatization campaigns, the withdrawal of privileges, abusive manipulations and distortions of existing laws, and a variety of additional illegal and extralegal mechanisms.

[28] The boomerang effect, which will be detailed in Chapter 4, refers to a strategy used by domestic CSOs to acquire the support and funding of international CSOs in an effort to put pressure on their own governments. This strategy was first coined and explored by scholars Margaret Keck and Kathryn Sikkink. *See* MARGRET KECK & KATHRYN SIKKINK, TRANSNATIONAL ADVOCACY NETWORKS IN INTERNATIONAL AND REGIONAL POLITICS (1999), available at http://courses.washington.edu/pbaf531/KeckSikkink.pdf; MARGRET KECK & KATHRYN SIKKINK, ACTIVISTS BEYOND BORDERS (1998).

including the decisions of regional and international human rights courts and the authoritative opinions issued by leading human rights experts (such as the UN Special Rapporteur on Peaceful Assembly and the Freedom of Association), were used as an interpretive guide when engaging in comparative legal analysis. Empirical documentation and trend analysis were used to evaluate, and debunk, the existing theories most often cited to explain the associational counter-revolution. And theory building, in conjunction with case studies, was used to illustrate the connection between the adoption of restrictive CSO laws and the growing perception among states that their place in the global order, and their national sovereignty specifically, are under threat by the rise of CSOs.

OUTLINE

This book documents, explores, and attempts to explain the spread of restrictive CSO laws in the world's strongest democratic states, the least likely category of states to engage in a global trend focused on undermining a core element of democracy. To understand the historical factors that gave rise to this trend, Chapter 2 traces the evolution and rise of CSOs from the end of WWII to the present, which includes an examination of the so-called "associational revolution," when the freedom of association was widely encouraged and supported, at least among the democracies of the world. During this period, CSOs reached their apex in terms of influence, funding, support, and ambition. Their rise, however, created a strain on traditional notions of national sovereignty, territorial integrity, and state exclusivity within the international policy and law-making spheres, ideas built into the fabric of the international order constructed after WWII. Fearing that this global order and their pinnacle place within it was being undermined, states began engaging in balancing behaviors against CSOs, which included the passage of restrictive CSO laws.[29] The attempt by states to reign in the rising influence of CSOs within both national and international politics led to what is referred to as the "associational counter-revolution," or the attempt by states to place restraints on the freedom of association in an effort to restrict the independence of CSOs.

After reviewing the associational revolution in Chapter 2, the associational counter-revolution is discussed in Chapter 3, which discusses and critiques the existing explanations for this reversal. Chapter 4 then advances a novel theory to explain the associational counter-revolution, which builds on the historical story of CSOs' rise presented in Chapter 3. This theory operates at the systemic or international level, unlike the other existing theories, which are largely focused on domestic level factors. By viewing the associational counter-

---

[29] Note that many other techniques are used by states as well, particularly authoritarian states. However, the focus of this book is exclusively restrictive CSO legislation.

revolution from the systemic level, a more uniform and holistic explanation is offered for why so many countries throughout the world, including ones we would least expect, are narrowing the independence of their CSO sectors through the passage of restrictive CSO laws. The theory offered in Chapter 4 is rooted in perhaps the oldest and most fundamental concept in all of international relations theory: balance of power theory.[30] This theory, which has ancient roots but was restated by Kenneth Waltz in the late 1970s, can help make sense of why the world's strongest democratic states began to feel threatened by CSOs following the turn of the twenty-first century. CSOs, which by the early 2000s had formed into many large-scale transnational movements and acquired new techniques to advance their goals, began to be perceived by states as threatening to their sovereignty. States began to perceive them not merely as legitimate critics or watchdogs but as enemies of the state or foreign agents intent on advancing malicious agendas at odds with the national interest.

Chapter 5 provides detailed empirical documentation of the associational counter-revolution in the world's strongest democratic states, presenting the number, typology, spread, and timing of adopted restrictive CSO laws between 1990–2018. The empirical data presented is entirely original; it does not build on existing databases or studies, as (at the time of writing) none exist that specifically examine democratic states. As such, this chapter fills an important gap in the existing literature on the associational counter-revolution, which tends to focus only on authoritarian-learning or low or middle-income countries, and on only one particular type of law (foreign funding laws). This chapter close examines three case studies, Bolivia, India and Poland, to exemplify how the balance of power theory, transnational advocacy networks, and the boomerang strategy can help to explain why strong democratic states now feel threatened by CSOs.

Chapter 5 examines the key implication, or consequence, of the associational counter-revolution, which is that it is contributing to, and potentially fueling, global democratic decay. By undermining a core aspect of democracy, an independent civil society sector, the passage of restrictive CSO laws undermines a foundational element of any democracy. Though often presented as two separate global trends, the associational counter-revolution and global democratic decay, the two closely parallel each other and are undoubtedly linked. Though more research is needed to ascertain the many factors fueling the widespread democratic backsliding seen around the globe, the stigmatization

---

[30] Steven Lobell, *Balance of Power, in* OXFORD BIBLIOGRAPHIES (Aug. 2019) (stating that "[t]he balance of power is one of the oldest and most fundamental concepts in international relations theory.")

of CSOs as malicious actors and the undermining of their autonomy is presented as a key factor contributing to this disturbing trend.

Chapter 7 concludes by examining the changing nature of international politics, which has been significantly impacted by the rise of non-state actors, notably including CSOs. It offers a new paradigm for thinking about international relations as a realm that encompasses a much broader array of actors than only states, challenging other legal scholars and political scientists to participate in re-thinking the traditional concepts and paradigms we use to understand international affairs. Many of these concepts remain rooted in the idea that the state is the only relevant actor in the international arena; that the state alone makes, performs, and enforces international policies and law. But this is no longer the case. CSOs, among other non-state actors, are now actively involved in shaping our national and international agendas, drafting and enforcing international law, and conducting the important work of transnational relations. Understanding how states are pushing back against this new reality, which will shape and define international relations in the centuries ahead, forms the focus of this book.

CHAPTER 2:

THE ASSOCIATIONAL REVOLUTION

We are in the midst of a global 'associational revolution' that may prove to be as significant to the latter 20th century as the rise of the nation-state was to the latter 19th.[1]

This chapter traces the rise of CSOs from WWII to roughly 2000, a period of enormous growth for CSOs – numerically, financially, and otherwise – known as "the associational revolution."[2] As the second half of the twentieth century unfolded, a variety of historical forces were set in motion that positioned CSOs to rise in importance and influence at the global level. As they became more entrenched in global and national politics, their ambitions grew, and they pushed for greater and greater involvement. By the twenty-first century, their rising status began to register with states who felt increasingly threatened that their national and international agendas, indeed their very sovereignty, were being compromised by the new and elevated roles played by CSOs in both the national and international spheres. While a similar story could be told about a variety of other non-state actors such as transnational corporations, terrorists, or subnational actors such as global cities, this book focuses exclusively on CSOs. It narrows in on the particular reasons why they uniquely began to be viewed by the world's strongest democratic states, which had historically championed their independence, as something to be feared and contained.

THE CENTRALIZATION OF GLOBAL POWER

The September 11th terrorist attacks in the United States, an event that requires no introduction despite the passage of nearly two decades, was an international event of enormous and lasting symbolic significance. While it is often identified as the prelude to the long and ongoing War against Terrorism, it, in fact, represented something more profound and of greater consequence.[3] The 9/11 attacks, which took place in the world's undisputed global superpower at that time, illustrated in grotesque form a decisive shift underway in global politics,

---

[1] Lester Salamon, *The Rise of the Nonprofit Sector*, 73 FOREIGN AFF. 109–22 (1994).

[2] This phrase was coined by Lester Salamon in *The Rise of the Nonprofit Sector*, 73 FOREIGN AFF. 109–22 (1994) [hereinafter Salamon 1994].

[3] Jeffery Goldberg, *The Real Meaning of 9/11*, THE ATLANTIC, Aug. 29, 2011.

a shift that dates back to World War II and is still in the process of evolution. [4] This shift, which will likely be a defining feature of the twenty-first century, involves the diffusion of global power to non-state actors.[5]

This diffusion of power involves the relinquishing of near-exclusive control over international relations by the world's states to a multitude of other non-governmental, sub-national, and transnational actors: NGOs, multinational corporations, intergovernmental organizations, local and state governments, terrorists, international criminal syndicates, citizen-led movements, and the many global cities whose economies are now larger than many industrialized nations, to name a few.[6] While the increasingly anachronistic state-based international system, which dates back nearly four centuries to the Peace of Westphalia in 1648, is not likely to disappear in the foreseeable future, it appears to be giving way, slowly, tumultuously, and not without a fight, to a more inclusive, decentralized, and diffuse model of global politics.

The nation-state model was first introduced as a more efficient and effective way to organize global affairs than the empires and large-scale political domains of bygone times, which in reality often consisted of multiple, overlapping, and conflicting authorities.[7] The far-flung, geographically enormous, and ethnically diverse empires that characterized the pre-Westphalian era, such as the Ottoman and Holy Roman Empires, had proven over time to be both inefficient and inept at conducting the important work of maintaining peace and trade among the dominant global actors. As time went on, the existing empires began to crumble into smaller and more contained units, the result of secessionist movements, internecine warfare, resource-depleting territorial conquests, and ongoing conflict between competing authority figures, notably including the Pope and the Emperor. Eventually, the nation-state, with its secular foundations and emphasis on national sovereignty and territorial integrity, was latched onto

---

[4] Christopher Layne, *The Unipolar Illusion Revisited*, 31 INT'L SECURITY 7–41 (Fall 2016).

[5] Alasdair Donaldson & Isabelle Younane, "A diplomatic deficit: the rise of non-state actors," the British Council, Feb. 2018.

[6] Richard Florida, *The Economic Power of Cities Compared to Nations*, CITYLAB, Mar. 16, 2017; Dana Rasgupta, *The Demise of the Nation-State*, THE GUARDIAN, Apr. 5, 2018; Yasmeen Serhan, *The Common Element Uniting Worldside Protests*, THE ATLANTIC, Nov. 19, 2019; Gary Younge, *Who's in Control – Nation States or Global Corporations*, THE GUARDIAN, June 2, 2014; Michael Vaughn, *After Westphalia, Whither the Nation State, its People and its Governmental Institutions?* (Paper presented at The International Studies Association Asia-Pacific Regional Conference, Sept. 29, 2011).

[7] Sagnik Guha, *Globalization and the State: Assessing the Decline of the Westphalian State in a Globalizing World*, 9 INQUIRIES J. 1–21 (2017).

as a way of organizing international and domestic affairs in a more efficient and less conflict-prone manner.[8]

The nation-state system rests on the core belief that the borders of each nation are sacrosanct and inviolable and that those living within those borders will cultivate a deep and lasting sense of attachment and loyalty to those borders. [9] This sense of exclusive commitment to one's nation rests on the foundational concept of national sovereignty, which requires that all authority resides within a single political leader (or governmental entity) tasked with representing that nation abroad.[10] Under the nation-state model, all international relations are expected to be conducted by and through the state, which is designated the exclusive representative of that nation in the international arena. This governance model was meant to both simplify and pacify the complicated, conflict-prone business of global politics. Gone were the days of multi-layered hierarchies, conflicting loyalties and heterogenous authorities, as was the norm during the pre-Westphalian era.[11] All power and leadership were to be centralized within the state and the state alone.

The nation-state model was chosen largely to ensure that all states respect the territorial boundaries of other states, the so-called non-interference principle.[12] This principle, which is considered critical to maintaining peace among and between the world's primary political units (states), when combined with a sense of nationalism among the people residing within each unit — considered critical to maintaining peace within a nation — was intended to reduce, or ideally eliminate, both domestic and international conflict.[13] Instead of warfare, territorial aggrandizement, and shifting loyalties, the hope was that states would focus their international relations on economic collaboration and transnational cooperation, with global peace and increased prosperity the hoped-for result. This Pollyanna model of international governance prevailed and took root throughout the globe, proving generally

---

[8] HENDRIK SPRUYT, THE SOVEREIGN STATE AND ITS COMPETITORS (1996).

[9] *Nationalism, in* STANFORD ENCYCLOPEDIA OF PHILOSOPHY (rev'd Dec. 2014), available at https://plato.stanford.edu/entries/nationalism/.

[10] Anthony McGrew, *Globalization and Global Politics, in* THE GLOBALIZATION OF WORLD POLITICS: AN INTRODUCTION TO INTERNATIONAL RELATIONS (J. Baylis et al. eds., 6th ed. 2014).

[11] MARIA T. SLYS, EXPORTING LEGALITY: THE RISE AND FALL OF EXTRATERRITORIAL JURISDICTION IN THE OTTOMAN EMPIRE AND CHINA (2014); LISA IDZIKOWSKI, THE RISE AND FALL OF THE ROMAN EMPIRE (2017).

[12] Niki Aloupi, *The Right to Non-Intervention and Non-Interferences*, 4 CAMBRIDGE INT'L L.J. 566–87 (2015).

[13] ERNST GELLNER, NATIONS AND NATIONALISM (2009); BENEDICT ANDERSON, IMAGINED COMMUNITIES: REFLECTIONS ON THE ORIGINS AND SPREAD OF NATIONALISM (Rev. ed. 2006).

successful as a model for organizing domestic and international affairs in the centuries following 1648.[14] International trade between the nations increased, feelings of nationalism surged, and large-scale global warfare, at least for a time, ceased.[15]

However, this system came to a catastrophic halt in the twentieth century. World War I (WWI) erupted, resulting in nearly 40 million casualties, closely followed two decades later by World War II (WWII), the deadliest conflict in all of human history when nearly 3% of the global population perished.[16] Following these two horrific inter-state wars, when the Hobbesians of the world appeared prescient, the nation-state model suddenly appeared weak.[17]

THE DIFFUSION OF GLOBAL POWER

As an attempt to maintain the nation's pinnacle place in global politics, and in an effort to prevent future world wars, a new international political and legal world order was created and installed by the victors of WWII, a system primarily designed to prevent subsequent state-on-state violence. The new post-WWII international order had a twofold purpose. The first was to reinforce and further entrench the centralization of power within the state and the inviolability of state borders, which were codified into the United Nations (UN) Charter and institutionalized within the United Nations and the other international organizations built to enforce the Charter's ideals.[18] The second goal was far more idealistic. As it turns out, it was consequential, unleashing as it did a fundamental, albeit unforeseen and inadvertent, transformation in the constituent units that comprise the international political order. This was the legal prohibition against the use of force, which was codified in Article 2(4) of the UN Charter. According to Article 2(4):

> All members shall refrain in their international relations from the threat
> or use of force against the territorial integrity or political independence

---

[14] Xuew Li & Alexander Hicks, *World Polity Matters: Another Look at the Rise of the Nation-State across the World, 1816–2001*, 8 AM. SOC. REV. 596–607 (June 2016).

[15] Roland Axtmann, *The State of the State: The Model of the Modern State and Its Contemporary Transformation*, 25 INT'L POL. SCI. REV. 259–79 (July 2004).

[16] U.S. CENSUS BUREAU, INTERNATIONAL PROGRAMS: HISTORICAL ESTIMATES OF WORLD POPULATION, available at https://web.archive.org/web/20130306081718/https://www.census.gov/population/international/data/worldpop/table_history.php.

[17] Thomas Hobbes, in his famous poem *Leviathan* from 1651, described the "natural state of mankind" as "solitary, poor, nasty, brutish, and short."

[18] UN Charter, 1 U.N.T.S. XVI (Oct. 24, 1945), http://www.unwebsite.com/charter.

of any state, or in any other manner inconsistent with the purposes of the United Nations.[19]

While prohibiting interstate force had been attempted once before – in the aftermath of WWI with the passage of the Kellogg-Briand Pact, officially named the "General Treaty for Renunciation of War as an Instrument of National Policy" – this attempt ended in spectacular failure when it did nothing to prevent the militarism that culminated in WWII.[20] While its failure is largely attributed to a lack of enforcement mechanisms, and more generally, a lack of commitment to its realization, the Kellogg-Briand Pact is also credited for planting the conceptual seeds for Article 2(4).[21]

Yet, it took WWII, the installation of a new international framework, and the buy-in of the world's most militarily and economically powerful nations for the prohibition against the threat or use of force as an instrument of international relations to be realized in any real sense. While this prohibition, to be sure, did not eliminate acts of international aggression among and between nations, it nevertheless significantly transformed how international relations are conducted.[22] No longer was the threat or use of force for the purpose of territorial aggrandizement, capturing or maintaining colonial possessions, recouping unpaid debts, or resolving diplomatic spats acceptable. With two specific exceptions (self-defense and UN Security Council authorization in response to a "threat to peace, breach of peace and act of aggression"),[23] the use of force was, for the first time in the history of the nation-state system (with the short and failed exception of the Kellogg-Briand Pact period), deemed illegal under international law.[24]

---

[19] *Id.* The preamble of the UN Charter also reinforces the commitment to end acts of state aggression, stating that "armed force shall not be used, save in the common interest." OONA HATHAWAY & SCOTT SHAPIRO, THE INTERNATIONALISTS: HOW A RADICAL PLAN TO OUTLAW WAR REMADE THE WORLD (2017) [hereinafter HATHAWAY & SHAPIRO 2017].

[20] Stephen Walt, *There's Still No Reason to Think the Kellogg-Briand Pact Accomplished Anything*, FOREIGN POL'Y, Sept. 29, 2017.

[21] W. Michael Reisman, *Article 2(4): The Use of Force in Contemporary International Law*, 78 PROC. ANN. MEETING (AM. SOC. INT'L L.) 74–87 (Apr. 12–14, 1984).

[22] HATHAWAY & SHAPIRO 2017.

[23] UN Charter, Art. 51 (allows for individual and collective self-defense); Chapter VII (allows the Security Council to use force to end a "threat to peace, breach of peace and act of aggression.").

[24] Oona A. Hathaway & Scott J. Shapiro, *Making War Illegal Changed the World. But It's Becoming too Easy to Break the Law*, THE GUARDIAN, Sept. 14, 2017.

So began a new and unprecedented era in political history when diplomacy could no longer (legally) be accomplished using either the threat or use of force.[25] The arsenal of tools available to states when engaging in international diplomacy dramatically shrank following the ratification of the UN Charter in 1945. States were now legally limited to using only non-aggressive means to advance their foreign policy goals – economic sanctions, reputational pressure, proportionate reprisals, and the like.[26] While this prohibition did nothing to prevent conflict within state borders, including civil wars, genocide, and domestic terrorism, the new international order successfully reduced interstate wars – the kind of wars resulting in noticeable reductions in the human population and catastrophic destruction.[27]

With the adoption of the UN Charter, the value and emphasis placed on state sovereignty, which forms the conceptual core of the international political and legal framework still in place today, was significantly strengthened. No longer was colonialism (or versions of colonialism), which had been practiced for centuries leading up to the UN Charter's ratification, a legally permissible option; state sovereignty and territorial integrity were prioritized above all else. The United States, which became an increasingly influential superpower on the global scene following WWII, also served to strengthen the anti-colonial ethos that infused the new world order. The European powers, devastated by both world wars and depleted from the many independence struggles occurring within their far-flung colonial possessions, were eclipsed as the US rose in influence and material power.[28] The US's global ascendancy, in addition to triggering the Cold War with the Soviet Union, allowed the US to more expansively spread its anti-colonial and pro-democracy values to a global audience.[29]

---

[25] Again, with the exception of self-defense and Chapter VII of the UN Charter. According to Article 51 of the UN Charter, "Nothing in the present Charter shall impair the inherent right of collective or individual self-defense if an armed attack occurs against a member of the United Nations, until the Security Council has taken the measures necessary to maintain international peace and security." Article 42 of the UN Charter enables the Council to use force to maintain or restore international peace and security if it considers non-military measures to be or to have proven inadequate.

[26] ROBERT E. SCOTT & PAUL B. STEPHAN, THE LIMITS OF LEVIATHAN: CONTRACT THEORY AND THE ENFORCEMENT OF INTERNATIONAL LAW (2006).

[27] STEVEN PINKER, THE BETTER ANGELS OF OUR NATURE: WHY VIOLENCE HAS DECLINED (2012).

[28] Charles Krauthammer, *The Unipolar Moment*, 70 FOREIGN AFF. 23–33 (1990/1991).

[29] SOVEREIGNTY, STATEHOOD, AND STATE RESPONSIBILITY (Christine Chinkin & Freya Baetens eds., 2015).

THE END OF COLONIALISM, THE EXPLOSION OF NEW STATES, AND THE RISE OF CSOS

Following WWII and the ratification of the UN Charter, the former colonizing states (primarily European) began withdrawing from their colonial territories. Many nations and territories throughout the Middle East, Africa, and parts of Asia regained their independence after being deprived of it for decades, and in some cases, centuries.[30] By the 1960s, the colonial era – which began in the 1500s, intensified and gained momentum in the 1700s and 1800s, and by the early twentieth century had resulted in the vast majority of the world being under the dominion of one European power or another – had come to a decisive end.[31] The result was the proliferation of new states – most of them weak, devastated, and poverty-stricken – which were ill-prepared to handle the many challenges involved in independent governance.[32] When the UN Charter came into existence on October 24, 1945, 51 member-states signed on.[33] By 1960, that number had nearly doubled, and by 1980, a mere 35 years later, it had tripled. Today, UN membership stands at 193.[34]

This explosion in new states led to many new challenges. The international community, particularly the economically powerful states, struggled to determine how to best assist the fragile new states, which were naturally suspicious of any

---

[30] As one example, the British colonized India for nearly 200 years. *See* Peter Marshall, *The British Presence in India in the 18th Century*, BBC, Feb. 17, 2011. *See also* Zach Beauchamp, *500 years of European Colonialism in one Animated Map*, VOX, Jan. 15, 2015.

[31] In some cases, colonialism extended beyond or well into the 1960s. For example, France continued fighting to maintain Algeria as its colonial possession until 1962, and Portugal did not abandon its African colonies until 1974. *See* Max Fisher, *Map: European Colonialism Conquered Every Country in the World but Five*, VOX, Feb. 24, 2015.

[32] COUZE VENN, THE POST COLONIAL CHALLENGE: TOWARDS ALTERNATIVE WORLDS (2006); Patrick Williams, *Problems of Post-Colonialism*, 16 POST-COLONIALISM, RACISM & CULTURAL DIFFERENCE 91–102 (Mar. 1993).

[33] As has always been, and remains the case today, the actual number of states was only slightly higher.

[34] About the UN, United Nations Website, available at https://www.un.org/en/about-un/index.html. Many place the total number of states slightly higher, at 195 or even 1997, depending on how certain territories, such as Taiwan and the Palestinian territories, are classified. Growth in UN Membership 1945–Present, United Nations, available at https://www.un.org/en/sections/member-states/growth-united-nations-membership-1945-present/index.html (last visited Apr. 18, 2020). *See also* World Atlas, which puts the total number of states at 195, available at https://www.worldatlas.com/articles/how-many-countries-are-in-the-world.html; and Countries of the World (2008–2020), puts this number at 197, available at https://www.countries-ofthe-world.com/how-many-countries.html.

foreign involvement, while still appearing to be respectful of their territorial integrity and newfound sovereignty.

Yet, as the national governments in many of the newly independent states failed to provide for the basic needs of their citizenry, a vacuum quickly emerged. This vacuum was filled, in many instances, by civil society organizations – churches, local community groups, and non-governmental organizations, among others.[35] However, because the domestic civil society organizations in many of the newly independent states were just as weak and underdeveloped as their national governments, there was an opening for international CSOs, particularly those based in the more prosperous, developed states. International CSOs, unlike national governments, could more easily enter other countries, especially formerly colonized territories, who were often sensitive to outside governmental involvement.[36] Unlike state actors, non-governmental organizations were unbound by the new rules of international relations, and while they still required governmental permission to enter a foreign country, such permission was typically forthcoming in the post-colonial era when distrust of outside states ran high. As a result, CSOs proliferated and spread like wildfire in the post-war decades, especially following the Cold War in the 1990s. Perceived as a less threatening foreign actor than foreign governments, international CSOs were widely accepted in post-colonial states, and indeed in most states.[37] So began the proliferation of global civil society.[38]

THE RISE & SPREAD OF GLOBAL CIVIL SOCIETY

While the origins of CSOs can be traced back to at least the 1700s, their numbers exponentially rose in the aftermath of WWII and the installation of the new political and legal world order.[39] The Union of International Associations, which has tracked the number of international CSOs since 1907, registered the existence of a mere 832 international CSOs in 1951, shortly after the UN Charter

---

[35] CRITICAL MASS: THE EMERGENCE OF GLOBAL CIVIL SOCIETY (James Walker & Andrew Thomason eds., 2008).

[36] James Walker and Andrew Thompson (Eds.), *The Emergence of Global Civil Society* (Wilfrid Laurier University Press, 2008).

[37] EDUARDO SZAZI, NGOS: LEGITIMATE SUBJECTS OF INTERNATIONAL LAW 27 (2012).

[38] JAN AART SCHOLTE, GLOBAL CIVIL SOCIETY: CHANGING THE WORLD? (CSGR Working Paper No. 31/99, May 1999); Szazi 2012.

[39] Steve Charnovitz, *Two Centuries of Participation: NGOs and International Governance*, 18 MICH. J. INT'L L. 183 at 190 (1997).

was adopted.[40] By 1985, this number had skyrocketed to nearly 21,000, and by 2006, it had reached over 50,000 (see Figure 2.1).[41] Today, the number of CSOs, including both domestic and international CSOs, is estimated to be around ten million.[42]

Figure 2.1: Number of INGOs from 1950–2005. Source: E. Turner, "Why has the number of International Non-Governmental Organizations Exploded since 1960?", The Journal of Theoretical and Mathematical History 1(1) (2010), at 82.

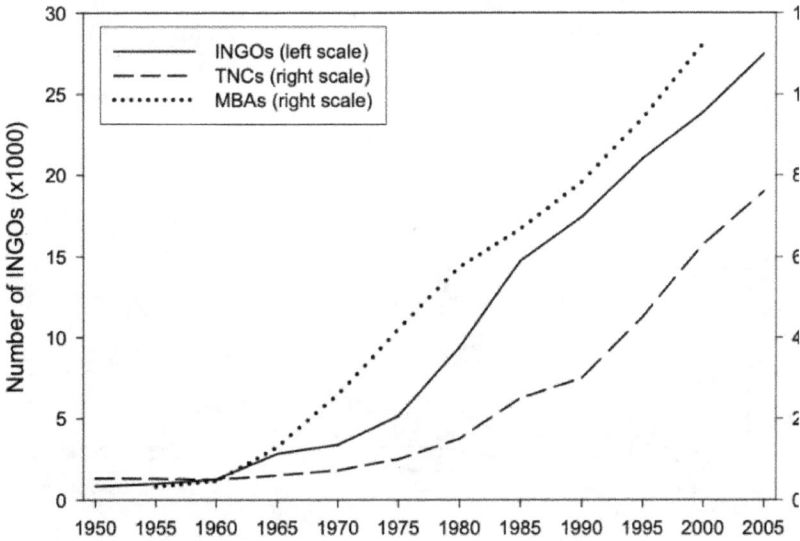

Another way to track the rise of CSOs is to examine the number of CSOs that have applied for consultative status in the UN's Economic and Social Council (ECOSOC), which is permitted under Article 71 of the UN Charter. In 1948, the number of CSOs with consultative status was a mere 40; in 1968, this number had risen to 180; and by 2012, it was over 3,500. Today, nearly 5,500 CSOs have consultative status in ECOSOC (see Figure 2.2).[43]

---

[40] Edward Turner, *Why Has the Number of International Non-Governmental Organizations Exploded since 1960?*, 1 J. THEORETICAL & MATHEMATICAL HIST. 81–92 (2010).

[41] *Id.*

[42] *Facts and States about NGOs Worldwide*, NON-PROFIT ACTION, May 2020, available at http://nonprofitaction.org/2015/09/facts-and-stats-about-ngos-worldwide/.

[43] UN Department of Economic and Social Affairs, NGO Branch, *Consultative Status*, available at https://esango.un.org/civilsociety/displayConsultativeStatusSearch.do?method=search&sessionCheck=false (last visited Apr. 18, 2020).

Figure 2.2: The # of NGOs to receive consultative status by the UN's Economic and Social Council from 1945–2015. Source: Peter Willetts, The Growth in the Number of NGOs in Consultative Status with the Economic and Social Council of the United Nations, 2015, available at http://www.staff.city.ac.uk/p.willetts/NGOS/NGO-GRPH.HTM.

The Growth in the Number of ECOSOC NGOs

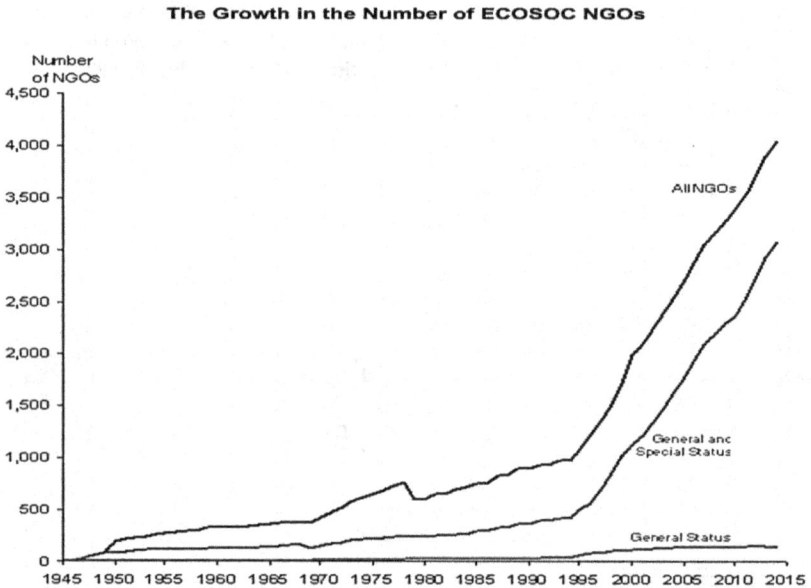

Data from individual countries similarly confirm the rising numbers of domestic CSOs, as well as their rising importance, especially in former colonial territories.[44] By 2004, CSOs in Ghana, Zimbabwe, Kenya, Sri Lanka, and elsewhere were providing over 40% of all healthcare and education in the country.[45] According to one report, by the turn of the new century, CSOs were providing necessary services and support to 20% of the world's poor.[46] However measured, the rise of international and domestic CSOs has been exponential since 1945, when the ratification of the UN Charter inadvertently contributed to this result.[47]

---

[44] Lauren MacLean, *Neoliberal Democratisation, Colonial Legacies, and the Rise of the Non-State Provision of Social Welfare in West Africa*, 44 REV. AFR. POL. ECON. 358–80 (2017).

[45] MICHAEL EDWARDS, CIVIL SOCIETY (2004).

[46] ALAN FOWLER, CIVIL SOCIETY, NGDOS AND SOCIAL DEVELOPMENT: CHANGING THE RULES OF THE GAME (UNRISD Occasional Paper 1, 2000).

[47] SASKIA BRECHENMACHER & THOMAS CAROTHERS, EXAMINING CIVIL SOCIETY LEGITIMACY (Carnegie Endowment for International Peace, May 2, 2018).

As the Cold War ended and the new millennium approached, the number of international CSOs involved in advocacy work, notably including democracy promotion, backed and funded by the democratic victors of the Cold War (primarily including the United States), caused the number of international CSOs to balloon further. According to Douglas Rutzen, a leading expert of global civil society who leads the International Center for Not-for-Profit Law, a human rights organization focused on strengthening the legal framework for CSOs around the globe:

> The decade before the new millennium was witness to a remarkable expansion of democratic reform and civil society empowerment. With the fall of the Berlin Wall, remarkable associational growth and the rise of the Internet, political, technological, and social factors converged to create an era of civic empowerment.[48]

This "era of civic empowerment," also referred to as the "associational revolution," saw the numbers, funding, and support for CSOs escalate to unprecedented new heights.[49] By the early 2000s, it was claimed that if CSOs were a country, they would have the fifth largest economy in the world.[50] Not only were international CSOs largely welcomed in the many states where they worked, but they also became a key way in which the United States and the former colonizing powers could channel their resources and indirectly advance their agendas abroad.[51]

THE ASSOCIATIONAL REVOLUTION

The term 'associational revolution' was coined in 1994 by Lester Salamon, a leading expert on global civil society in *Foreign Affairs*. According to Professor Salamon:

> A striking upsurge is under way around the globe in organized voluntary activity and the creation of private, nonprofit or nongovernmental organizations. From the developed countries of North America, Europe

---

[48] ICNL, A MAPPING OF EXISTING INITIATIVES TO ADDRESS LEGAL CONSTRAINTS ON FOREIGN FUNDING OF CIVIL SOCIETY (July 1, 2014) at 1.

[49] International Center for Not-for-Profit Law, *On Aid Barriers Aid Barrier and the Rise of Philanthropic Protectionism: A Conversation with Douglas Rutzen*, NGO SOURCE, Sept. 30, 2015, https://www.ngosource.org/blog/on-%e2%80%9caid-barriers-and-the-rise-of-philanthropic-protectionism%e2%80%9d-a-conversation-with-douglas-rutzen-international-center-for-not-for-profit-law-icnl [hereinafter Rutzen 2015].

[50] LESTER SALAMON ET AL., GLOBAL CIVIL SOCIETY: AN OVERVIEW (2003).

[51] RICHARD YOUNGS, RETHINKING CIVIL SOCIETY AND SUPPORT FOR DEMOCRACY (Carnegie Endowment for International Peace, 2015).

and Asia to the developing societies of Africa, Latin America and the former Soviet bloc, people are forming associations, foundations and similar institutions to deliver human services, promote grass-roots economic development, prevent environmental degradation, protect civil rights and pursue a thousand other objectives formerly unattended or left to the state.[52]

Salamon goes on to describe the "immense" scope and scale of the associational revolution, which he attributes to a variety of factors, including profound social and technological change and a "long-simmering crisis of confidence in the capability of the state."[53] Salamon, like various others who have assessed the rise of what he refers to as "the associational sector,"[54] focuses heavily on the diminishing ability of states to satisfy the needs of their citizens and the declining levels of confidence and trust among citizens toward their state in explaining the rise of CSOs.[55] CSOs, in many countries, began to act as gap-fillers and need providers, filling in where the state was absent. As more nimble, flexible, and narrowly focused alternatives to states, unfettered by partisan politics at the domestic level and power politics at the international level, CSOs were viewed by many as more capable and trustworthy than their national governments. This shift in perceptions was so "sweeping" in scope that it was thought to resemble the third wave of democratic political revolutions that rocked the developing world in the 1970s and 1980s.[56]

The associational revolution essentially began when the cold war ended in the early 1990s when democracy – and the United States, specifically – emerged

---

[52] Salamon 1994 at 50.

[53] *Id.* at 50–51.

[54] The "associational sector" and the "associational" revolution are referring to the freedom of association, the fundamental human right that undergirds civil society's existence. The freedom of association, which is one of the most basic rights enjoyed by people, is the right to form and participate in groups, whether formal or informal. *See* "The Freedom of Association," International Center for Not-for-Profit Law, available at https://www.icnl.org/our-work/freedom-of-association (defining freedom of association as: "The right to freedom of association enables individuals to come together to pursue shared interests and achieve common goals – to act collectively to improve their lives. It protects registered and unregistered groups alike, including civil society organizations, cooperatives, religious associations, political parties, trade unions, and online associations. Whether they seek to form a large advocacy organization or an informal group for hobby enthusiasts, individuals exercise this right by forming groups.")

[55] *E.g.,* Douglas Rutzen & Cathy Shea, *The Counter-Associational Revolution,* ALLIANCE, 2006; Douglas Rutzen, Aid Barriers and the Rise of Philanthropic Protectionism, 17 INT'L J. NOT-FOR-PROFIT L. (2015) [hereinafter Rutzen 2015].

[56] Salamon 1994 at 51.

victorious. CSOs were viewed by the United States and their allies as trustworthy vehicles for proselytizing and institutionalizing the virtues of democracy worldwide. As a result, international CSOs became the recipients of massive state-backed financial and material support by the United States and other democracies.[57] CSOs, especially those engaged in democracy promotion work, flush with funding and strongly supported by the democratic states of the world, ventured abroad in order to perform their services and advocate on behalf of their missions.[58]

CSOs fully seized this hopeful moment in their history: they proliferated both domestically and internationally, successfully fought for involvement in traditionally state-based international organizations, and inserted themselves at all levels of global and domestic affairs.[59] The extraordinary rise in the number and visibility of CSOs around the globe lead certain political scientists to notice "a dramatic shift in the institutional landscape" of global politics, with CSOs playing larger and more visible roles in shaping international agendas.[60] In the heyday of the associational revolution, some even referred to CSOs as "second superpowers,"[61] who would usher in a significant "power shift" in global politics.[62] A writer for *Foreign Affairs* declared that the "steady concentration of power in the hands [of states that] began with the Peace of Westphalia, is over, at least for a while," concluding that power was now shifting to CSOs.[63] Professor Salamon, quoted above, similarly predicated that the "associational revolution" would prove to be "as significant to the latter twentieth century as the rise of the nation-state was to the latter nineteenth."[64]

---

[57] RICHARD LUGAR, NONGOVERNMENTAL ORGANIZATIONS AND DEMOCRACY PROMOTION: GIVING VOICE TO THE PEOPLE – A REPORT TO MEMBERS OF THE COMMITTEE ON FOREIGN RELATIONS (U.S. Senate 109th Congress, 2nd Session, 2006).

[58] Rutzen 2015.

[59] Sudarsana Kundu, *Women's Rights Struggle as Restrictions Deepen Globally*, DIPLOMATIC COURIER BLOG (Sept. 20, 2017); Ann Towns, *Norms and Social Hierarchies: Understanding International Policy Diffusion "From Below"*, 66 INT'L ORG. 179–209 (2012); Charli Carpenter, *Vetting the Advocacy Agenda: Network Centrality and the Paradox of Weapons Norms*, 65 INT'L ORG. 69–102 (2011); Brian Greenhill, *The Company You Keep: International Socialization and the Diffusion of Human Rights Norms*, 54 INT'L STUD. Q. 127–45 (2010).

[60] *Id.*

[61] JAMES F. MOORE, THE SECOND SUPERPOWER REARS ITS BEAUTIFUL HEAD (Berkman Center for Internet & Society, Harvard Univ., Mar. 31, 2003).

[62] Jessica T. Mathews, *Power Shift*, 76 FOREIGN AFF. 50–66 (1997).

[63] *Id.*

[64] Salamon 1994 at 52.

At the domestic level, CSOs proved capable of compelling states to make important policy and legal changes to institutionalize domestic watchdog institutions,[65] adopt specific policies,[66] enact and rescind legislation,[67] and amend long-standing constitutional provisions.[68] They also inspired large-scale social movements that led to radical shifts in deeply-entrenched political and cultural norms,[69] and held governments to account when citizens acting on their own, treaty commitments, foreign states, and international organizations did not or could not.[70] They also repeatedly named and shamed states into making important policy and structural changes, such as withdrawing from colonial territories,[71] replacing long-standing incumbents,[72] ending the

---

[65] Dongwook Kim, *International Nongovernmental Organizations and the Global Diffusion of National Human Rights Institutions*, 67 INT'L ORG. 505–39 (2013).

[66] Amanda Murdie & Alexander Hicks, *Can International Nongovernmental Organizations Boost Government Services? The Case of Health*, 67 INT'L ORG. 541–73 (2013) [hereinafter Murdie & Hicks 2013].

[67] Benjamin Brake & Peter J. Katzenstein, *Lost in Translation? Nonstate Actors and the Transnational Movement of Procedural Law*, 67 INT'L ORG. 725–57 (2013).

[68] DAVID COLE, ENGINES OF LIBERTY: THE POWER OF CITIZEN ACTIVISTS TO MAKE CONSTITUTIONAL LAW (2016).

[69] The US alone provides many examples. Environmental CSOs in the US sparked the environmental movement in the 1980s, and CSOs were also instrumental in catalyzing and leading the campaign to franchise women, the civil rights movement, and the marriage equality campaign, among others. Although arguably not as successful, the Black Lives Matter campaign has led to many legal and regulatory changes that have increased oversight and accountability of police officers, such as requirements for video camera installation in police cars. According to Salaman Lester, who wrote a landmark article on the rise of the non-profit sector in *Foreign Affairs* in 1994, "[v]irtually all of America's major social movements, for example, whether civil rights, environmental, consumer, women's or conservative, have had their roots in the nonprofit sector" (see p. 109). Globally, one can point to the abolitionist movement, the campaign to end Apartheid, the bans on landmines and wars of aggression within international law, the movement to end the proliferation of nuclear weapons, and most recently, the #MeToo movement as examples of successful CSO-led advocacy campaigns (Klotz 2002; Price 1998).

[70] Emilie Hafner-Burton, *Sticks and Stones: Naming and Shaming the Human Rights Enforcement Problem*, 62 INT'L ORG. 689–716 (2008).

[71] Algeria is just one example: here, coalitions of citizens banned together to form groups that fought their French colonial masters in the late 1950s to early 1960s, which eventually forced the French to withdraw and led to Algeria's independence in 1962.

[72] Danielle Meltz, Civil Society in the Arab Spring: Tunisia, Egypt, and Libya (Thesis, University of Colorado, Boulder, 2016).

institution of slavery, committing to the prohibition against torture,[73] and even abandoning powerful weapon systems.[74]

At the global level, as the twenty-first century dawned, CSOs had become essential to accomplishing international development goals,[75] instigators of norm creation and change,[76] agents of socialization,[77] key diffusers of global human rights norms,[78] recognized actors within international law,[79] and catalysts of transformational shifts in global politics.[80] They were key actors in the global effort to end Apartheid in South Africa;[81] leading movements to ban wars of aggression, landmines, and nuclear weapons within international law;[82] and launched global campaigns to raise awareness of violence against women, the most recent manifestation of this being the #MeToo Movement which was named Time Magazine's "Person of the Year" in 2017.[83] The International Campaign to Abolish Nuclear Weapons, also in 2017, became yet

---

[73] The Convention against Torture was largely the result of Amnesty International's decade-long campaign against torture. *See* Peter Willets, *The Role of NGOs in Global Governance*, WORLD POL. REV., Sept. 27, 2011.

[74] Michael Horowitz & Julia Macdonald, *Will Killer Robots Be Banned? Lessons from Past Civil Society Campaigns*, LAWFARE, Nov. 5, 2017; JOEL QUIRK, THE ANTI-SLAVERY PROJECT: FROM THE SLAVE TRADE TO HUMAN TRAFFICKING (2011); Richard Price, *Reversing the Gun Sights: Transnational Civil Society Targets Land Mines*, 52 INT'L ORG. 613–44 (1998).

[75] Sudarsana Kundu, *Women's Rights Struggle as Restrictions Deepen Globally*, DIPLOMATIC COURIER, Sept. 20, 2017.

[76] Ann Towns, *Norms and Social Hierarchies: Understanding International Policy Diffusion "From Below"*, 66 INT'L ORG. 179–209 (2012).

[77] Brian Greenhill, *The Company You Keep: International Socialization and the Diffusion of Human Rights Norms*, 54 INT'L STUD. Q. 127–45 (2010).

[78] KECK & SIKKINK 1998.

[79] EDUARDO SZAZI, NGOS: LEGITIMATE SUBJECTS OF INTERNATIONAL LAW (2012) [hereinafter SZAZI 2012].

[80] OONA HATHAWAY & SCOTT SHAPIRO, THE INTERNATIONALISTS: HOW A RADICAL PLAN TO OUTLAW WAR REMADE THE WORLD (2017) [hereinafter HATHAWAY & SHAPIRO 2017].

[81] Audie Klotz, *Transnational Activism and Global Transformations: The Anti-Apartheid and Abolitionist Experiences*, 8 EUR. J. INT'L REL. 49–76 (2002).

[82] HATHAWAY & SHAPIRO 2017; Richard Price, *Reversing the Gun Sights: Transnational Civil Society Targets Land Mines*, 52 INT'L ORG. 613–44 (1998); Matthew Bolton, *A Brief Guide to the New Nuclear Weapons Ban Treaty*, JUST SECURITY, July 14, 2017.

[83] Sophie Gilbert, *The Movement of #MeToo*, THE ATLANTIC, Oct. 16, 2017; Mala Htun & S. Laurel Weldon, *The Civic Origins of Progressive Policy Change: Combating Violence against Women in Global Perspective, 1975–2005*, 106 AM. POL. SCI. REV. 548–69 (2012). What I mean here is an enormous success in bringing visibility and awareness to the issue of sexual assault and violence against women, not unfortunately, in solving the problem.

another in the long list of CSOs to be awarded the Nobel Peace Prize,[84] an international prize originally created for the state-centric purpose of recognizing those who have "done the most or the best work for fraternity between nations, for the abolition or reduction of standing armies and for the holding and promotion of peace congresses."[85] In sum, as the twenty-first century unfolded, CSOs, fueled by the momentum of the 1990s, began pushing the traditional boundaries of the state-civil society divide, becoming more assertive and involved in all levels of politics.

CONCLUSION

The end of the twentieth century witnessed the golden age for civil society, a time of great optimism in the potential of democracy and the power of technology, people, and their organizations to serve the state's interests, particularly democratic states. However, as the twenty-first century dawned, states were beginning to feel threatened by the rising participation and influence of CSOs in national and international politics. No longer were CSOs simply serving as gap-fillers, providing development aid and services to the destitute where the state fell short. They were beginning to lead revolutions, overthrow long-standing incumbents, successfully lobby for their agendas at the United Nations, and in general, actively get involved in matters and institutions that had historically been the preserve of states alone.

By the mid-2000s, many states began to fear that their exclusive and pinnacle spot in the global order was at risk, and they began pushing back. So began the "associational counter-revolution," which refers to the attempt by state actors to reverse the gains made by CSOs during the associational revolution. Chapter 3 examines this counter-revolution in more detail and outlines and critiques the existing theories that have been offered to explain it. It then posits that the existing explanations, which all operate at the domestic level and focus mainly on non-democratic (or weakly democratic) states, fail to adequately explain this trend, which is now observed in all parts of the world, including in the world's strongest democratic states.

---

[84] Nobel Peace Prize, *International Campaign to Abolish Nuclear Weapons*, FACT, available at https://www.nobelprize.org/prizes/peace/2017/ican/facts/.
[85] *Nobel Peace Prize, in* THE OXFORD DICTIONARY OF TWENTIETH CENTURY WORLD HISTORY.

CHAPTER 3:

THE ASSOCIATIONAL COUNTER-REVOLUTION

Every revolution has its counter-revolution – that is a sign the revolution is for real.

C. Wright Mills, Listen Yankee (1960)

This chapter details the counter-reaction of states to the rising influence of CSOs, the so-called "associational counter-revolution."[1] This counter-reaction has manifested in many different ways by many different states over the past two decades. However, in the world's strongest democratic states, it has largely occurred through the passage of restrictive CSO laws. After detailing and confirming the existence of this counter-trend, the chapter then turns to the existing explanations posited to understand this phenomenon.

The rising influence of CSOs at the domestic and especially the global levels, as detailed in Chapter 2, eventually triggered states to take notice. This recognition unleashed a powerful state-led counter-trend, the so-called "associational counter-revolution," whereby states attempted to reverse the gains made by CSOs throughout the associational revolution of the 1990s.[2] Various methods have been used to accomplish this goal, including violence, harassment, stigmatization campaigns, and cooptation. However, an increasingly popular tactic of choice by states, especially democratic states, is the law. The law is a less costly, even if perhaps more time-consuming, strategy that can lead to the weakening of civil society (or the lessening of their independence from the state) but with less risk of international outcry.[3] Beginning roughly in 2005, a

---

[1] Douglas Rutzen & Cathy Shea, *The Counter-Associational Revolution*, ALLIANCE, Sept. 1, 2006 [hereinafter Rutzen & Shea 2006]. This term originates from this article.
[2] *Id.*
[3] Chaudhry 2016. The violent assault against CSOs is an enormous problem worldwide. Certain groups, such as Global Witness, which focuses on environmental civil society actors, as well as Civicus, track incidents of violence and other crimes inflicted on civil society actors, including targeted murder of CSO leaders, violent attacks, disappearances of activists, unlawful detentions, public vilification, forcible closures of CSOs, and other illegal acts. Recent research by Civicus confirms in its "Anatomy of the Global Crackdown" on civil society that activists being detained, protest disruption, and excessive force are still the predominate ways in which this crackdown is done. See their visual of this here: https://monitor.civicus.org/globalfindings0417/. I acknowledge the enormity of this

cascade of new restrictive CSO laws began to appear in one state after another. This phenomenon is so alarming in scope and spread that it is often referred to by civil society activists and human rights attorneys as the "closing space" trend; referring to the elimination of spaces, literal and figurative, within society for CSOs to freely voice their opinions and carry out their activities.[4]

Through the passage of legislation imposing new restrictions on the ability of CSOs to form, operate, access funding, and assemble, what I refer to as "restrictive CSO laws," governmental actors are attempting to gain more control over the non-governmental sector. First identified as a systematic and global problem in 2006,[5] the seemingly contagious associational counter-revolution reached "crisis" proportions by 2014[6] and "emergency" status by 2017,[7] according to global civil society watchdogs. Human rights defenders describe this global phenomenon in apocalyptic, even hysteric, terms: as a "disturbing" and "alarming" "existential threat" to civil society;[8] a "global contagion" with unstoppable and incurable force, which "threatens the viability of civil society organizations ... vital to holding governments accountable and advancing human rights;"[9] an all-out "global war" on non-governmental organizations;[10] and an attempt to "choke out" civil society altogether.[11] Hyperbole aside, a concerted attempt by an increasing number of states to stem or reverse civil society's growing strength and influence through the passage of restrictive laws began in earnest shortly after the turn of the twenty-first century and has been gaining momentum ever since.[12]

---

problem, but it is not the focus of my research, which is specifically focused on the use of the *law* to restrict the autonomy of CSOs. I hope, in future research, to broaden my inquiry to include these other tactics used by states to repress the work of CSOs.

[4] MARIA STEPHEN, RESPONDING TO THE GLOBAL THREAT OF CLOSING CIVIC SPACE: POLICY OPTIONS (U.S. Institute of Peace, 2017); ALEX TIERSKY & EMILY RENARD, CLOSING SPACE: RESTRICTIONS ON CIVIL SOCIETY AROUND THE WORLD AND U.S. RESPONSES (Congressional Research Services, 2016); Wolff & Poppe 2015; Carothers & Brechenmacher 2014.
[5] Carl Gershman & Michael Allen, *New Threats to Freedom: The Assault on Democracy Assistance*, 17 J. DEMOCRACY 36–51 (Apr. 2006); Thomas Carothers, *The Backlash Against Democracy Promotion*, 85 FOREIGN AFF. 55–68 (2006).
[6] Carothers & Brechenmacher 2014.
[7] CIVICUS, MONITOR: TRACKING CIVIC SPACE (2017), available at https://monitor.civicus.org/.
[8] M. KIAI, CIVIL SOCIETY'S RIGHT TO SEEK, RECEIVE AND USE RESOURCES: HUMAN, MATERIAL AND FINANCIAL (UN Special Rapporteur on Peaceful Assembly and Association A/HRC/23/39, 2013).
[9] CENTER FOR STRATEGIC AND INTERNATIONAL STUDIES, STRENGTHENING CIVIL SOCIETY (2017).
[10] *The Global War against NGOs*, WASHINGTON POST, Dec. 10, 2015.
[11] Kenneth Roth, *The Great Civil Society Choke Out*, FOREIGN POLICY, Jan. 27, 2016.
[12] Rutzen 2015; Carothers & Brechenmacher 2014; Rutzen & Shea 2006; Dupuy et al. 2016; Chaudhry 2016; Schuman 2017; Tiersky & Renard 2016; Wolff & Poppe 2015.

The small handful of organizations that closely track legal developments pertaining to global civil society has confirmed this trend. The International Center for Not-for-Profit Law (ICNL), a global leader in tracking civil society legal developments around the world, documented more than fifty countries that either enacted or considered legal measures as restricting civil society between 2004 and 2010.[13] Between 2012 and 2015, ICNL reported on another ninety such laws that had been proposed or enacted; and by May 2018, they were reporting on the existence of 144 restrictive CSO laws and regulations that had been proposed or adopted by seventy-two countries, or roughly forty percent of all states.[14] An article published by ICNL's president, Douglas Rutzen, in 2015 stated that the number of restrictive legal initiatives proposed or adopted began to double each year beginning in 2012;[15] and an internal ICNL document, which tracks a broader array of legal instruments, reveals even higher numbers: the emergence of 400 state-led legal initiatives (laws, decrees, regulations, key policies, and the like) that impose new restrictions on CSOs proposed or adopted since 2012.[16] ICNL's vice president for legal affairs, David Moore, described the spate of restrictive CSO laws worldwide as "a paradigm shift" for global civil society, which has seen its freedom to operate free from government control significantly erode since the new century began.[17]

Civicus, another organization that closely tracks developments affecting global civil society, maintains a regularly updated virtual map visually depicting the ever-expanding closing space phenomenon. A cursory glance at this map reveals that countries with "narrow" or "open" environments for CSOs, the least restrictive categories, comprise a slim minority of countries worldwide, while

---

[13] Rutzen 2015 at 3.

[14] International Center for Not-for-Profit Law, *Effective Donor Responses to the Challenge of Closing Civic Space*, Apr. 2018, at 9, available at http://www.icnl.org/news/2018/Effective%20 donor%20responses%20FINAL%201%20May%202018.pdf [hereinafter International Center for Not for Profit Law 2018]. The distinction between a "proposed" and "enacted" law is a crucial one, as I address in the "key definitions" section below (located in the broader Research Design section). My research will focus on adopted laws, though I am attempting to gather information on proposed laws (and proposal dates) as well. If I am able to collect enough data on these proposals, I hope to expand my inquiry to include both. Also discussed below in the "key definitions" section is what precisely I mean by "laws," which I expand to include anything that carries the force of law, such as certain policy pronouncements and executive decrees.

[15] Rutzen 2015 at 4.

[16] These mostly include adopted laws (including amendments to existing laws), but also include proposed laws, official policy statements, official regulations, and executive decrees, a broader category of legal initiatives than those captured in the other lower figures.

[17] Michael Schuman, *An Increasingly Uncivil World*, US NEWS, July 31, 2017 [hereinafter Schuman 2017].

countries with "closed," "repressed," or "obstructed" civil society environments comprise the vast majority.[18] According to Civicus, only four percent of the human population currently lives in a country where civil society freely operates, while in 111 countries, well over half of all states, CSOs are under "serious attack."[19] Though Civicus tracks all types of challenges faced by CSOs, including legal, illegal, and extralegal challenges, their empirical data similarly confirm the "viral-like spread of new laws" snaking their way around the globe that attempt to minimize the autonomy and increase government oversight of CSOs.[20] According to their 2017 report, "when it comes to the freedom of association [the cornerstone freedom underlying the existence of CSOs] far more disenabling laws and policies than enabling ones are being introduced."[21]

The few scholars who have examined the closing space phenomenon not only confirm the spread of restrictive CSO laws around the globe, what some have referred to as the "regulatory offensive,"[22] but also their negative, and in some cases devastating, consequences.[23] A variety of reports suggest that the percentage of states that have adopted restrictive CSO laws, notably including laws that restrict CSOs' ability to access foreign funding, has risen sharply since 2013.[24] Moreover, a mounting body of evidence suggests the dire consequences that such laws are having on CSOs, which in some contexts is leading to the collapse of entire sectors of civil society altogether.[25] A 2013 study published by Darin Christensen and Jeremy M. Weinstein in the *Journal of Democracy* examined the spread of a particular type of restrictive CSO legislation — restrictive foreign

---

[18] Civicus Monitor, *World Map – CIVICUS – Tracking Conditions for Citizen Action* (2019), available at https://monitor.civicus.org/ [hereinafter Civicus Monitor 2019].

[19] *Id.*

[20] Harriet Sherwood, *Human Rights Groups Face Global Crackdown "Not Seen in a Generation"*, THE GUARDIAN, Aug. 26, 2015; Carothers & Brechenmacher 2014.

[21] Civicus, *State Of Civil Society Report 2017* at 3. "Disenabling" is a term often used by civil society activists to describe laws, and other instruments, that create an environment not conducive to a robust, independent civil society sector. For CSOs to flourish and reach their full potential, according to civil society activists, states should create an "enabling environment" conducive to their success, which would include a legal and regulatory framework that encourages and permits their independence and growth.

[22] Dupuy et al. 2015 at 420, 423.

[23] Dupuy & Prakash 2017; Chaudhry 2016.

[24] Samantha Laufer, *A Difference in Approach: Comparing the US Foreign Agents Registration Act with Other Laws Targeting Internationally Funded Civil Society*, 19 INT'L J. NOT-FOR-PROFIT L. 5 (2017); Schuman 2017; Rutzen 2015.

[25] Kristen Chick, *Egypt's Civil Society Is on Life Support*, FOREIGN POL'Y, Dec. 13, 2017; Dupuy et al. 2015; Charles Digges, *"Foreign Agent" Law Has Put 33 Percent of Russia's NGOs out of Business*, BELLONA, Oct. 20, 2015 [hereinafter Digges 2015]; Carothers & Brechenmacher 2014.

funding laws — and found that at least 26% of the UN's current 193 member states either prohibit or restrict CSOs' access to foreign funding.[26] Another 2017 study, building on the work of Christensen and Weinstein, found that the adoption of restrictive CSO foreign funding laws not only negatively impacts CSOs but the adopting states too: indeed, adopting this type of law was associated with a 32% decline in bilateral aid received by the state in subsequent years.[27] More recently, a study released in 2020 charted the significant rise in legal restrictions on CSOs from roughly 1997 on, which has corresponded with a leveling off of their numerical growth globally (see Figure 3.1).[28]

Figure 3.1: Charting the rising number of (legal) restrictions on CSOs and the total number of CSOs worldwide from the 1990s to 2017. Source: Marlies Glasius et al., "Illiberal Norm Diffusion: How Do Governments Learn to Restrict Nongovernmental Organizations?" *International Studies Quarterly* 64, at 459.

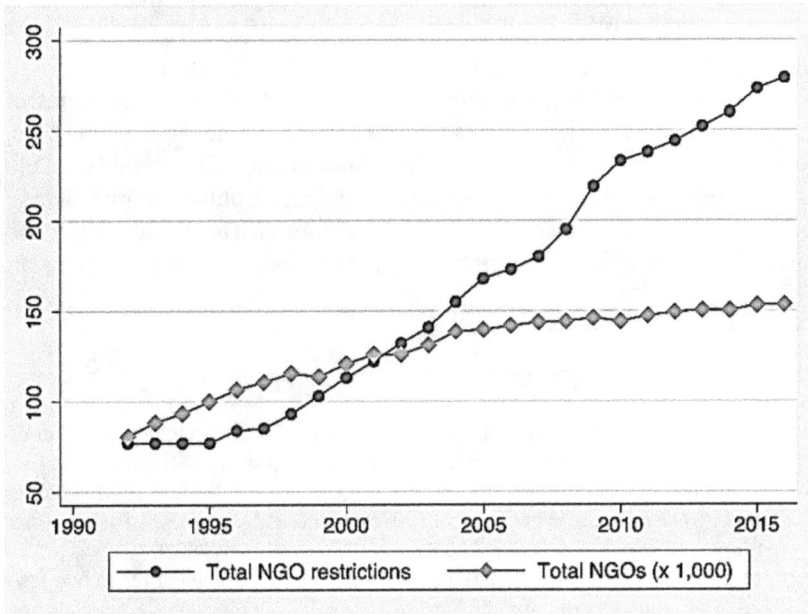

---

[26] Darin Christensen & Jeremy M. Weinstein, *Defunding Dissent: Restrictions on Aid to NGOs*, 24 J. DEMOCRACY 77–91 (2013).

[27] Dupuy & Prakash 2017.

[28] Marlies Glasius et al., *Illiberal Norm Diffusion: How Do Governments Learn to Restrict Nongovernmental Organizations?*, 64 INT'L STUD. Q. 453–68 at 458 (2020) (stating that "[f]rom 1997 onward, the number begins to rise considerably every year and continues to rise during the 2000s as the total growth in the number of NGOs begins to level off") [hereinafter Glasius et al. 2020].

RESTRICTIVE CSO LAWS IN DEMOCRATIC STATES

The adoption of restrictive CSO laws is puzzling in the context of democratic states, which, as previously discussed, historically funded and supported a robust and independent civil society. Yet, such laws have been appearing, and increasingly so, in democracies in recent years.[29] While restrictive CSO laws vary in scope, intensity and content, they share a common goal at their core: the extension of additional *governmental* control over the *non-governmental* sector. Restrictive CSO laws are defined more by their intent than their particular labels or precise contents, although specific provisions can and are a way of identifying them, as further explored below.[30] In general, restrictive CSO laws transfer additional levels of control and oversight over CSOs to government actors. They complicate or burden CSOs' ability to freely form, operate, access funding (especially foreign funding), engage in certain activities, and dissolve.

Some recent examples of what one study referred to as 'the governmentalizing of non-governmental organizations" through the adoption of new types of restrictive CSO laws will help to illustrate the points made above.[31] In June 2018, Hungary's parliament adopted a package of laws, colloquially referred to as the "Stop Soros" laws, due to their specific targeting of philanthropist George Soros, who supported a variety of pro-immigrant NGOs in Hungary at the time.[32] This package of laws imposed a variety of onerous new restrictions on

---

[29] Their research findings (and this particular quote) are summarized in this *Washington Post* article: Kristen Bakke et al., *Governments Around the World Are Restricting Rights, Using the Pandemic for Cover*, WASHINGTON POST, May 6, 2020 [hereinafter Bakke et al. 2020]. The articles behind this shorter piece include: K. Bakke et al., *When States Crack Down on Human Rights Defenders*, 64 INT'L STUD. Q. 85–96 (2020); Hannah M. Smidt et al., *Silencing Their Critics: How Government Restrictions Against Civil Society Affect International "Naming and Shaming"*, 51 BRIT J. POL. SCI. 1270–91 (2021).

[30] Different scholars and practitioners have different ways of labeling restrictive CSO laws. The International Center for Not-for-Profit Law (ICNL), for example, which is one of the global leaders in tracking CSO laws, labels and identifies them in one way; while CIVICUS and Freedom House tend to refer to them using slightly different language. Scholars also employ different labels and terms, which can make it difficult to cross-compare research findings and conclusions. As a former contractor for ICNL, I tend to adopt their labeling, which I also trust due to ICNL's depth of experience and knowledge on this topic. The term "lifecycle law" in particular, I borrow from ICNL's vocabulary.

[31] DAVID CRAIG & DOUG PORTER, DEVELOPMENT BEYOND NEOLIBERALISM?: GOVERNANCE, POVERTY REDUCTION AND POLITICAL ECONOMY (2006).

[32] Bill No. T/333 amending certain laws relating to measures to combat illegal immigration. This package of laws includes three laws – the Law on the social responsibility of organizations

CSOs, including a 25% tax for those organizations suspected of assisting migrants, new criminal penalties for organizations (and individuals) associated with facilitating the entry of asylum seekers, and additional new authorities given to government agencies to register, penalize, and ban organizations who support 'illegal immigration,' which can include distributing informational materials or helping refugees fill out asylum requests.[33] A multitude of global human rights organizations, migrant groups, multilateral organizations, UN officials, and civil society activists condemned the passage of these "draconian" laws and called for their immediate repeal.[34] A year before, in June of 2017, Hungary similarly passed a new law, which many compare to Russia's restrictive 2012 Foreign Agent Law, requiring CSOs that receive approximately $28,000 or more of their funding from abroad, no matter the source, to label themselves as "funded from abroad" on all publications.[35] In the Hungarian context, this label is extremely stigmatizing and degrading to the sub-sector of CSOs that it most directly impacts, including anti-corruption and human rights organizations.[36] Similar laws were passed in Israel in 2016 and India in 2010, the latter of which has had devastating consequences for many CSOs, particularly human rights and environmental CSOs.[37]

In India, the 2010 Foreign Contribution Regulation Act, amended to impose additional restrictions in 2015, requires CSOs to apply for and receive explicit governmental permission before receiving any funds from abroad, whether from governmental or private sources. The government can deny permission for vague and broad reasons such as "activities not conducive to the [country's] national interest," and has used this law routinely to place CSOs on

---

supporting illegal migration; the Law on Immigration Financing Duty; and the Law on Immigration Restraints – all adopted in June 2018.

[33] Reuters, *Hungary Passes Anti-Immigrant "Stop Soros" Laws*, THE GUARDIAN, June 20, 2018.

[34] *E.g.*, Amnesty International, *Hungary: Draconian Anti-NGO Law Will Be Resisted Every Step of the Way*, AMNESTY INT'L USA, June 20, 2018; Pablo Gorondi, *Council of Europe Experts: Hungary Must Repeal Anti-NGO Law*, AP NEWS, June 22, 2018.

[35] Transparency Bill Act (LXXVI of 2017), adopted in June 2017.

[36] Yasmeen Serhan, *Hungary's Anti-Foreign NGO Law*, THE ATLANTIC, June 13, 2017; Christian Keszthelyi, *President Áder Signs NGO Law into Effect*, BUDAPEST BUS. J., June 16, 2017.

[37] Melissa Cyrill & Adam Pitman, *FCRA Compliance in India: How 24,000 NGOs Lost Their License*, INDIA BRIEFING NEWS, Sept. 28, 2017; Jonathan Lis, *Despite Global Criticism, Israel Approves Contentious "NGO Law"*, HAARETZ, July 11, 2016. Since Prime Minister Narendra Modi took office in 2014, the 2010 law has reportedly been used to strip over 24,000 CSOs of their operating licenses, a number that continues to increase.

government watchlists, strip CSOs of their operating licenses, and force them to dissolve voluntarily.[38]

In the US in 2017, a policy was adopted requiring foreign CSOs that provide health care services to women and children to first sign a pledge promising not to perform any abortion-related activities, including those that involve educational opportunities or counseling, in order to receive any amount of US health aid.[39] This requirement has had a significant chilling effect on many NGOs that provide healthcare to impoverished families around the world and are dependent, for their existence, on US foreign aid.[40] According to one affected NGO, this policy, which not only implicates sexual and reproductive health services, including abortion, but also affects the provision of nutrition and maternal health services and the ability to reach a sub-sector of women who are victims of gender-based violence.[41] One study found that at least 1,275 foreign NGOs and nearly 500 US NGOs have been negatively impacted, and specifically, their speech and activities curtailed, by this US policy.[42]

In October of 2017, the Polish parliament approved a law that consolidates all power over CSO funding into the hands of a single individual appointed by the Prime Minister; this individual now entirely controls the distribution of CSO funding, no matter the source, foreign or domestic.[43] Under the new law,

---

[38] Melissa Cyrill & Adam Pitman, *FCRA Compliance in India: How 24,000 NGOs Lost Their License*, INDIA BRIEFING NEWS, Sept. 28, 2017.

[39] Human Rights Watch. 2018. "Trump's 'Mexico City Policy' or 'Global Gag Rule.'" Questions and Answers. Human Rights Watch. Under the expanded Mexico City Policy, described as the "global gag rule" passed by previous republican administrations but this time "on steroids," adopted by President Trump in January of 2017, foreign CSOs wishing to receive any amount of global US health funding, must first sign a pledge promising to not engage in any abortion-related activities whatsoever, including counseling or education

[40] VANESSA RIOS, CRISIS IN CARE: YEAR TWO IMPACT OF TRUMP'S GLOBAL GAG RULE (2019).

[41] Amy Lieberman, *Two Years in, Report Finds "Global Gag Rule" Cuts Access to Health Care*, DEVEX, June 5, 2019.

[42] KELLIE MOSS & JENNIFER KATES, HOW MANY FOREIGN NGOS ARE SUBJECT TO THE EXPANDED MEXICO CITY POLICY? (2017). In addition to the expanded Mexico City Policy, thirty-five US states have proposed or adopted 100 laws imposing new restrictions on individuals' and CSOs' ability to protest in the past three years. See the US Protest Law Tracker, International Center for Not-for-Profit, available at http://www.icnl.org/usprotestlaw tracker/ (last accessed June 6, 2019).

[43] *State Department Urged to Press Duda to Veto Harmful Legislation, Protect Polish NGOs*, HUMAN RIGHTS FIRST, Oct. 5, 2017. While some CSOs, particularly certain types of CSOs such as human rights and other advocacy organizations operating in countries inhospitable to the causes they are advocating, have historically relied on government funding for their existence,

government actors get to exclusively decide which CSOs receive funding and at what level, effectively giving them the ultimate power over which CSOs survive, thrive, or dissolve. Many fear that this will lead to a passive and fearful CSO sector that simply parrots the government's agenda in an attempt to maintain organizational existence, which naturally relies on access to funding.[44]

In Australia, in June of 2018, the Australian parliament passed the Foreign Influence Transparency Scheme Bill, which bans donations from foreign sources not only for political parties but also for those classified as "political campaigners." Charities and unions were exempted from this provision after a spirited campaign and the onslaught of domestic and international criticism that the law received, but other types of CSOs not registered as either a charity or a union are theoretically still covered by this new restrictive law. Australian CSO organizations are extremely worried about this unpopular bill, which has been described as "startling" in scope and as expected to have an "adverse impact on many organizations."[45]

In Italy, after a restrictive policy was adopted by the government in 2017, various humanitarian CSOs dedicated to rescuing migrants trying to traverse the Mediterranean sea without adequate protection along the Italian coast had their rescue vessels impounded, their staffs investigated for human trafficking, and their assets were frozen after attempting to help undocumented immigrants safely come to shore.[46] And a 2015 law in Austria bans Islamic organizations – and only Islamic organizations – from accessing any foreign funds whatsoever, engaging in any fundraising efforts outside the county, using any version of the Quran other than the state-approved version (which is in German), and from espousing any opinions that contradict "a positive

---

and while this implicates a debate about the genuine independence of such organizations, what I am focused on here are not government funds, which a CSO can voluntarily choose to apply for and receive, but laws that attempt to control the distribution of funding to CSOs altogether (including from non-governmental sources) and that require all or certain kinds of funds meant for CSOs, such as foreign funds, to first flow through the government, which then gets to decide which CSOs get access to the funding and by how much. This type of law would constitute a "restrictive CSO law" for my purposes, rather than an a law dictating how a CSO could apply for and receive government funding, which in my view, preserves and maintains a CSO's autonomy.

[44] Goran Buldioski, *EU Must Confront Poland and Hungary*, EU OBSERVER, Nov. 21, 2017.

[45] Paul Karp, *Coalition's Foreign Agents Bill Attacked for Overreach and Curtailing "Freedoms of Expression"*, THE GUARDIAN, Jan. 18, 2018.

[46] John Lysa, *Government Attacks on Humanitarian Organizations and Human Rights Rising*, DEVEX, June 6, 2019.

fundamental view towards [Austria's] state and society."[47] In June 2018, Austria's right-wing government, which came to power in December 2017, announced its plans to shut down seven mosques and expel up to 60 imams for violating the restrictive and vague provisions of this bill.[48] These are just a few of the many examples of restrictive CSO laws adopted in historically strong democratic states in recent years, which will be carefully documented and mapped in the following chapter.[49]

THE NEGLECT OF DEMOCRACIES IN THE EXISTING LITERATURE

The above discussion leads to a puzzle in need of explanation: why would democratic states participate in a global trend that undermines their democratic credentials, threatens a long-established principle of democratic governance, and goes against their long-standing support for an autonomous civil society sector? Existing studies and reports that have examined the associational counter-revolution often note, but without further examination, that democracies are increasingly participating in this global trend.[50] Those studies that do attempt to go beyond mere description, often narrow their scope to examine only one type of law (typically foreign funding laws),[51] one type of state (typically developing, low and middle-income states or states that engage in egregious human rights violations involving physical integrity), and only certain kinds of CSOs (usually human rights and other advocacy NGOs).[52] The

---

[47] Amendment to the 1912 Law on Islam.

[48] *Austria to Shut Down Mosques, Expel Foreign-funded Imams*, REUTERS, June 8, 2018 (reporting by Francois Murphy & Ali Kucukgocmen; editing by Robin Pomeroy).

[49] CIVICUS Monitor: Tracking Civic Space. Civicus, an international NGO based in Johannesburg, South Africa, closely tracks the imposition of restrictive measures on civil society organizations around the globe. Their reporting reveals that the vast majority of countries around the world have cracked down on their civil society sector in some shape or form, in some cases more intensively than others, but overall, that the environment for CSOs in these countries has deteriorated when compared to earlier times.

[50] JONAS WOLFF & ELENA POPPE, FROM CLOSING SPACE TO CONTESTED SPACES: RE-ASSESSING CURRENT CONFLICTS OVER INTERNATIONAL CIVIL SOCIETY SUPPORT (NO. 137) (2015) [hereinafter WOLFF & POPPE 2015]; Carothers & Brechenmacher 2014; SARAH E. MENDELSON, WHY GOVERNMENTS TARGET CIVIL SOCIETY AND WHAT CAN BE DONE IN RESPONSE (Center for Strategic & International Studies, Apr. 2015).

[51] Dupuy et al., *Hands Off My Regime!*; Darin Christensen & Jeremy M. Weinstein, *Defunding Dissent: Restrictions on Aid to NGOs*, 24 J. DEMOCRACY 77–91 (2013) [hereinafter Christensen & Weinstein 2013].

[52] Kristen M. Bakke et al., *When States Crack Down on Human Rights Defenders*, 64 INT'L STUD. Q. 85–96 (Mar. 2020); Dupuy & Prakash 2017; Dupuy et al. 2016; Chaudhry 2016; Christensen & Weinstein 2013.

small but growing list of academic studies presents additional limitations too: one is an unpublished dissertation;[53] one performs only "simple tests" in order to access the "facial validity" of the proposed explanations and is explicitly "not focused on identifying causal effects," which means that their conclusions are little more than educated hunches as to what is really going on;[54] and all of them explicitly exclude established, wealthy, consolidated democratic states from their review.[55]

The academic neglect of the counter associational revolution with respect to democratic states among political scientists, particularly among IR scholars,[56] is perplexing given the existing (and enlarging) bodies of literature on CSOs pertaining to their rising influence in both domestic and international politics;[57] their participation in transnational advocacy networks, which can amplify their influence over states with their "boomerang" effects;[58] their rising status in international law, inter-governmental organizations, and traditionally state-dominated global events, such as major UN conferences;[59] and the internal dynamics, organizational structures, and external incentives that shape their agendas.[60] Testifying to the increasingly robust literature on CSOs is the recent emergence of a much more nuanced and critical body of scholarship on CSOs, which are no longer assumed to be the unquestioned 'paragons of virtue' they were once thought to be.[61] Yet, political scientists, who

---

[53] Chaudhry 2016.

[54] Christensen & Weinstein 2013 at n.5.

[55] Chaudhry 2016 at 13; Dupuy et al. 2016; Dupuy & Prakash 2017.

[56] I am still accessing if comparative politics scholars have considered the closing space phenomenon.

[57] Elizabeth A. Bloodgood & Emily Clough, *Transnational Advocacy Networks*, 35 Soc. Sci. Computer Rev. 319–35 (2017) [hereinafter Bloodgood & Clough 2017]; Murdie 2014; Murdie & Hicks 2013; Brian Greenhill, *The Company You Keep: International Socialization and the Diffusion of Human Rights Norms*, 54 Int'l Stud. Q. 127–45 (2010).

[58] This refers to the ability of CSOs to amplify the pressure exerted on their own government by allying with CSOs in other states, forming a transnational network. *See* Bloodgood & Clough 2017; Audie Klotz, *Transnational Activism and Global Transformations: The Anti-Apartheid and Abolitionist Experiences*, 8 Eur. J. Int'l Rel. 49–76 (2002); Keck & Sikkink 1998; Keck & Sikkink 1999.

[59] Sarah Stroup & Wendy H. Wong, *The Agency and Authority of International NGOs*, 14 Perspectives on Politics 138–44 (2016); Szazi 2012; Mala Htun & S. Laurel Weldon, *The Civic Origins of Progressive Policy Change: Combating Violence against Women in Global Perspective, 1975–2005*, 106 Am. Pol. Sci. Rev. 548–69 (2012).

[60] James McGann, *The Power Shift and the NGO Credibility Crisis*, 11 Brown J. World Aff. 159–72 (2005).

[61] Murdie 2014; McGann 2005; Mendelson & Glenn 2002; Cooley & Ron 2002; Carothers 1999.

clearly have the tools to assess the associational counter-revolution thoroughly, have largely failed to notice it.[62]

The lack of scholarly attention to what appears to be an international trend led by states in response to the rising power of a non-state actor, typically a topic of paramount interest and concern among IR scholars, is all the more perplexing given that this phenomenon is predicted by various IR theories. Classical and structural realists, who are fixated on balance of power concerns, would expect states to rebalance, or push back against, a growing international imbalance in the distribution of global power or threats to their exclusive sovereignty.[63] CSOs, which have successfully fought for participation alongside states in many international arenas and often act as 'gap-fillers' performing roles and offering services traditionally provided by states, should, according to realists, trigger a reaction by states (which indeed they have, as my research will highlight). Similarly, constructivists, who are interested in questions of identity and ideology in the shaping of global politics, should be intrigued by a phenomenon that raises fascinating questions about the changing identities and ideologies of many democratic states in the twenty-first century.[64] Constructivists would likely point to the enduring power of certain

---

[62] In a full-text search through six of the top IR Journals (*International Organization, International Security, International Studies Quarterly, World Politics, European Journal of International Relations,* and *APSR*), for all articles published since at least 1997 through to the present, the "closing space" phenomenon was mentioned in passing (not discussed) once within the text (*see* Bell et al. 2017 at 20) and was mentioned in the title of one reference contained within a footnote in one other (*see* Nuñez-Mietz & García Iommi 2017). *Foreign Affairs,* another leading IR journal, is an exception; there, one author in particular (Sarah Mendelson) has written various times on the closing space phenomenon ("Dark Days for Civil Society" and "Putin Outs the NGOs"), and others, such as Daniel Wilkinson, have discussed the ways in which individual states are cracking down on individual types of civil society activists, such as environmentalists ("Ecuador's Authoritarian Drift: Correa Cracks down on Environmental Activism"). In *International Organization,* arguably the leading IR journal, a search through all issues published since 1997 for the term "civil society organizations" yielded zero results, while a search for "civil society" turned up two articles. One pertains to a civil society success (the banning of landmines campaign), and the other only tangentially discusses civil society, and even then, it mostly addresses civil society's positive contributions to society; neither address state-led efforts to restrict the autonomy of CSOs. In *International Security,* one article specific to Russia, (*Russians' Rights Imperiled: Has Anyone Noticed?* by Sarah Mendelson, the same author mentioned above) briefly addresses Putin's attempts to manipulate and harass the civil society.

[63] KENNETH WALTZ, THEORY OF INTERNATIONAL POLITICS (2010).

[64] Alexander Wendt, *Anarchy Is What States Make of It,* 46 INT'L ORG. 391–425 (Spring 1992).

international norms, such as state sovereignty, as well as the global wave of populist, hyper-nationalist leaders and parties who have risen to power in many democratic states in recent years, to explain why states are pushing back against transnational non-state actors who endorse causes that often transcend state boundaries and national interests. Yet, to my knowledge, neither realist nor constructivist IR scholars have taken on the challenge of explaining this exceedingly relevant and intellectually fascinating puzzle, which implicates both power politics and ideological concerns.[65]

Many of the existing explanations of the associational counter-revolution come from participants in global civil society, such as civil society activists and human rights attorneys, as well as a small handful of experts affiliated with think tanks or policy organizations.[66] These individuals are understandably preoccupied with empirical realities rather than theory building and tend to focus on the more extreme legislative examples adopted by the more high-profile authoritarian states such as Russia, Egypt, and China.[67] While the spread of similar laws in democratic states is often acknowledged, their focus tends to be on understanding why individual states adopted a particular restrictive law or on tracking, rather than assessing and explaining, the broader trend.[68] Moreover, these dedicated practitioners, who are often on the front lines of this trend, are typically focused more on combating this growing phenomenon than explaining, mapping or theorizing its causes. Yet, the rich empirical-based assessments provided by civil society activists, combined with the insightful studies conducted by the small but growing number of scholars who have examined this topic, offer important insights for understanding the spread of restrictive CSO laws into democratic states.

EXISTING EXPLANATIONS

A careful review of the existing theories reveals an overwhelming focus on domestic level causes and the most extreme cases, despite widespread claims that the phenomenon being explained is global in scope and pertains to states

---

[65] I am still evaluating whether comparative politics scholars have similarly failed to examine the closing space phenomenon. Based on my preliminary research, it seems likely that area studies experts, who specialize in a particular country or region, have noticed this and commented on it, but as with IR scholars, not attempted to map its causes in a systematic way. *See, e.g.*, MARC M. HOWARD, THE WEAKNESS OF CIVIL SOCIETY IN POST-COMMUNIST EUROPE (2003).

[66] Wolff & Poppe 2015; Carothers & Brechenmacher 2014; Rutzen & Shea 2006.

[67] Carothers & Brechenmacher 2014.

[68] ICNL Civic Freedom Monitor 2017; Civicus Monitor 2019.

of all types.[69] For example, Kendra Dupuy, James Ron, and Aseem Prakash, who have published extensively on this topic, focus heavily on domestic political competition. They argue that governments are more likely to pass restrictive CSO legislation when the regime in power's political chances in an upcoming election are threatened.[70] By restricting CSOs' access to foreign funding, they argue, incumbent officials undermine a core source of support for their political opponents, which they believe to be foreign-funded CSOs. Political Scientists Jeremy Christensen and Darin Weinstein similarly find that governments are more likely to adopt laws restricting CSOs' access to foreign funding when they feel vulnerable to domestic challenges, notably including electoral challengers.[71] More recently, Kristin Bakke, Neil Mitchell, and Hannah Smidt, in a paper examining the ongoing global crackdown on human rights defenders by human rights violating states, focus heavily on the desire by states to silence the voices of those who seek to expose their human rights abuses.[72] It's a "familiar story," they state in an op-ed written in the *Washington Post* summarizing their research findings: "governments seek to stop the flow of inconvenient information about their performance failures and wrongdoings" by passing restrictive CSO laws.[73] The authors further conclude that CSOs "remind governments of their obligations enshrined in international treaties, including environmental and human rights obligations" and threaten to report lapses in these obligations to the international community. Such reporting could then trigger retaliation and/or damage to the state's international reputation.[74] Rather than complying with their international treaty obligations, the authors conclude, many states are instead choosing to silence those who will likely report on their lack of compliance.

Despite the many insights and useful analyses offered by the above scholars, their theories tend to apply only to human rights violating regimes and to government watchdog-type organizations. Christensen and Weinstein, for example, focus on Rwanda, Uganda, Belarus and Kazakhstan as their case studies;[75] Kendra Dupuy, James Ron and Aseem Prakash focus on resource-

---

[69] Chaudhry 2016; Christensen & Weinstein 2013 at 79; Rutzen & Shea 2006; Moore 2006.

[70] Dupuy et al. 2016.

[71] Christensen & Weinstein 2013.

[72] Bakke et al. 2020.

[73] Kristen M. Bakke et al., *Governments around the World are Restricting Rights: Using the Pandemic for Cover*, WASHINGTON POST, May 6, 2020, https://www.washingtonpost.com/politics/2020/05/05/governments-around-world-are-restricting-rights-using-pandemic-cover/.

[74] *Id.*

[75] Christensen & Weinstein 2013.

strapped developing countries, such as Kenya and Ethiopia;[76] and Bakke, Mitchell and Smidt focus on repressive regimes known for their human rights abuses, such as Egypt and Nigeria.[77] In other words, the few scholars who have examined the closing space phenomenon tend to focus on the obvious examples, the countries we most expect to adopt legislation restricting the ability of CSOs to operate freely.

In addition to these thoughtfully crafted explanations, five factors are most often suggested by those attempting to explain the spread of restrictive CSO laws. These include: (1) the ideological/ partisan orientation of the executive in power at the time of the restrictive CSO law's adoption; (2) the ideological/partisan affiliation of the dominant legislative group in power at the time of the law's adoption; (3) recent large-scale citizen-led uprisings; (4) fear of terrorism; and (5) the influence of a neighboring state. In the sections below, each of these explanations is examined with respect to the world's strongest democratic states. As the analysis reveals, none of these commonly cited explanations hold much explanatory value when applied to this subset of states.

THE IDEOLOGICAL ORIENTATION OF THE EXECUTIVE

A variety of recent reports have highlighted the rise of far-right leaders in democratic states in recent years, variously described as illiberal, hyper-nationalist, authoritarian-leaning, or populist, such as in Turkey, India, Israel, Poland, Hungary, the Philippines, and the US. Some reports have linked this rise to identifiable declines in a whole range of global freedoms,[78] while some have specifically linked the election of these leaders to increased repression of civil society.[79] According to a 2017 report commissioned by the European Union's Subcommittee on Human Rights, which concluded that the spread of restrictions on CSOs has assumed "an unprecedented depth and seriousness in recent years":

> The closing space [phenomenon] is part of a general authoritarian pushback against democracy, but it is not only that. Neither is it simply a crusade against human rights defenders. The phenomenon counts

---

[76] *E.g.*, Kendra E. Dupuy et al., *Who Survived? Ethiopia's Regulatory Crackdown on Foreign-Funded NGOs*, 22 REV. INT'L POL. ECON. 419–56 (2014) [hereinafter Dupuy et al. 2015].

[77] Hannah M. Smidt et al., *Silencing Their Critics: How Government Restrictions Against Civil Society Affect International "Naming and Shaming"*, 51 BRIT J. POL. SCI. 1270–91 (2021).

[78] Timbro Populism Index 2017; Puddington 2017; Freedom House 2017; Civicus 2017.

[79] Schuman 2017; Jones 2017; Roberto Stefan Foa & Yascha Mounk, *The Danger of Deconsolidation: The Democratic Disconnect*, 27 J. DEMOCRACY 5–17 (2016).

many causal drivers, in part linked to the world's authoritarian turn, in part the reflection of an emboldened anti-Western social agenda.[80]

While this report focuses on various factors to explain the closing space trend, it repeatedly emphasizes and repeats the "authoritarian turn" seen throughout the globe in recent years to try and explain why this trend is happening and spreading so widely.[81]

There is indeed an intuitive appeal to this argument. Recent studies suggest that when far-right populist leaders, who tend to elevate national sovereignty and national security above all other concerns, come to power in democratic states, they tend to do things more typical of authoritarian leaders: violate minority rights, put pressure on independent media outlets, and undermine independent institutions, such as the courts.[82] Anecdotal reports suggest that they tend to adopt restrictive CSO legislation as well. Poland, Hungary, Israel, Turkey, and the US are just four examples that readily come to mind where far-right leaders came to power and, under their watch, restrictive CSO laws were subsequently adopted. In each of these countries, their leaders are described as hyper-nationalist, populist, and/or far-right with respect to their ideological orientation. Each has openly voiced fear of foreign influence in domestic politics and elections.

Moreover, when each of these countries adopted a restrictive CSO law, it was justified at least in part on nationalistic grounds, suggesting that the nationalist leanings of the executive could have been part of the reason for its adoption.[83] Yet, Germany and Bolivia offer counterexamples. Chancellor Angela Merkel, a conservative leader who has not been associated with the wave of illiberal far-right leaders elected in recent years, oversaw a constitutional amendment to Germany's Basic Law in June 2017, which will impose additional new funding restrictions on a subset of civil society.[84] And Evo Morales, the far-left-leaning President of Bolivia from 2006 to 2019, oversaw the adoption of four restrictive CSO laws. Despite the oft-made assumption that the rise of illiberal leaders is

---

[80] Shrinking Space for Civil Society: The European Union Response (Directorate-General for External Policies, Policy Department, European Parliament, 2017) at 11 [hereinafter EU Response 2017].

[81] *Id.* at 5, 9, 11, and 12.

[82] Foa & Mounk 2016 at 15.

[83] Serhan 2017; Buldioski 2017; Cyrill & Pitman 2017; Lis 2016.

[84] Interestingly, this amendment was justified precisely on the grounds that it would prevent the further spread of illiberal democracies in Europe, adding additional perspective and nuance to the discussion of what constitutes a restrictive CSO law, as further discussed below. *See* Daly 2017b.

connected to the passage of restrictive CSO laws, to my knowledge, this theory has never been empirically verified.

DOES THE EXECUTIVE'S IDEOLOGICAL ORIENTATION MATTER?

The short answer to the above question is no. To determine whether there was a connection between the passage of a restrictive CSO law and the ideological orientation of the executive, the party and ideological affiliation of the executive in power (at the time a restrictive CSO law was adopted) was identified using the Database of Political Institutions (DPI); a reputable database published annually by the World Bank.[85] Two of DPI's measures were used for this: the first codes each executive's party affiliation as "left," "center," or "right"; and the second codes each executive leader as either nationalistic or not. Usefully, the DPI deals explicitly, but carefully, with labels such as "liberal," "progressive," "authoritarian," and "xenophobic," and has a way of coding for each. See Appendix 1 for how each of the 59 democratic countries reviewed in this book was coded.[86]

Based on existing reporting and the anecdotes discussed above, many would suspect that those leaders who are categorized as both "right" and "nationalist," what will be referred to as "hyper nationalist," would be more likely to push for and oversee the passage of a restrictive CSO law.[87] This hypothesis naturally presupposes that executive leaders have some level of influence over the legislative process, which varies in accuracy depending on the state and their specific law-making procedures in place. While in most democratic countries,

---

[85] World Bank 2015. According to DPI's website, located at http://econ.worldbank.org/WBSITE/EXTERNAL/EXTDEC/EXTRESEARCH/0,,contentMDK:20649465~pagePK:64214825~piPK:64214943~theSitePK:469382,00.html, nearly "3,000 studies have used this database so far as a source of institutional and political data in their empirical analysis," which gives me confidence in its accuracy. This assurance is important given the vulnerability to bias inherent in labeling a regime's ideology.

[86] For a full discussion of how the list of strong democracies was chosen, see Chapter 5. Most of the appendices also include the full list.

[87] In two cases, I differ with the the the DPI's determination. It does not classify Victor Orban or Donald Trump as a nationalist, which is deeply perplexing. But virtually all accounts, and by Orban's and Trump's explicit rhetoric, they are both nationalists. Many articles, scholarly and in the popular media, confirm both to be true. Orban is a leader that explicitly elevates Hungary's national interests above all else including international alliances. He looks inward, is exclusionary toward migrants, and actively endorses Hungarian nationalism. The same can be said, without reservation, about Donald Trump except with respect to the United States. This is problematic and if there was another database to look to, I would have, but for now, the DPI is all I could find.

the legislative branch is an independent branch of the government, the law-making process itself does not have the same level of independence from the executive. Indeed, executive leaders tend to have some amount, and often a significant amount, of influence over which bills do and do not get adopted into law. In certain countries, such as the United States, executives are essential to the law-making process through their veto power.[88] This empirical reality makes it all the more probable that hyper-nationalist executives could explain the spread of restrictive CSO laws in the world's strongest democratic states. But what does the empirical data actually reveal?

As Figure 3.2 below makes clear, the vast majority of the restrictive CSO laws adopted were passed while a *non*-hyper-nationalist executive was in power. Put another way, most of the restrictive CSO laws adopted in strong democracies were *not* adopted under a hyper-nationalist executive. Only 14% of the laws, 12 out of the 86 restrictive CSO laws collected, were adopted under the watch of a hyper-nationalist leader.

Figure 3.2: No. of Restrictive CSO Laws adopted by Hyper-Nationalist Executive.

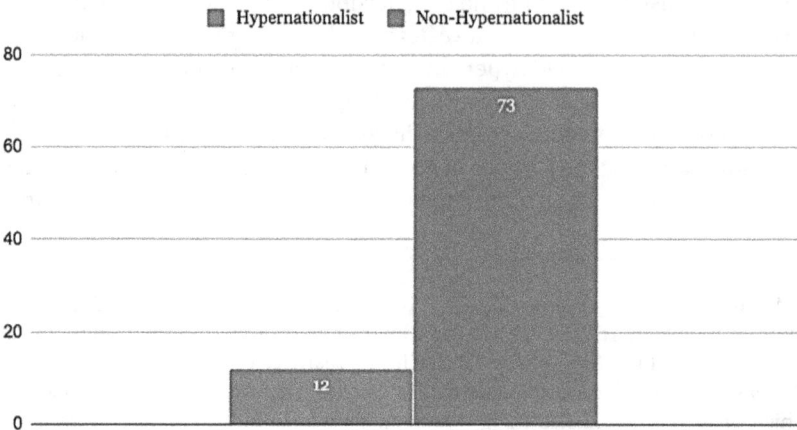

Moreover, the restrictive CSOs laws adopted while a hyper-nationalist executive was in power occurred in only six countries: Belgium, Croatia, Hungary, Macedonia, Panama, and the United States.

This finding debunks one of the more common assumptions inhering in discussions of the associational counter-revolution, particularly discussions surrounding democratic countries' participation in this trend. It is no longer

---

[88] ELLIOT BULMER, PRESIDENTIAL VETO POWER (2nd ed. 2017), available at https://www.idea.int/sites/default/files/publications/presidential-veto-powers-primer.pdf; *How Laws are Made*, U.S. GOV'T, available at https://www.usa.gov/how-laws-are-made.

accurate to claim that the spread of restrictive CSO laws is tied to the election of hyper-nationalist executive leaders. Despite the election of illiberal and hype-nationalist regimes in many democratic states over the past decade and a half, this trend cannot, at least on its own, explain the adoption of restrictive CSO laws. Restrictive CSO laws are not only adopted when far-right, hyper-nationalist regimes, or even conservative or right-leaning regimes, are in power. Quite to the contrary, twenty-six of the restrictive CSO laws identified for this project[89] were adopted under an executive that identifies with the left, and nine others were adopted under a centrist or "left of center" regime, for a combined total of 31% or roughly one-third (again, see Appendix 1 for coding results).[90] While a majority of the laws – 49 to be exact, close to 60%– were adopted while a right-leaning executive was in power, 40% were adopted by regimes that cannot be classified as on the political "right," thereby challenging one of the most common assumptions underlying analysis of the closing space trend. In short, the adoption of restrictive CSO laws, while a bit more typical of right-leaning governments, is a bipartisan legal phenomenon. Such laws are adopted under the watch of nationalistic and non-nationalistic leaders, as well as left-leaning, right-leaning, and centrist leaders.[91]

PARTISAN AFFILIATION OF THE DOMINANT PARTY IN POWER

The question of whether there is a connection between the party affiliation of the dominant party in the legislative branch, the branch primarily responsible for law-making, and the passage of a particular type of law seems almost too obvious to ask. Naturally, the dominant party will push through the laws that they want, and the minority party will have less influence over law-making in general. Yet, when doing a global analysis of laws, particularly when examining the passage of one type of law, one can take a broader view to ascertain whether right-leaning or left-leaning parties are more likely to adopt certain types of laws. Stereotypes and assumptions abound in these types of discussions, yet rarely if ever, are they actually empirically confirmed, as before with executive leaders. Another assumption running throughout much of the closing space literature, which goes hand-in-hand with the assumption assessed in the previous section, is that restrictive CSO laws are pushed forward and passed by

---

[89] These laws are discussed in Chapter 5, and individually listed in Appendix 7.

[90] The left leaning leaders were in: Australia (2013), Austria (2015), Bolivia (2007, 2008, and 2 laws in 2013); Denmark (2017); France (2015, 2016, and two in 2017); Greece (2016); and India (2010). The centrists were in: Croatia (2014, 2015); Ireland (2001, 2009); and Italy (2017).

[91] To view the data compiled for this section, go to: https://docs.google.com/spreadsheets/d/1zA1Nk_lvKFNexze7tVecHrylsvva__f4RDG_N_xX9fg/edit?usp=sharing.

right-leaning legislatures who are less favorable to an independent civil society. Yet, as before, this claim is often made but rarely verified.

Once again, using the Database of Political Institutions published by the World Bank, each legislature was coded based on the dominant party in power when a restrictive CSO law was adopted. Legislatures responsible for passing such laws were coded as either "left," "right," or "centrist" (see Appendix 2). Similar to the findings presented above pertaining to executive leaders, restrictive CSO laws are adopted by both left *and* right-leaning legislatures alike, though not in equal numbers. As before, legislatures dominated by those on the right are more likely than legislatures dominated by the left to pass such laws: 50 of the restrictive CSO laws (or 58%) were adopted by right-leaning parliaments, 28, or one-third of the laws were adopted by a left-leaning lawmaking body. Another eight laws (or 9%) were adopted by lawmaking bodies dominated by a centrist party. Combined, over 40% of the restrictive CSO laws were adopted by a left or centrist legislative branch, once again defying expectations and conventional thinking on the topic (see Figure 3.3).

Figure 3.3: % of Restrictive CSO Laws adopted by Dominant Party.

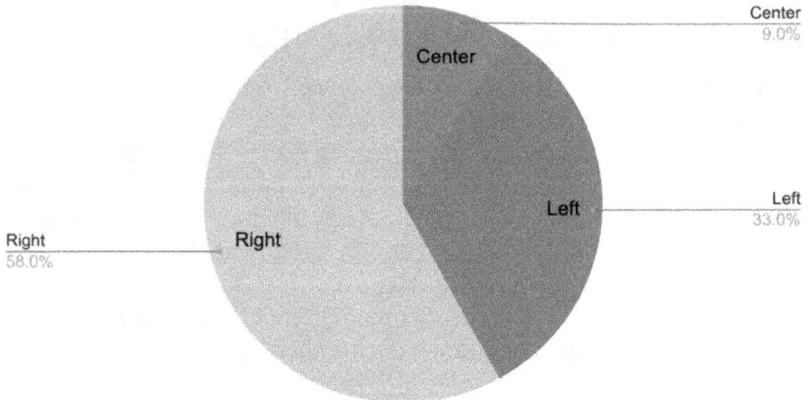

Moreover, only 15 of the 86 laws adopted, or 17%, were adopted by what could be characterized as "hyper-nationalist" congresses, similar to the figure associated with hyper-nationalist executives (see Figure 3.4). Once again, the associational counter-revolution, and specifically its spread into the world's strongest democratic states, cannot be said to be a trend only furthered by the far-right or the so-called 'hyper-nationalists' of the world. Indeed, all sides of the political spectrum, including the middle, have participated in its spread.[92]

---

[92] To view the data I compiled for this section, go to: https://docs.google.com/spreadsheets/d/15JPwFsHEMSuoGr4OHbm4gfe0-iFQp6_N-x_XoyY65h0/edit?usp=sharing.

Figure 3.4: No. of Restrictive CSO Laws Adopted by a Hyper-nationalist Legislative Branch.

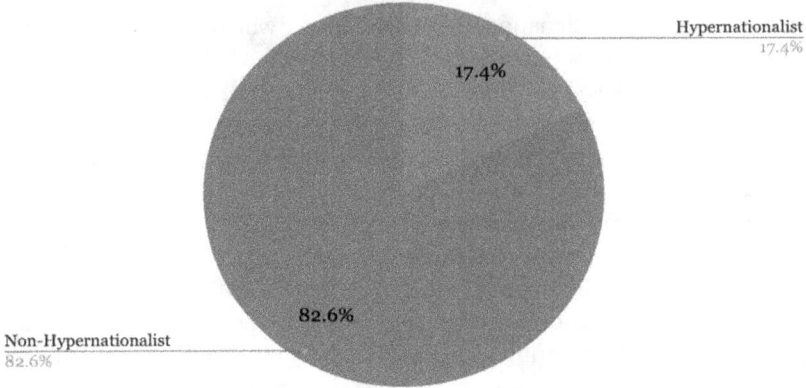

FEAR OF DOMESTIC UPRISINGS / PROTEST

Another explanation often posited for the closing space phenomenon points to a series of revolutions and large-scale protest movements that swept parts of the globe beginning in the early part of the twenty-first century, including the "color revolutions" in Eastern Europe in 2003–2005 and later, the Arab Spring uprisings of 2010–2012.[93] In most cases, these uprisings resulted in the overthrow or replacement of an existing incumbent, oftentimes a long-standing incumbent who had been in power for decades.[94] In the aftermath of both series of revolutions, there was, in fact, a significant uptick in the number of restrictive CSO laws adopted around the globe and, in many cases, a fear of similar revolutions occurring within a country's borders was openly voiced as a justification for those laws' passage.[95] According to civil society expert Thomas Carothers, a "backlash" against international NGOs and foreign funding for local groups began in earnest following the "color revolutions" in Georgia, Ukraine, and Kyrgyzstan.[96] Carothers, puzzled by the sudden uptick in restrictive CSO legislation in the aftermath of these uprisings, asked, "[a]re [these governments] generally afraid that relatively modest Western democracy-training programs and financial aid for often weak civic and political groups will

---

[93] Rutzen 2015; Schuman 2017.
[94] Koesel & Bunce 2013.
[95] Rutzen 2015.
[96] Carothers 2006.

undermine their hold on power, or is this fear just a convenient justification for repressive measures they would take anyway?"[97]

According to this explanation, these revolutions, which in many cases were organized, led and/or supported by CSOs, revealed the full extent of the power and influence achieved by civil society, particularly those backed by foreign support.[98] Incumbents, fearful of the ability of foreigners to manipulate domestic politics via foreign-funded CSOs, and specifically to inspire, fund, and push them to rise up in protest, began cracking down on the latter's ability to operate and, notably, receive foreign support.[99] Advocates of this explanation can point to two powerful empirical facts: in the six years following the color revolutions, between 2004 and 2010, more than fifty countries around the world enacted or considered measures restricting civil society; and in the aftermath of the Arab Spring uprisings, between 2012 and 2015, more than ninety such laws were proposed or enacted.[100]

Existing research on protest activity and state-civil society relations suggests that states are not irrational in fearing the potential of CSOs to catalyze domestic unrest.[101] Recent scholarship suggests that the presence and density of NGOs both within a state and in the geographic neighborhood of a state are linked to increases in the occurrence of domestic non-violent, anti-government protest movements, while the presence of international human rights organizations in a country increases the level of *both* non-violent and violent protests within that state.[102] Interestingly, this body of research also finds that the presence of human rights organizations in neighboring states can increase the level of non-violent protest activity within another state.[103] Some IR scholars have suggested that we now live in an "age of rage," in which protest movements have become more numerous and geographically widespread than in the past.[104] Existing data points to a spike in global protest activity in the 2011–2012 period, followed by a lull, and then a renewed intensification in 2015–2016. According to political scientist and protest expert Richard Youngs:

> While much debate among [IR] experts has focused on the shift in power away from the West to rising economies, equally significant is the

---

[97] *Id.* at 62.

[98] Chaudry 2016.

[99] Rutzen 2015.

[100] *Id.* at 3.

[101] Murdie & Bhasin 2010; Taylor 2002; Schock 2005.

[102] Murdie & Bhasin 2010 at 6.8.

[103] Haines 2006; Murdie & Bhasin 2010.

[104] Youngs 2017.

nascent era of witnessed bouts of protest. Today's wave of protests is relatively unique, however, in effecting all regions of the world, with similar patterns of revolt spanning diverse national and cultural contexts. The ubiquity and frequency of large-scale mobilizations is sufficient to denote a structural shift in how citizens confront power and in how global civil society organizes in pursuing its concerns. [105]

Many of the non-academic reports and policy analyses that have examined the broader closing space phenomenon anecdotally link the passage of restrictive CSO laws to large-scale citizen-led uprisings. Ethiopia, Egypt, Russia, Zimbabwe, Canada, and India, though not all democracies, are just a few of the countries that experienced large-scale protest activity prior to adopting a restrictive CSO law.[106] The theory here is that after witnessing the power of civil society-led protest activity to disrupt the status quo in other countries, states, fearing the potential of civil society to do similar things within their own borders, choose to adopt restrictive CSO laws in order to minimize this possibility. In certain instances, particularly following the color revolutions, a variety of states (such as Russia, China, Iran, Belarus, Kazakhstan, Venezuela, and others) openly voiced their determination to prevent such uprisings from occurring within their borders.[107] But whether these things are actually linked – domestic uprisings and the passage of restrictive CSO laws; and/or high-profile uprisings in other countries and the passage of restrictive CSO laws – has never, to my knowledge, been empirically confirmed, and the anecdotal reports that exist typically cite examples from authoritarian states.

IS PROTEST ACTIVITY LINKED TO PASSAGE OF RESTRICTIVE CSO LAWS?

Unfortunately, unlike with legislative branch party affiliation or executive ideological orientation, there does not appear to be one single data source that tracks and measures global protest activity. However, there are various sources that, when patched together, can provide information regarding the volume of protest activity in the years preceding the passage of any particular restrictive CSO law. The Global Database of Events, Language and Tone (GDELT) is one such source; it tracks protest events, as well as many other events, beginning in 1979.[108] GDELT is a real-time, AI-led and governed database that virtually

---

[105] *Id.*

[106] Human Rights Watch 2013; ICNL 2017; Ram 2014.

[107] Rutzen 2015; Mendelson 2015.

[108] I emailed with Dr. Richard Youngs at the University of Warwick who is an expert on global protest and currently writing a book on the topic. When asked which database he relied on for some of his previous articles on protest, he confirmed that there is "no one

monitors and maps what it claims to be "the world's news media from nearly every corner of every country in print, broadcast, and web formats, in over 100 languages, every moment of every day." Using its data, researchers have created chronologies of global protest activity and intensity and attempted to glean broad global patterns and trends. One such researcher found that between January 1979 and April 2014, GDELT recorded over 2.4 million episodes of protest around the globe, with three key moments of particular protest intensity: 1980, 2006 and 2011.[109] The latter two correspond to the color revolutions and the Arab Spring uprisings, while 1980 corresponds to protests linked to the Iranian Revolution and the resulting oil embargo, which had rippled effects throughout the world. My empirical mapping of the global spread of restrictive CSO laws into the world's strongest democratic states, as presented in Chapter 5, reveals a small spike in the passage of restrictive CSO legislation in 2007 and again in the early 2010s following the color revolutions and the Arab Spring uprisings. However, the largest spike occurred in 2016 and 2017, long after these high-profile protest movements, or rather, long enough after these events to make any solid conclusions about their connection with the passage of restrictive CSO laws in far-away democratic states shaky at best.

GDELT provides a "protest intensity" score, which tracks how prevalent worldwide protest has been month-by-month since 1979. It is calculated by taking the total number of protests each month and dividing it by the total number of all events recorded in GDELT for that month (this corrects, it claims, for the exponential rise in media coverage over the last 30 years and the imperfect nature of computer processing of the news). This data was useful in identifying whether there is any connection between key moments of high protest intensity in the world and passage of restrictive CSO laws, though naturally, this information is only correlative, not causal. To provide more nuanced and fine-textured protest data specific to each country that I reviewed, two other sources were relied upon: first, a report published by the Economist Intelligence Unit in 2015 that examines protest movements from 2009–2014, a much smaller but nevertheless useful timeframe than the one examined in Chapter 5 (1990–2018); and second, the Nonviolent and Violent Campaigns and Outcomes Data Project (NAVCO), based at the University of Denver, which catalogues major nonviolent and violent resistance campaigns

---

single, reliable data source" for protest activity; instead, it must be cobbled together. He steered me toward the GDELT, but noted that it can be difficult to use, and suggested the 2015 report by the Economist Intelligence Unit described below, which is useful in characterizing protest activity but covers only 2009–2014.
[109] Kalev 2014.

around the globe from 1900–2011.[110] While the latter database doesn't cover the full scope of my timeframe either, it usefully catalogues protest activity for a longer time period than the Economist Intelligence Unit report. When pieced together, these two sources cover the majority of the temporal scope that I reviewed and convey useful correlative information about the connection between protest activity and the passage of restrictive CSO laws.

As discussed in Chapter 4, the years of most intense legislative activity with respect to the passage of restrictive CSO laws occurred in 2015, 2016, and 2017, all of which are more than two years outside the parameters of either the Color Revolutions that swept parts of Europe and the Arab Spring uprisings, which swept through much of the Middle East and North Africa. As such, while one cannot conclude with certainty that these large-scale and high-profile protests did not influence the passage of those laws adopted in the years just following them, one can conclude that other explanatory factors must be at work given the distance from these events and the passage of most of the restrictive CSO laws adopted in the world's strongest democratic states. In the two years following the Color Revolutions, I found only two restrictive CSO laws adopted in strong democratic states, while in the two years following the Arab Spring protests, from 2012–2014, I located only sixteen laws. Again, while one cannot eliminate that these global events influenced the passage rate of these eighteen laws, clearly they do not hold much explanatory value given that the vast majority of the restrictive CSO laws adopted in the world's strongest democratic states were adopted years after (or before) either of these large-scale protest events.

Yet, it could nevertheless still be true that protest activity occurring *within* a state's borders prompted a state to propose and then adopt a restrictive CSO law on the belief that restricting the autonomy of the CSO sector would help to reign in their protest capabilities or potential. To determine if there is any truth to this claim, it was critical to examine those democracies that did *not* adopt a restrictive CSO law and to identify whether protest activity had occurred there in addition to examining whether protest activity occurred in those states where at least one restrictive CSO law has been adopted. If protest activity is just as prevalent in democracies that have not adopted a restrictive CSO law, then one cannot conclude with any causal certainty that protest activity is connected to the passage of such laws.

So what does the empirical record reveal using the sources cited above and looking at all countries that qualified as a strong democracy, whether they

---

[110] Their website is available at https://www.du.edu/korbel/sie/research/chenow_navco _data.html.

adopted a restrictive CSO law or not? Basically, the data reveals a muddled picture, with some countries with lots of protest activity adopting a restrictive CSO law and others not; and conversely, with some countries showing low levels of protest activity adopting restrictive CSO laws and others not adopting any such laws. More specifically, of the twenty-four democracies that did *not* adopt a restrictive CSO law between 1990 and 2018,[111] many have experienced repeated large-scale protests, casting doubt on the claim that there is a causal connection between protests and the passage of restrictive CSO laws. Chile is one such example; it has experienced near-constant protest activity, and in many cases, large-scale protest activity every year since 1990, with the exception of 2017. Indeed, the protest data sources reveal it experienced over 145 large protest events in the time frame examined. Cyprus and Ecuador are similar: Cyprus witnessed 120 large-scale protests since 1990, and Ecuador nearly 150.[112] Yet, none of these three countries has adopted a restrictive CSO law.

On the contrary, a variety of democratic states that have adopted at least one restrictive CSO law did so in the complete absence of protest activity or the aftermath of only a very small number of protests. Australia, which has adopted six restrictive CSO laws, as well as Belgium, Canada, and Finland, which have each adopted at least one such law, are all examples that fall into the no or very-low protest activity in the lead up to these laws passage category. That said, those states with the highest number of protests, which include France, Germany, Greece, Kenya, and Thailand, all adopted restrictive CSO laws in the two years following large-scale protests. See Appendix 3 for a full listing of how many protests were recorded for each of the world's strongest democratic states, whether or not they have adopted a restrictive CSO law, using the sources discussed above.

Despite these muddled findings, the overarching finding to emerge from the protest data is clear: one cannot claim with any level of empirical veracity or confidence that protest activity is casually connected to the passage of restrictive CSO laws. In fact, states that experienced large-scale protest activities in the years leading up to the passage of a restrictive CSO law, and those that did not, passed restrictive CSO laws at roughly the same rates.[113]

---

[111] These include: Albania, Cape Verde, Chile, Comoros, Costa Rica, Cyprus, Czech Republic, Ecuador, Estonia, Iceland, Jamaica, Japan, Luxembourg, Madagascar, Mauritius, Mongolia, Netherlands, Portugal, Slovenia, Sweden, Taiwan, and Trinidad and Tobago.

[112] DAVID CLARK & PATRICK REAGAN, MASS MOBILIZATION PROTEST DATA (2016).

[113] To view the data I compiled for this section, go to: https://docs.google.com/spreadsheets/d/1_3O7sw6u7DarLMB4ds0OWHlabwc0pWkBP1mzPcicF00/edit?usp=sharing.

FEAR OF TERRORISM

Many reports suggest that restrictive CSO laws are passed due to rising fear of foreign and/or domestic terrorism. Some specifically point to the September 11th terror attacks in New York as the key moment that inspired the closing space phenomenon to take off.[114] In the wake of the 9/11 attacks, then-President George W. Bush, as well as other world leaders, in fact, made various comments specifically linking CSOs, terrorism, and terrorist financing, which the influential Financial Action Taskforce reinforced with its own declaration that CSOs were particularly vulnerable to money laundering by terrorists.[115] Moreover, in the wake of the 9/11 attacks, the UN Security Council passed at least two resolutions urging, and in some cases requiring, all UN member states to enact strong counterterrorism legislation,[116] which contribute to "a flood of new and revised [counterterrorism] laws" in most nations around the world.[117] Many of these new counterterrorism laws indirectly, and in some cases directly, imposed new restrictions on CSOs, a topic worthy of a book unto itself.[118] Various reports confirm that counterterrorism laws have indeed made it more difficult for CSOs to operate in the years since the September 11th attacks by imposing additional restrictions, reporting obligations, and bureaucratic hurdles.[119]

The timing of the associational counter-revolution, which seems to have emerged in the early 2000s, makes the 9/11 attacks – and concerns regarding global terrorism more generally – a possible catalyst for the closing space phenomenon, and one that applies just as much to democracies as non-democracies, both of which have been impacted by terrorism. Indeed, we know from media reports that states, including democratic states, often cite terrorism as a relevant factor when passing restrictive CSO laws.[120] However, this explanation isn't compelling with respect to the broader array of non-

---

[114] Sherwood 2015; Rutzen 2015.

[115] Bush 2011; Open Society Institute 2015.

[116] These include Security Council Resolution 1373 (2001), which urged countries to implement a number of measures intended to enhance their legal and institutional ability to counter terrorist activities at home, in their regions and around the world; and Security Council Resolution 1624 (2005), calling on states to prevent incitement to commit terrorism. For more information, see the Security Council's Counter-Terrorism Committee's website, available at: https://www.un.org/sc/ctc/about-us/.

[117] Human Rights Watch 2012.

[118] BEN HAYES, THE IMPACT OF INTERNATIONAL COUNTER-TERRORISM ON CIVIL SOCIETY ORGANIZATIONS: UNDERSTANDING THE ROLE OF THE FINANCIAL ACTION TASK FORCE (Analysis 68, Apr. 2017).

[119] Open Society Institute 2015.

[120] Serhan 2017.

counterterrorism-related civil society laws that have been adopted by democratic states specifically, particularly the ones adopted in recent years. Many states, when adopting (non-counterterrorism-related) restrictive CSO laws, do so in a context where terrorism is not a paramount concern, such as Poland and Hungary, and/or where counter-terrorism and criminal laws, which typically include CSOs within their jurisdictional reach, are already securely in place, which includes virtually all states under my purview. Moreover, the phenomenon I am trying to explain – the passage of restrictive CSO laws in the world's strongest democratic states – gained momentum in the past five to ten years, not in the years following the 9/11 attacks, making this explanation increasingly tenuous. Yet, fear of terrorism is cited enough in discussions of the closing space trend to warrant closer examination. Similar to the other explanations evaluated in this chapter, this justification for the passage of restrictive CSO laws is often anecdotally cited but without any empirical verification.

The reason why many commentators frequently point to increasing fears of terrorism when seeking to explain the introduction of restrictive civil society laws is likely linked to the fact that state actors, when lobbying for the adoption of restrictive CSO laws (notably including those having nothing to do with counter-terrorism on their face), often cite terrorism concerns, among other national security-related concerns, in their advocacy campaigns.[121] For example, when Hungary passed a restrictive CSO law in June of 2017, President Orbán announced that the law was designed in part to prevent NGOs from engaging in money laundering by terrorists.[122] Yet, when Orbán made this assertion, Hungary already had counterterrorism and money laundering statutes securely in place, which would encompass any terrorism-related acts performed by CSOs operating within their borders. Moreover, there were no discernible links between CSOs and terrorists or financial irregularities at that time (or since), and there was no attempt made to establish such links.[123] Moreover, Hungary has a very low risk of terrorism and always has; it has not had anything nearing the 9/11 attacks that occurred in New York City or the more recent terrorist attacks in Europe, such as in Paris. Indeed, Hungary was recently categorized as having the "lowest impact of terrorism" by the Global

---

[121] Though a non-democratic example, Egypt provides the quintessential example here. In the name of combating terrorism, President Sisi has engaged in a number of repressive acts, including pushing for the successful adoption of an extremely restrictive CSO law, which has effectively put Egyptian civil society "on life support" (Chick 2017).
[122] Serhan 2017.
[123] Buldioski 2017.

Terrorism Index for the fifth straight year in a row,[124] making it highly questionable whether their spate of recently adopted restrictive CSO laws was truly motivated by terrorism-related concerns. In the most relevant study I could locate, which focused largely on developing states, the authors specifically found that the adoption of one type of restrictive CSO law, foreign funding laws, were not associated with or motivated by the 9/11 attacks, suggesting that at least one category of restrictive CSO legislation, laws that prohibit or limit CSOs' access to foreign funding and support, is motivated by something other than concerns about terrorism.[125]

Does Fear of Terrorism Spur Passage of Restrictive CSO Laws?

To test whether there is, in fact, a connection between the passage of a restrictive CSO law in one of the world's strongest democratic states and terrorist attacks, I relied on the Global Terrorism Database (GTD), which is considered to be the most comprehensive dataset on global terrorism in existence.[126] The GTD, which is based at the University of Maryland's Department of Criminology and Criminal Justice, is an open-source database that includes information on terrorist events from 1970 to 2017. Its data is relatively granular: for each terrorist incident discovered, information is included on the date and location of the incident, the weapons used, the nature of the target, the number of casualties, and, when identifiable, the group or individual responsible.[127] This database allowed me to identify when and if terrorist acts occurred in the world's 59 strongest democratic countries in the two years preceding (and including) the year that a restrictive CSO law was adopted (see Appendix 4).

As with the above explanations, the research here can only reveal a correlative, not a causal connection, between terrorist acts and the passage of restrictive CSO laws. It's important to note that motivation cannot be directly known, only surmised. If a restrictive CSO law is passed in the aftermath of a terrorist incident, unless the legislative history or the law itself indicates a specific motivation for the law, it cannot be said with certainty why a given law was proposed and then adopted. Yet, correlative data is nevertheless useful in illuminating data and trends worthy of additional investigation. Indeed, causal connections usually begin by first establishing correlation; and at times, establishing a connection between two things, even if not causal, is enough to

---

[124] Global Terrorism Index 2017 at 10.

[125] Dupuy & Prakash 2017 at 12.

[126] The Global Terrorism Database is publicly available online at https://www.start.umd.edu/gtd/.

[127] See Overview of the GTD, available at https://www.start.umd.edu/gtd/about/.

56 Chapter 3

prove a point. Establishing a connection between the passage of a restrictive CSO law and an environmental factor is enough, for example, to raise awareness among civil society observers and activists so that they are ready and prepared to act when that particular trigger occurs again.

The first finding to emerge from the data eliminates the argument that the spread of restrictive CSO laws in democratic states was inspired by the September 11th attacks, as various theorists and civil society observers have suggested.[128] As Figure 3.4 below reveals, and as has been stated several times, most of the restrictive CSO laws adopted in the world's strongest democratic states have appeared in the last few years, not following 9/11, which occurred in 2001. In fact, only five such laws could be located.[129]

Figure 3.5: Terrorist Incidents vs. Year of CSO Law Adoption.

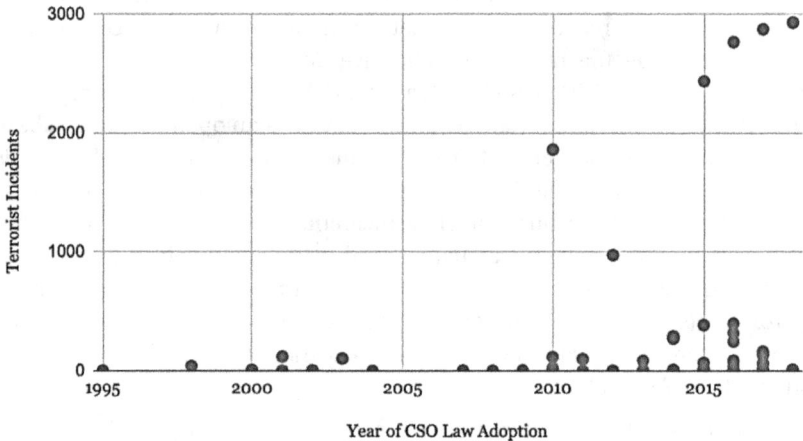

Year of CSO Law Adoption

What is also striking from the data is that with the exception of Cape Verde and Mongolia, for which no data was available, as well as Montenegro and Mauritius, in all of the countries that did *not* pass a restrictive CSO law between 1990–2018, terrorist incidents occurred, and sometimes in extremely high

---

[128] BEN HAYES, THE IMPACT OF INTERNATIONAL COUNTER-TERRORISM ON CIVIL SOCIETY ORGANIZATIONS: UNDERSTANDING THE ROLE OF THE FINANCIAL ACTION TASK FORCE (Analysis 68, Apr. 2017). "In the Name of Security | Counterterrorism Laws Worldwide since September 11." https://www.hrw.org/report/2012/06/29/name-security/counterterrorism-laws-worldwide-september-11; Open Society Institute. 2015. "The Impact of Financial Action Task Force Recommendations on Non-Profit Organizations in Central and Eastern Europe and Central Asia."
[129] These include restrictive CSO laws adopted in Belgium (2002), New Zealand (2002), Peru (2002), and the United States (2001 and 2003). See Appendix 7 for the complete list of laws.

numbers, such as in Chile (548 terrorist attacks), Ecuador (104), and Japan (237).

Terrorism, like protest, seems to be an ever-present global activity, which similarly makes it difficult to draw any firm conclusions about its connection with the associational counter-revolution in democratic states. Yet, some findings nevertheless jump out. For example, in those states that had an extremely high number of terrorist attacks in the temporal scope that was reviewed (1990–2018) – India, Israel, South Africa, and Kenya – all showed particularly high levels of terrorist acts in the years preceding passage of their restrictive CSO laws, and each of these countries adopted more than one restrictive CSO law. Also, the country with the highest number of terrorist attacks in proportion to their population size, Israel, adopted the highest number of restrictive CSO laws, and many of these laws, when passed, were justified on national security grounds.[130] Yet, other countries that adopted multiple restrictive CSO laws, such as Australia, the US, Poland, Hungary, Croatia, and Bolivia, experienced very few terrorist attacks in the years leading up to the passage of their laws.

The basic conclusion that can be drawn from all of these conflicting findings is that one cannot claim that the associational counter-revolution is a result of a nation's fear of terrorism and their attempt to reign in the voluntary, non-governmental sector to prevent manipulation by would-be terrorists. At the very least, other factors are also driving this trend, with terrorism possibly being only one among them.[131]

NEIGHBORHOOD EFFECTS

Finally, many reports also anecdotally link the passage of a restrictive CSO law in one state with the adoption of a similar law in another state, often a nearby state.[132] The associational counter-revolution has been described as a "global contagion,"[133] a "contagion growing in intensity,"[134] and as a global trend with a "contagion effect."[135] It is also described as a trend that spreads through learning or mimicry, with states learning from or mimicking the acts of other

---

[130] LAWS DESIGNED TO SILENCE: THE GLOBAL CRACKDOWN ON CIVIL SOCIETY ORGANIZATIONS 25, 44 (Amnesty International, 2019), available at https://reliefweb.int/sites/reliefweb.int/files/resources/ACT3096472019ENGLISH.PDF.

[131] To view the data that I compiled for this section, go to: https://docs.google.com/spreadsheets/d/1gE9ZdpETJ5GlvVeV80otra6_6vc5hguLvcJKpjUWJjM/edit?usp=sharing.

[132] Carothers & Brechenmacher 2014; CIVICUS 2017b.

[133] Center for Strategic and International Studies 2017.

[134] Mendelson 2015.

[135] Rutzen 2012; Grabel 2013.

states when determining how to regulate their civil society sector. According to one report:

> Governments pursuing pushback [against CSOs] are clearly learning from and copying each other. Rhetoric about the dangers of foreign subversion in the form of civil society assistance migrates quickly across borders. Debates within national legislatures over restricting access to external funding for NGOs, for example, frequently refer to measures passed in other countries. This learning often occurs within regions – such as the former Soviet Union, where Putin's example has resonated widely, and South America, where Chávez's denouncements of U.S. assistance attracted followers. But copycat actions have also spanned regional lines.[136]

Another report similarly writes:

> The phenomenon's acceleration has been facilitated by the fact that governments seeking to inhibit civil society groups have learned from each other, for example by copying and implementing nearly identical restrictive legislative measures, analysts suggest.[137]

References to different diffusion processes at work, whether through learning, copying or contagion, are common in the existing reports on the closing space phenomenon. With the exception of one study that concluded that "there is no empirical evidence that restrictive [CSO] laws are spreading through processes of diffusion,"[138] this claim is often touted and assumed but rarely backed by empirical data.

ARE DEMOCRATIC STATES ADOPTING RESTRICTIVE CSO LAWS BECAUSE OF THEIR NEIGHBORS?

To examine whether neighborhood effects could be playing a role in the adoption of restrictive CSO laws in democratic states, an assessment was performed to determine whether any geographically neighboring states adopted a restrictive CSO law in the two years preceding passage of their own restrictive CSO law. To the extent possible, all "neighbors" were examined for whether they had adopted a restrictive CSO law, irrespective of their political structure (i.e., whether they are classified as a democracy or not). In all cases,

---

[136] Carothers & Brechenmacher 2014.

[137] Tiersky & Renard 2016.

[138] Dupuy et al. 2016 at 306. This study is narrowly focused on foreign funding laws and developing states only. So perhaps diffusion processes could be detected if the inquiry were broadened to include other types of laws and developed democracies?

unless the state was an island (like Australia), an "immediate" neighbor is defined as a state that physically borders the state under review. For Island nations, like Australia, the countries closest in proximity were considered "neighbors" (see Appendix 5 for full results).

With the sole exception of South Africa, every strong democratic state that adopted a restrictive CSO law had at least one neighbor who had already adopted a restrictive CSO law, and in many cases, they had more than one neighbor who had done so. However, this was largely also true among those states that have *not* adopted a restrictive CSO law. Indeed, only three of the 24 democracies that have not adopted a restrictive CSO law (Jamaica, Comoros and Madagascar) did not have a single neighbor that had adopted a restrictive CSO law. The clear finding to emerge from this data-gathering exercise was the ubiquity with which these types of laws have spread, confirming was is often reported on by civil society observers operating on the front lines and the few scholars to have examined this trend. However, what also emerges is the lack of explanatory power attached to this often-made claim, namely that restrictive CSO laws are adopted because of the influence of a neighboring state. Though additional research is needed to fully ascertain whether neighbors have any real influence, the claim that restrictive CSO law adoption can be explained by neighborhood effects cannot be empirically supported, at least with respect to the world's strongest democratic states.[139]

CONCLUSION

Various explanations are often posited for the associational counter-revolution, which, as previously discussed, is generally examined in the context of authoritarian leaning and/or lower-income countries, never democratic ones. Yet, when these explanations are applied to democratic states, they generally do not hold up to empirical scrutiny. To quickly recap the empirical findings presented above:

First, it is often assumed that restrictive CSO laws are adopted only by hyper-nationalist, far-right-leaning executives, such as Orban in Hungary, Bolsonaro in Brazil, or Trump in the United States. In reality, however, only 14% of these laws were adopted under the watch of a "hyper-nationalist" leader. Instead, restrictive CSO laws are adopted while right, left, and center-leaning executives are in power, even if right-leaning governments do so slightly more often than those on the left or in the center.

Second, similar to the above findings, the dominant legislative party in power is also not predictive of whether a restrictive CSO law will be adopted.

---

[139] See Appendix 5 for documentation of neighborhood effects.

Restrictive CSO laws are adopted by both left and right-leaning legislatures alike, though as with the executive, legislatures with right-leaning majorities are more likely than left-leaning legislatures to pass such laws (58% of the time).

Third, the recent spate of restrictive CSO laws in the world's strongest democratic states does not seem to correspond with either the color revolutions of the early 2000s or the Arab Spring protests, which began in 2010. The years of most intensive legislative activity with respect to restrictive CSO laws occurred between 2015 and 2017, not in the immediate aftermath of either of these two trans-national, high-profile protest events. When protest activity within a state's borders is examined, the findings are mixed: many states with large-scale protests did not adopt a restrictive CSO law in the two years following these internal protests, while some did. Moreover, numerous democratic states adopted a restrictive CSO law despite a total absence of domestic protest activity. Yet, a clear finding to emerge from this empirical review is that the globe has experienced a dramatic increase in protest activity in recent years, making it very difficult to make any causal claims about the connection between the passage of CSO laws and protest activities.

Fourth, the belief that the September 11th terrorist attacks set the spread of restrictive CSO laws in motion also does not hold up to empirical scrutiny, at least with respect to democratic states. Very few restrictive laws (only five out of nearly 90) were adopted in democratic states in the years immediately following the 2001 attacks. With respect to other large-scale terrorist attacks, many countries that experienced such attacks (including some that experienced terrorist incidents in extremely high numbers, such as Ecuador, Chile and Japan) have yet to adopt a restrictive CSO law. The only conclusion that can be drawn with certainty with respect to the connection between terrorism and the passage of restrictive civil society laws is that one can no longer rely on the overly simplistic explanation that the closing space trend began in response to the 9/11 terrorist attacks – at least not as it pertains to the world's democracies.

Fifth, excepting only one state (South Africa), every democratic state that adopted a restrictive CSO law had at least one neighbor who had already adopted such a law, and in many cases, that state had more than one neighbor who had done so. Yet, mudding the ability to make any firm conclusions, especially causal conclusions, about neighborhood effects, many states with neighbors that adopted restrictive CSO laws did *not* adopt a restrictive CSO law. Indeed, only Jamaica, Comoros and Madagascar did not have a single neighbor that adopted a restrictive CSO law. As before, further qualitative analysis is necessary to determine the extent to which neighborhood effects and diffusion are playing a role in the global closing space trend.

As the above findings reveal, many of the conventional understandings and assumptions associated with the closing space trend, when applied to democratic states, do not hold up to empirical review. While the explanations reviewed above are perhaps helpful in explaining the passage of individual laws in certain national contexts, they are unable to explain the trend as a whole. For this, a higher-order theory is needed, one that looks to exogenous, international factors, rather than the domestic level, idiosyncratic details associated with the passage of individual laws.

CHAPTER 4:

EXPLAINING THE ASSOCIATIONAL COUNTER-REVOLUTION IN THE WORLD'S STRONGEST DEMOCRATIC STATES

Beginning in the 1990s, an imbalance in the overall global balance of power began to emerge slowly. CSOs grew in numerical, rhetorical, and economic strength, but more importantly, they became savvier in their abilities to disrupt and shape both national and international agendas. By the early 2000s, CSOs were routinely engaging in, or interfering with, activities traditionally left to states alone. This imbalance became more pronounced in the early years of the twenty-first century and reached crisis – or balance-worthy – proportions by 2010. States, fearing that their national sovereignty and primacy within the international system were increasingly threatened by the increased influence of non-state actors, notably including CSOs, began imposing restrictions on their ability to operate independently.

This chapter draws on the balance of power theory, the literature on transnational advocacy networks (TANs) and the "boomerang effect," and the power of framing to explain why so many states, notably including the world's strongest democratic states, have been adopting restrictive CSO laws (as part of a broader campaign to impose restrictions on CSOs) since roughly 2005. At the end of the day, democratic states are states triggered to engage in counterbalancing behaviors when they feel that their national sovereignty or their place of primacy within the international order is under threat. However, given that democratic states tend to be concerned with maintaining their international reputation as upholders of democratic values, they tend to frame CSOs in ways that justify the imposition of restrictive CSO laws – as malicious actors, foreign agents, or extremists intent on undermining the national interests and sovereignty of the state. By framing CSOs as threatening to the state's very existence, the world's strong democracies have narrowed the autonomy of their civil society actors through the legislative process while averting (or attempting to avert) accusations that they are undermining their democratic credentials.

BALANCE OF POWER THEORY

Balance of power theory, as articulated by Kenneth Waltz in his oft-assigned and cited 1979 book *Theory of International Politics*, seems an odd and misplaced theory to apply here.[1] First, the balance of power theory has largely been debunked by more nuanced minded international relations theorists, such as Jack Levy, Helen Milner, Colin Elman, William Wohlforth, and John Vasquez, the latter of whom referred to balance of power theory as a "degenerating research program" with little empirical support or real-life application.[2] By 2004, Waltz himself was devoting much of his professional time and energy to combating the claim that balance of power theory, and realism more generally, are entirely obsolete.[3] Second, the balance of power, perhaps more than any other theory of international relations, is entirely state-centric; indeed, it is uniquely fixated on the world's most militarily and economically powerful nations, the world's hegemons.[4] CSOs, needless to say, are neither states nor hegemons: they do not and cannot harness the economic potential of nations, at least the world's wealthiest nations, nor do they command armies, arsenals of weaponry, or jurisdiction over state-sized pieces of territory. Yet, this seemingly anachronistic theory, which was articulated at a time when it was inconceivable that non-state actors would acquire the levels of influence over states that we see today, nevertheless offers a clarifying prism through which to view the associational counter-revolution.[5]

Waltz, who focused on explaining why "dissimilar units behave in similar ways," rejected the approach taken by many of his colleagues who looked for "unit-level" explanations to explain international phenomena; a practice he

---

[1] KENNETH N. WALTZ, THEORY OF INTERNATIONAL POLITICS (1979) [hereinafter WALTZ 1979].

[2] Helen Milner, *The Assumption of Anarchy in IR: A Critique, in* NEOREALISM AND NEOLIBERALISM 143–69 (David A. Baldwin ed., 1993); Colin Elman, *Horses for Courses: Why Not Neorealist Theories of Foreign Policy?*, 6 SECURITY STUD. 7–53 (1996); William Wohlforth, *The Stability of a Unipolar World*, 24 INT'L SECURITY 5–41 (Summer 1999); Stephen Brooks & William Wohlforth, *Hard Times for Soft Balancing*, 30 INT'L SECURITY 72–108 (Summer 2005); John Vasquez, *Realist Paradigm and Degenerative versus Progressive Research Programs: An Appraisal of Neotraditional Research on Waltz's Balancing Proposition*, 91 AM. POL. SCI. REV. 899–912 (Dec. 1997); REALISM AND THE BALANCING OF POWER (John Vasquez & Colin Elman eds., 2002).

[3] Kenneth N. Waltz, *Structural Realism After the Cold War, in* AMERICAN UNRIVALED: THE FUTURE OF THE BALANCE OF POWER (G. John Ikenberry ed., 2004).

[4] *E.g.*, CHRISTOPHER LAYNE, THE PEACE OF ILLUSIONS: AMERICAN GRAND STRATEGY FROM 1940 TO THE PRESENT (2007).

[5] Barry Buzan & Richard Little, *Waltz and World History: The Paradox of Parsimony*, 23 INT'L REL. (Sept. 2009); WALTZ 1979 at 74.

disparagingly referred to as "reductionism."[6] Similar to Waltz's conclusion, the analysis presented in the previous chapter revealed that unit-level explanations, at least on their own, are unable to explain why over half the world's strongest democratic states have adopted restrictive CSO laws. While these unit-level factors can be useful in explaining the passage of individual laws in individual countries, they are unable to explain the broader trend as a whole. To explain why so many states are engaging in broadly similar behavior, a higher-order international-level theory is needed.

To be sure, one sacrifices precision and nuance when moving to a higher-level theoretical framework, a common criticism of balance of power theory.[7] Yet, such a framework, at least as applied here, brings surprising clarity, and therefore predictability, to an otherwise perplexing global phenomenon. Balance of power theory, which forms the bedrock of classical realist theory and is considered by some to be "one of the most important concepts of international politics," was first articulated long before Waltz's time.[8] It shows up, though not explicitly, in the writings of Thucydides from the 5th century BCE and Machiavelli in the 1480s, and explicitly in David Hume's essay *Of the Balance of Power* from 1742, the latter of which claims that balance of power theory "is founded so much on common sense and obvious reasoning, that it is impossible it could altogether have escaped antiquity."[9] This ancient-turned-modern theory of international relations, which was re-articulated and popularized by Waltz in 1979, predicts that the world's most powerful states will compete for the top spot in the international order, the so-called hegemon. As one state climbs this hierarchical political ladder by amassing more military and financial power, other states with comparable power try to counter or match that state's increased power in an attempt to preempt the rise of a single hegemon. This competition for hegemony continues until a general balance forms among the most powerful states, leading to a generally equal distribution of global power among the world's strongest states.

This theory, which beautifully explained the decades-long Cold War (as well as the various periods of intense competition and warfare throughout history between the leading European powers), rests on four assumptions. First, the international system is anarchical, meaning it has no central governing authority

---

[6] *See* WALTZ 1979, Chapter 3, *Reductionist and Systemic Theories.*

[7] *E.g.*, Helen Milner, *The Assumption of Anarchy in IR: A Critique, in* NEOREALISM AND NEOLIBERALISM 143–69 (David A. Baldwin ed., 1993).

[8] Morten Andersen, *Balance of Power, in* ENCYCLOPEDIA OF DIPLOMACY (Feb. 27, 2018) at 1.

[9] *Id. See also* DAVID HUME, OF THE BALANCE OF POWER: ESSAY VII, available at https://david hume.org/texts/empl2/bp.

to offer protection to individual states. Second, states seek to maintain their national sovereignty. Third, power competition is an ever-present fact of international politics; and fourth, states will continually try to prevent other states from gaining more power.[10] The fundamental goal of balance of power politics is two-fold: first, preventing any one state from becoming a solitary hegemon; and second, maintaining the sovereign independence and primacy of states within the international system.[11]

Most balance of power theorists, as well as the balance of power critics, have focused on the former goal, preventing hegemony.[12] This is understandable given that this theory was formulated (in its modern manifestation) during the Cold War when global leadership was carefully balanced (and competed for) between the United States and the Soviet Union. This bipolar period in modern political history was then succeeded by what is retrospectively referred to as the "unipolar moment," when the United States took the decisive lead in global affairs. This was a period of intense interest in the single hegemon idea, and while it lasted only briefly (just over a decade according to most analysts), it seemed, for that "moment" at least, to debunk balance of power theory, which predicts that unipolarity will never occur.[13] William Wohlforth, for example, writing in the late 1990s and early 2000s at the peak of America's global hegemony, criticized balance of power theory as no longer having any explanatory relevance due to the unipolarity that had come to define the international order.[14] According to critics of the balance of power theory, the

---

[10] WALTZ 1979 at 74.

[11] *Id.*

[12] *E.g.*, Christopher Layne, *Rethinking American Grand Strategy: Hegemony or Balance of Power in the Twenty-First Century*, 15 WORLD POL'Y J. (Summer 1998); ROBERT KEOHANE, AFTER HEGEMONY (1984); G. Ikenberry, *From Hegemony to Balance of Power: The Rise of China and America Grand Strategy in East Asia*, 23 INT'L J. KOREAN UNIFICATION STUD. 41–63 (2014).

[13] *E.g.*, HAL BRANDS, MAKING THE UNIPOLAR MOMENT: FOREIGN POLICY AND THE RISE OF THE POST-COLD WAR ORDER (2016); Amitav Acharya, *From the Unipolar Moment to a Multiplex World,* YALE GLOBAL (July 2014); Charles Krauthammer, *The Unipolar Moment,* WASHINGTON POST, July 20, 1990, available at https://www.washingtonpost.com/archive/opinions/1990/07/20/the-unipolar-moment/62867add-2fe9-493f-a0c9-4bfba1ec23bd/; Keir A. Lieber & Gerard Alexander, *Waiting for Balancing: Why the World Is Not Pushing Back*, 30 INT'L SECURITY 109–39 (Summer 2005).

[14] Stephen Brooks & William Wohlforth, *Hard Times for Soft Balancing*, 30 INT'L SECURITY 72–108 (Summer 2005).

unipolarity that emerged in the 1990s eliminated the need for the balance of power politics, and with it, the veracity of the theory that underlies it.[15]

With the benefit of hindsight, we know now that those critics who condemned balance of power theory to the dustbin of history around the turn of the new century were wrong.[16] The unipolar American "moment" was just that – brief and transitory; just a stepping stone toward another multipolar world order. By the early 2000s, the political science world was all abuzz with talk of "multipolarity," which, like bipolarity, is what balance of power theory predicts.[17] Indeed, one of the core insights of the realist research agenda, which is based in part on the balance of power theory, is that the international order will always devolve back to one of these two default orientations – bipolarity or multipolarity – in order to prevent a unitary hegemon.

BALANCE OF POWER THEORY AND CSOS

It was during the brief unipolar moment in modern IR history that civil society experienced its golden age, as detailed in Chapter 2. And this was not coincidental. The US, already reliant on CSOs to perform much of its development work and distribute much of its development aid, perceived CSOs – after the Cold War ended – as a less controversial way to disseminate its democratic ideals and institutions throughout the globe; especially in developing and post-communist states.[18] CSOs were upheld as a "cornerstone of American foreign policy" and as essential to the promotion of human rights and democracy worldwide.[19] The US, which has always rhetorically

---

[15] William Wohlforth, *The Stability of a Unipolar World,* 24 INT'L SECURITY 5–41 (Summer 1999).
[16] Michael Mastanduno, *Preserving the Unipolar Moment: Realist Theories and U.S. Grand Strategy after the Cold War,* 21 INT'L SECURITY 49–88 (Spring 1997); William Wohlforth, *The Stability of a Unipolar World,* 24 INT'L SECURITY 5–41 (Summer 1999); Stephen G. Brooks & William C. Wohlforth, *American Primacy in Perspective,* 81 FOREIGN AFF. 20–33 (July/Aug. 2002); UNIPOLAR POLITICS: REALISM AND STATE STRATEGIES AFTER THE COLD WAR (Ethan B. Kapstein & Michael Mastanduno eds., 1999); AMERICA UNRIVALED: THE FUTURE OF THE BALANCE OF POWER (G. John Ikenberry ed., 2002).
[17] ROBERT KEOHANE, AFTER HEGEMONY: COOPERATION AND DISCORD IN THE WORLD POLITICAL ECONOMY (2005).
[18] JUDE HOWELL & JENNY PEARCE, *CIVIL SOCIETY AND DEVELOPMENT: A CRITICAL EXPLORATION* (2001); Sada Aksartova, *Why NGOs? How American Donors Embraced Civil Society After the Cold War,* 8 INT'L J. NOT-FOR-PROFIT L. (May 2006) [hereinafter Askartova 2006].
[19] HUMAN RIGHTS: A CORNERSTONE OF US FOREIGN POLICY, US Department of State, December 8, 2005, available at https://2001-2009.state.gov/documents/organization/57932.pdf; "Fact Sheet: Support for Civil Society," the US White House, Office of the Press Secretary, Sept. 23,

condemned colonialism, did not want to appear as a modern-day colonizer forcing its values and institutions on the world, especially in the weaker and fragile states of the world that had already endured centuries of colonialism. As such, CSOs were used as a middleman, becoming the distributors of US aid, the disseminators of American-style democracy, and the builders of American institutions abroad.

Given that the US dominated the international bully pulpit for nearly a decade during the unipolar moment, its ideas and endorsements took hold and spread, eventually being endorsed by other democracies and international organizations as well.[20] One of them was the importance and value of an active and independent civil society. According to one scholar of global civil society, "the end of the Cold War made civil society the central idea of the 1990s."[21]

The unprecedented levels of financial, material, and vocal support transferred to CSOs throughout the 1990s eventually translated into political influence and international ambition. Soon enough, CSOs were not only serving abroad as development aid providers and democracy promoters but as international diplomats, lobbyists, and advocates for their own particular causes and agendas independent of any national government.[22] They began actively lobbying at the United Nations, routinely showing up at high-profile international events and conferences, fully utilizing their participatory rights under international law (such as Article 71 of the UN Charter), independently allying with international organizations, and in general, acting as independent international actors with their own agendas and missions autonomous from any national governments.[23] In effect, the unipolar moment in global politics served to empower and elevate the role of CSOs in ways never seen before or since.

Yet, shortly after the turn of the twenty-first century, the growing independence of CSOs – particularly those that advocated for agendas at odds with those endorsed by the world's most powerful states– was beginning to

---

2013, available at https://obamawhitehouse.archives.gov/the-press-office/2013/09/23/fact-sheet-us-support-civil-society.

[20] UN SYSTEM AND CIVIL SOCIETY: AN INVENTORY AND ANALYSIS OF PRACTICES (Background Paper for the Secretary-General's Panel of Eminent Persons on United Nations Relations with Civil Society, May 2003).

[21] Askartova 2006.

[22] Peter Willets, *The Role of NGOs in Global Governance*, WORLD POL. REV., Sept. 27, 2011.

[23] Chrystie F. Swiney, *The Counter-Associational Revolution: The Rise, Spread and Contagion of Restrictive Civil Society Laws in the World's Strongest Democratic States*, 43 FORDHAM INT'L L.J. 399 (2020).

register with states. The extensive closing space literature has detailed the various ways in which authoritarian and low and middle-income countries started pushing back against CSOs, including through the passage of restrictive civil society laws.[24] However, as Chapter 5 fully documents, this trend has touched states of all types and varieties, including fully democratic states. By 2010, many of the world's states – and over 50% of the world's democracies – were actively trying to contain the growing influence, ambitions and autonomy of their civil society sectors, in a sharp reversal of what was seen in the 1990s and early 2000s.[25]

Balance of power theory can help to make sense of this perplexing phenomenon. As noted above, the balance of power theory advances a second core insight, which is often overshadowed by the preoccupation with hegemony. This insight – that balancing behaviors are also triggered when there is a perceived threat to a state's national sovereignty or place of primacy within the international system – is applicable to the associational counter-revolution.[26] As discussed in Chapter 2, the current international order rests squarely on the concept of state sovereignty, which designates the state as the preeminent actor in global affairs.[27] The global order created after World War II envisions states as the dominant international envoys on the global stage, responsible for international trade, international policy formation, international law-making, and international alliances, organizations, and courts. This world order never envisioned anything more than a passive role for CSOs, as is clear from Article 71 of the UN Charter.[28]

Yet, since the turn of the twenty-first century, CSOs have become actively involved in many (traditionally) state-only organizations and activities, as the

---

[24] *E.g.*, Kendra E. Dupuy et al., *Who Survived? Ethiopia's Regulatory Crackdown on Foreign-Funded NGOs*, 22 Rev. Int'l Pol. Econ. 419–56 (2014); Thomas Carothers & Saskia Brechenmacher, Closing Space: Democracy and Human Rights Support Under Fire (Carnegie Endowment for International, 2014) [hereinafter Carothers & Brechenmacher 2014]; Wolff & Poppe 2015); Carothers & Brechenmacher 2014; Sarah Mendelson, Why Governments Target Civil Society and What Can Be Done in Response: A New Agenda (Center for Strategic and International Studies, 2015).

[25] *E.g.*, Rutzen & Shea 2006.

[26] Waltz 1979.

[27] A cursory review of the UN Charter will reveal the entire fixation on the state as the center of the global order.

[28] Article 71 of the UN Charter allows the UN's Economic and Social Council to "make suitable arrangements for consultation with non-governmental organizations which are concerned with matters within its competence."

previous chapter explored.[29] This has led certain states, especially the world's democratic states, to feel that their national sovereignty and place of primacy in the international order are under threaten. As the balance of power theory predicts, states are now counter-balancing against such threats and attempting to re-establish their dominant and exclusive position within both national and global politics; and one of the ways in which they are doing this is through the passage of restrictive CSO laws. Evidence that states perceive CSOs (especially certain types of CSOs) as threatening to their national sovereignty, and that this perception contributes to their decision to adopt restrictive CSO laws, can be found in the actual words expressed by national leaders around the time that such laws are proposed and adopted. These laws are often described as necessary for the sake of preserving the country's national sovereignty or defending their national interests, while CSOs are described as "foreign agents" or "foreign actors" intent on "meddling" in the country's internal affairs.[30] By framing CSOs and restrictive CSO laws in this way, states are framing CSOs' threats to the state and their sovereignty.

TRANSNATIONAL ADVOCACY NETWORKS

To help make further sense of why states have felt compelled to frame CSOs as threats to national security in need of containment, one can look to two phenomena specific to the rise of CSOs in the late twentieth century. These include the rise of transnational networks (TANs), which refer to large-scale coalitions of CSOs from across the world united by a particular cause or agenda, and the use of a particular strategy by CSOs and their TANs, the so-called "boomerang." The "boomerang strategy" or "boomerang effect" refers to the attempt by a CSO (or coalition of CSOs) based in one country to amplify their influence and to increase pressure on their national government by teaming up with foreign CSOs or TANs. Together, these then raise the profile of their issue

---

[29] *E.g.*, Raffaele Marchetti, *Global Civil Society*, INT'L REL., Dec. 28, 2016; RAFFAELE MARCHETTI, THE ROLE OF CIVIL SOCIETY IN GLOBAL GOVERNANCE (Report on the joint seminar organized by the EUISS, the European Commission/DG Research, and UNU-CRIS, Brussels, Oct. 1 2010); Lisa Jordan, *Civil Society's Role in Global Policy Making*, ALLIANCE, March 2003; Vesselin Popovski, *The Role of Civil Society in Global Governance*, *in* ENGAGING CIVIL SOCIETY: EMERGING TRENDS IN DEMOCRATIC GOVERNANCE 23–43 (Oct. 2013); Mor Mitrani, *Global Civil Society and International Society: Compete or Complete?*, 38 ALTERNATIVES: GLOBAL, LOCAL, POL. 172–88 (May 2013).

[30] Maria Tysiachniouk et al., *Civil Society under the Law "On Foreign Agents": NGO Strategies and Network Transformation*, 70 EUR.-ASIA STUD. 615–37 (2018).

and heighten the pressure on that national government to effectuate whatever change the CSO desires.[31]

An example of this can be found in China, where local environmental organizations have allied with the transnational environmental movement, which is comprised of hundreds of international and foreign-based CSOs, to put pressure on the Chinese government to adopt certain "green" policies.[32] Another example of this can be found in Russia, where local women's rights organizations have joined forces with the transnational women's advocacy movement to put pressure on the Russian government.[33] And a more recent example can be found in the United States, where the domestic based Black Lives Matter movement has joined a broader international advocacy movement focused on social and racial justice, which it hopes will amplify their influence in the US context.[34]

Through the formation of TANs, CSOs can amplify their voices, resources and impact through the simple power of numbers.[35] TANs, as large-scale coalitions of CSOs, united around a shared agenda, come together in order to communicate their joint agendas collectively, share information and resources, and co-strategize on how best to effectuate the desired change. Unlike states, TANs are "lighter on their feet" and "particularly apt for circumstances in which there is a need for efficient, reliable information" and where "there is a need for the exchange of commodities whose value is not easily measured."[36] TANs, as non-state actors, use a variety of non-traditional political tools to effectuate their desired change, including informational persuasion, advocacy campaigns, public shaming, empirical documentation, and publicizing.[37] Though TANs do

---

[31] MARGRET KECK & KATHRYN SIKKINK, ACTIVISTS BEYOND BORDERS 12 (1998); MARGRET KECK & KATHRYN SIKKINK, TRANSNATIONAL ADVOCACY NETWORKS IN INTERNATIONAL AND REGIONAL POLITICS (1999), available at http://courses.washington.edu/pbaf531/KeckSikkink.pdf;

[32] Jie Chen, *Transnational Environmental Movement: Impacts on the Green Civil Society in China*, 19 J. CONTEMP. CHINA 503–23 (2010).

[33] Valerie Sperling et al., *Constructing Global Feminism: Transnational Advocacy Networks and Russian Women's Activism*, 26 GLOBALIZATION & GENDER 1155–86 (Summer 2001).

[34] Andrea Castillo, *How Two Black Women in LA Helped Build Black Lives Matter from Hashtag to Global Movement*, L.A. *Times*, June 21, 2020.

[35] MARGRET KECK & KATHRYN SIKKINK, TRANSNATIONAL ADVOCACY NETWORKS IN INTERNATIONAL AND REGIONAL POLITICS (1999), available at http://courses.washington.edu/pbaf531/Keck Sikkink.pdf [hereinafter KECK & SIKKINK 1999]; MARGRET KECK & KATHRYN SIKKINK, ACTIVISTS BEYOND BORDERS (1998) [hereinafter KECK & SIKKINK 1998].

[36] W. Powell, *Neither Market nor Hierarchy, Network Forms of Organization*, in RESEARCH IN ORGANIZATIONAL BEHAVIOR 12 at 295–96, 303–04.

[37] KECK & SIKKINK 1999 at 95.

not always succeed in accomplishing their goals, when they do, "advocacy networks are among the most important sources of new ideas, norms, and identities in the international system."[38] According to political scientists Margret Keck and Kathryn Sikkink, who studied TANs in the late 1990s:

> At the core of [TAN] activity is the production, exchange, and strategic use of information. This ability may seem inconsequential in the face of the economic, political or military might of other global actors. But by overcoming the deliberate suppression of information that sustains many abuses of power, networks can help reframe international and domestic debates, changing their terms, their sites, and the configuration of participants.[39]

TANs, whose primary goal is to change the behavior of states and international organizations, are threatening to states in multiple ways. They increase access to resources and, relatedly, make international resources available to new or under-resourced actors in domestic struggles. They build new linkages between actors in civil societies across the world, empowering and strengthening their cause, and they raise the profile of their demand or cause, not only domestically but globally as well.[40]

THE BOOMERANG EFFECT

Another popular strategy employed by CSOs to challenge their government's agenda is something known as "the boomerang effect," which involves gaining international allies, such as the support of a TAN, to bring outsized and outside pressure on their own government.[41] Similar to forming into a TAN, the boomerang effect amplifies and inflates a CSO's domestic influence and power of persuasion by gaining international support from foreign actors, typically foreign CSOs.[42] However, studies reveal that this strategy can backfire. Reports

---

[38] KECK & SIKKINK 1998 at x.

[39] *Id.*

[40] *Id.* at 2.

[41] Sonia Cardenas, *The Boomerang Effect*, ERGA OMNES, Sept. 7, 2011.

[42] Frank den Hond & Frank G. A. de Bakker, *Boomerang Politics: How Transnational Stakeholders Impact Multinational Corporations in the Context of Globalization, in* A STAKEHOLDER APPROACH TO CORPORATE SOCIAL RESPONSIBILITY: PRESSURES, CONFLICTS, AND RECONCILIATION 281–298 (Adam Lindgreen et al. eds., 2016); Hagai Katz & Helmut Anheier, *Global Connectedness: The Structure of Transnational NGO Networks, in* GLOBAL CIVIL SOCIETY 2005/2006 240–65 at 247 (Marlies Glasius et al. eds. 2006); Emily McAteer & Simone Pulver, *The Corporate Boomerang: Shareholder Transnational Advocacy Networks Targeting Oil Companies in the Ecuadorian Amazon*, 9 GLOBAL ENVTL. POL. 1–30 (2009).

by Human Rights Watch document how certain states have cracked down on civil society activists in the aftermath of boomerangs, or out of fear that such activists might engage in a boomerang by allying with foreign activists or organizations to put a spotlight on the state's behavior, which the CSO hopes to change.[43] According to a study on transnational environmental networks, which have used the boomerang strategy:

> [W]hile the boomerang effect may help a domestic campaign in the short term, in the long run boomerangs may rebound and harm local NGOs as states frame this strategy as unpatriotic, seditious and contrary to national interests.[44]

The backfiring of boomerangs can be seen in Hong Kong today, where China has been retaliating against activists and organizations that have sought international support for their independence and human rights agenda.[45] Crackdowns have also been seen in places where local environmental CSOs have joined forces with the broader global network of environmental organizations to put pressure on their government to disengage from plans involving natural resource extraction or industrial development projects that would be damaging to the environment, as has been seen in Bolivia, India, Canada, Australia, and elsewhere.[46] When CSOs from Canada allied with foreign CSOs and activists to oppose a planned hydrocarbon pipeline in northern British Columbia, the government, led by Prime Minister Stephen Harper at the time, accused them of being "extremists" and "foreign agents" working to undermine Canada's national interests.[47] In Australia, when local

---

[43] Human Rights Watch, *Russia: Government vs Rights Groups: The Battle Chronicle*, May 22, 2017, https://www.hrw.org/russiagovernmentagainstrightsgroupsbattlechronicle; Human Rights Watch, *China: Events of 2015*, 2016, https://www.hrw.org/world-report/2016/country-chapters/china-and-tibet.

[44] Matejova et. al. 2018 at 3.

[45] Steven Meyers, *China Seeks to Retaliate after Trump Signs Hong Kong Sanctions Bill*, N.Y. TIMES, July 22, 2020.

[46] Jen I. Allan & Jennifer Hadden, *Exploring the Framing Power of NGOs in Global Climate Politics*, 26 ENVTL. POL. 600–20 (2017); Anna Stanley, *Resilient Settler Colonialism: "Responsible Resource Development," "Flow Through" Financing, and the Risk Management of Indigenous Sovereignty in Canada*, A48 ENV'T & PLAN. 2422–42 (2016).

[47] Peter O'Neil, *RCMP Claim of B.C. Anti-Pipeline Extremists Shocks Native, Environmental Leaders*, VANCOUVER SUN, Feb. 26, 2015; Shawn McCarthy, *CRA Audits Charitable Status of Tides Canada Amid Tory Attacks*, GLOBE & MAIL, May 7, 2012; Joe Oliver, *Canada's Elections Are Already Being Infiltrated by Foreign Interests and, Shockingly, It's All Legal*, FIN POST, May 16, 2017.

environmentalists joined up with TANs to oppose the government's plan to invest in the mining sector, the Prime Minister accused those involved of being driven by "a new breed of radical activism" led by "extremists," [48] which must be stopped before they "threaten the livelihoods of fellow Australians."[49] In the UK, environmental groups, including Greenpeace, were similarly labeled as "extremists" and placed on a radicalization watch list alongside neo-Nazi organizations and suspected terrorists.[50] And in the US, climate activist organizations were listed alongside mass murderers and white nationalist groups in an internal watch list maintained by the Department of Homeland Security.[51]

LEAP-FROGGING

Another strategy employed by CSOs to gain leverage over states at the international level is known as "leapfrogging," a term coined by legal scholar Yishai Blank, a scholar of local government law, to describe how cities have gained influence over international agendas and international law independent of their national governments.[52] Prior to Professor Blank's research, legal scholarship only ever focused on two dyads, or relationships: the local-national relationship or the national-international relationship; the local-international connection was never explored. This was in large part because of the way in which the international political and legal order is constructed, which, as previously discussed, designates national governments as the only relevant actors in global politics. However, Professor Blank, writing in the early 2000s, recognized that this no longer held true. He carefully documented the emergence of a third dyad had, the local-international dyad, whereby cities (and their networks) are now acting independently of their national governments to access and shape international politics and law all on their own.[53]

---

[48] LESTER FEDER ET. AL., AUSTRALIAN, UK & US GOVTS. INCREASINGLY CATEGORIZING NONVIOLENT ENVIRONMENTAL & LAND PROTESTORS AS EXTREMISTS & TERRORISTS (Business and Human Rights Resource Center, Jan. 22, 2020).

[49] J. Lester Feder, "Australia's Leader Called for a Crackdown on Environmentalists before Fires Broke Out, Buzz Feed News, Jan. 17, 2020.

[50] Vikram Dodd & Jamie Grierson, *Greenpeace included with neo-Nazis on UK counter-terror list*, THE GUARDIAN, Jan. 17, 2020.

[51] Adam Federman, *Revealed: US listed climate activist group as "extremists" alongside mass killers*, THE GUARDIAN, Jan. 13, 2020.

[52] Yishai Blank, *The City and the World*, 44 COLUM. J. TRANSNAT'L L. 875, 930 (2006).

[53] Yishai Blank, *Localism in the New Global Legal Order*, 47 HARV. INT'L L.J. 263, 266 (2006).

Blank's findings had profound implications for scholars of cities and local government law, leading to the emergence of a whole new body of law referred to as "international local government law."[54] However, while unknown to scholars of international relations and (until very recently) international law, his findings can similarly help to explain how CSOs have penetrated the traditionally states-only arena of international politics.[55] CSOs, like cities and their networks, have formed into strong and large-scale coalitions, or TANs, which are united and energized by a shared agenda. Together, they have learned how to "leapfrog" over their national governments to act as their own representatives in the international arena to advance their own independent ideas and concerns. They have forged independent relationships with international organizations, such as the World Bank, the International Monetary Fund, and the Organization for Economic Cooperation and Development, among others;[56] gained seats on UN committees and decision-making bodies, such as; gained recognition in multilateral agendas such as the Sustainable Development Goals and UN-Habitat;[57] and in general, acted as independent actors representing their specific interests in the halls of international policymaking.[58] Blank's insight that there could be a direct connection between the local and the global, unmediated by the nation-state, was novel at the time he developed this idea. In reality, however, this

---

[54] *E.g.*, Gerald Frug & David Barron, *International Local Government Law*, 38 URB. L.J. 1, 59 (2006); Ileana M. Porras, *The City and International Law: In Pursuit of Sustainable Development*, 36 FORDHAM URB. L.J. 537, 552–63 (2009); Chrystie Swiney & Sheila Foster, *Cities are Rising in Influence and Power on the Global Stage*, CITY LAB, Apr. 15, 2019.

[55] Chrystie Swiney, *The Urbanization of International Law*, 41 MICH. J. INT'L L. 227 (2020) [hereinafter Swiney, *Urbanization of International Law*, 2020].

[56] Barbara K. Woodward, *The Role of International NGOs: An Introduction*, 19 WILLAMETTE J. INT'L L. & DISP. RESOL. 203–31 (2011).

[57] African Civil Society Circle, The Role of Civil Society in Localizing the Sustainability Goals, Policy Brief, Global Public Policy Institute, Mar. 7, 2016, available at https://www.gppi.net/2016/03/07/the-roles-of-civil-society-in-localizing-the-sustainable-development-goals.

[58] Swiney, *Urbanization of International Law*, 2020. Though this article focuses on cities and city networks, the same ways in which cities have gained influence and access in international politics – by (1) forming into large networks; (2) allying with well-connected and well-resourced international organizations; (3) gaining inclusion in UN multilateral agendas; (4) mirroring state-based coalitions and their high-profile events; (5) harnessing the language of international law (especially international human rights and environmental law) to advance agendas at odds with their national counterparts; and (6) adopting resolutions, declarations, and voluntarily self-policed commitments – can be directly mapped onto CSOs. In fact, city networks are, in essence, a type of TAN.

connection was being forged on a much wider and broader scale, among the many CSOs and activist groups also attempting to access and influence the international policy and law-making worlds.

THE POWER OF FRAMING

Whether joining or forming a TAN, utilizing a boomerang, or leapfrogging over a national government to participate autonomously in international relations, CSOs forge connections with other foreign actors, typically other CSOs. By engaging in these three strategies, CSOs have been able to transcend national borders and acquire their own international allies and tools to advance their own agendas, entirely separate from the national governments that host them. While these strategies have been effective at helping them gain the influence they seek in the international and domestic arenas, they have also enabled states to frame CSOs as malevolent actors or "foreign agents" intent on undermining the state's national sovereignty.

Framing is a common tool used by states to stigmatize those they view as opposed or threatening to their interests.[59] According to political scientists Matejova, Parker and Peter (2018), states use framing "as an attempt at political manipulation, creating or inserting themselves into policy debates that shape the way in which the public understands specific issues."[60] Research on the power that framing has over individuals was spearheaded by Nobel Award winner Daniel Kahneman and his colleague Amos Tversky in the 1980s. Through a series of experimental studies, they showed how susceptible individuals are to mental shortcuts, which framing facilitates.[61] Contradicting rational choice theorists and economists who argued that people behave rationally and in predictable ways based on costs and benefits, research on the powerful influence of framing showed how susceptible people are to the ways in which issues are framed, whether "rational" or not.[62]

Political leaders seem to intuitively understand the "powerful effects" of framing.[63] Research shows that leaders use frames strategically to "focus

---

[59] Alex Mintz & Steven B. Redd, *Framing Effects in International Relations*, 135 SYNTHESE 193–213 (May 2003).

[60] Matejova et. al. 2018 at 3.

[61] Daniel Kahneman & Amos Tversky, *Rational Choice and the Framing of Decisions*, 59 J. BUS. 251–78 (Oct. 1986).

[62] Steve Rathje, *The Power of Framing: Its Not What You Say, its How you Say It*, THE GUARDIAN, July 20, 2017, https://www.theguardian.com/science/head-quarters/2017/jul/20/the-power-of-framing-its-not-what-you-say-its-how-you-say-it.

[63] *Id.*

attention" on "specific dimensions" of a particular issue and to highlight connections between issues and particular considerations, "increasing the likelihood that these considerations will be retrieved when thinking about an issue."[64] Psychologists and public opinion scholars have also recognized the power of framing to shape individuals' perceptions of events and actors,[65] especially when the framing is done by a trusted leader or an elite.[66]

By framing certain types of CSOs and TANs as unpatriotic extremists – or as radicals, terrorists, foreign agents, foreign actors, or enemies of the state, as they are variously labelled – government actors characterize CSOs as antagonistic to the interests of the state and the nation's sovereignty as a whole.[67] Such framing is used to justify the adoption of restrictive CSO laws, which are often presented as efforts to defend the state's sovereignty and/or national interests. In addition to garnering support for the passage of new legal restrictions on CSOs, labeling CSOs in these derogatory and stigmatizing ways can help to delegitimize the work of activists whose agendas are at odds with the state, distract law-makers from considering the democracy-promoting purposes of CSOs, and cause the public to distrust CSOs, which can lead to fewer donations and less support.[68]

---

[64] Stanley Feldman, *Answering Questions: The Measurement and Meaning of Public Opinion, in* POLITICAL JUDGEMENT: STRUCTURE AND PROCESS 267–68 (Milton Lodge & Kathleen M. McGraw eds., 1995).

[65] Tversky & Kahneman 1981; GEORGE LAKOFF, DON'T THINK OF AN ELEPHANT!: KNOW YOUR VALUES AND FRAME THE DEBATE (2004).

[66] Dennis Chong & James N. Druckman, *A Theory of Framing and Opinion Ormation in Competitive Elite Environments,* 51 J. COMM. (Feb. 2007); James N. Druckman & Kjersten R. Nelson, *Framing and Deliberation: How Citizens' Conversations Limit Elite Influence,* 47 AM. J. POL. SCI. 729–45, 729 (Oct. 2003) (stating that "the last twenty years of public opinion research demonstrates that citizens base tmany of their opinions on what they hear from elites"); GEORGE LAKOFF, DON'T THINK OF AN ELEPHANT!: KNOW YOUR VALUES AND FRAME THE DEBATE (2004).

[67] Miriam Matejova et al., *The Politics of Repressing Environmentalists as Agents of Foreign Influence,* 72 AUST. J. INT'L AFF. 145–62 (2018); Maria Tysiachniouk et al., *Civil Society under the Law "On Foreign Agents": NGO Strategies and Network Transformation,* 70 EUR.-ASIA STUD. 615–37 (2018).

[68] Press Release, Amnesty International, Hungary: Plan to Brand NGOs has Some Echoes of Russia's Foreign Agents Law, Apr. 7, 2017; Gerald Steinberg, *The Issues Behind Israel's NGO Law,* LAWFARE, Jan. 6, 2016.

CASE STUDIES

In order to exemplify how the balance of power theory, in conjunction with transnational advocacy networks, boomerangs, leap-frogging, and framing, can be used to explain why so many of the world's strongest democratic states have adopted laws narrowing the scope of autonomy for those CSOs operating within their borders, three case studies are presented below. Through case studies on Bolivia, India and Poland, each of which has adopted multiple restrictive CSO laws, we can closely examine why and how individual states have adopted legal restrictions on their civil society sectors in recent years.

The case study methodology, which is well known among political scientists and legal scholars, is used to illustrate the broader trends and patterns identified through meticulous empirical work.[69] The case study approach is appropriate in the context of synergistic research, or research that relies on insights, methods and scholarship drawn from different fields. Given that the research contained in this book relies on legal tools, methods, and scholarship, as well as those of political science and international relations specifically, case studies are useful in more concretely illustrating and synergizing the insights drawn from both.[70]

CASE STUDY #1: BOLIVIA

If the commonly held assumptions posited for why the closing space trend is sweeping the globe were true – an increase in hyper-nationalist executive leaders, the rise of far-right leaning legislatures, an increase in protest activity, fear of terrorism, or neighborhood effects – then Bolivia would be a most unlikely case for participating in this trend. Indeed, when their four restrictive CSO laws were adopted between 2007 and 2013, a far-left, populist leader who endorsed socialism and indigenous rights was in power (Evo Morales), the parliament was dominated by members of the far-left Movement for Socialism party (the party of Evo Morales), and there were very few incidents of protest (less than 10 in the two years preceding passage of each of the restrictive CSO laws, one of the lowest figures among the cases reviewed) or of terrorism (4 or less, also one of the lowest among the cases reviewed) in the years preceding passage of their restrictive CSO laws. While Peru, one of its neighbors, passed a

---

[69] *E.g.*, Sarah Bush, *International Politics and the Spread of Quotas for Women in Legislatures*, 65 INT'L ORG. 103–37, at 126 (2011).

[70] *E.g.*, SARAH MENDELSON, WHY GOVERNMENTS TARGET CIVIL SOCIETY AND WHAT CAN BE DONE IN RESPONSE: A NEW AGENDA (Center for Strategic and International Studies, 2015) at 7; Stephen Chaudoin et al., *International Systems and Domestic Politics: Linking Complex Interactions with Empirical Models in International Relations*, 69 INT'L ORG. 286 (2015).

restrictive CSO law in 2002, this law (the Law on the Creation of the Peruvian Agency for International Cooperation) is entirely dissimilar from any of the four laws adopted in Bolivia, so it's hard to conclude that the Bolivian laws were inspired by the earlier Peruvian one. Moreover, as the previous chapter revealed, given that virtually all the states reviewed, whether they adopted a restrictive CSO law or not, are bordered by a neighboring state that had previously adopted a restrictive CSO law, it is difficult to draw any conclusions, or make any causal claims, about the influence of neighborhood effects on the adoption of restrictive CSO laws in Bolivia.

President Morales' election was part of the "pink tide" that saw the rise of left-leaning leaders elected into the highest positions of power in countries throughout Latin America in the early 2000s, a trend that, in recent years, has sharply reversed course.[71] Morales, the first indigenous leader of Bolivia, was elected on a far-left platform that promoted the rights of the vulnerable and marginalized, specifically including the indigenous communities, as well as poverty reduction, the nationalization of natural resources, and increased taxes on the wealthy. Morales rose to power in the 1990s after founding and heading the *Movimiento al Socialismo,* or the Movement Toward Socialism; a movement focused on defending the rights of rural farmers, peasants and the indigenous throughout Bolivia. Morales' election to the highest office in the country was widely celebrated by the marginalized and left-leaning communities of Bolivia, hopeful that he would restore a sense of equality, justice, and progressivism to their lives.[72]

Shortly after Morales was elected, a constitutional referendum was held, and a new constitution, infused with leftist values, was adopted. Environmentalists, the indigenous, human rights advocates, and activists who rejected privatization and free-market economic policies all rallied around Morales, hopeful of the progressive changes to come. However, tensions soon emerged once Morales revealed his development plan for the country, which included massive infrastructure and construction projects that would impose severe environmental and social costs on the same communities that elected him. One project, in particular, a proposed 182-mile highway that would have cut directly through the Amazon rainforest, which encompasses indigenous territory located within a protected national park, was particularly offensive to the communities that lived there, as well as to environmental and human rights activists and CSOs operating in Bolivia. Those living in the affected territories

---

[71] Nick Caistor, *Latin America: The Pink Tide Turns,* BBC, Dec. 11, 2015.
[72] Alexandra Ellerbeck, *Red Tape or Repression: NGOs Fight for a Place in the New Bolivia they helped Evo Morales Create,* May 22, 2015 [hereinafter Ellerbeck 2015].

(known as the *Territorio Indigena y Parque Nacional Isiboro-Secure*) joined forces with various environmental CSOs to stop the project from moving forward. As time went on, more and more CSOs joined the cause, including international and foreign-based CSOs, who together formed a TAN, which mounted a massive opposition campaign against Morales' development agenda.[73] Using the boomerang strategy to put pressure on the Morales government and leapfrogging over the national government to reach out to foreign supporters to gain allies, this transnational advocacy campaign was ultimately successful, leading Morales to cancel the project entirely and declare the area an "untouchable" zone.[74]

However, this campaign triggered a major backlash by the Morales administration, which used a variety of tactics, including the law, to smear and diminish the specific CSOs involved, as well as civil society activists more generally. Individual CSOs were publicly named and shamed, and in some cases, forcibly shut down or expelled from the country; foreign CSOs were especially targeted. For example, IBIS Dinamarca, a Danish environmental CSO that had provided resources and support to the Confederation of Indigenous Peoples of Bolivia (CIDOB), a consortium of CSOs focused on indigenous rights based in Bolivia, for many years, was banned from entering the country in December 2013.[75] IBIS was given a 48-hour warning to leave the country after working in Bolivia on environmental justice issues since the 1960s. According to a report by Amnesty International, the Bolivia government accused IBIS of meddling in the state's internal affairs and sowing divisions among the Bolivian people.[76] According to the Minister of the Presidency:

> [IBIS] is doing political work against the government. We are tired of tolerating IBIS's political interference in Bolivia, we are tired of tolerating IBIS's promotion of internal conflict among the indigenous organizations themselves ... Just as IBIS is leaving today, other non-

---

[73] Nicole Fabricant, *Performing Indigeneity in Bolivia: The Struggle Over the TIPNIS*, in INDIGENOUS LIFE PROJECTS AND EXTRACTIVISM: ETHNOGRAPHIES FROM SOUTH AMERICA (Cecilie Vindal Odegaard & Javiera Rivera Andia eds., 2019) [hereinafter Fabricant 2019]; Carmelo Ruiz, *Bolivian Vice President García Linera vs NGOs: A Look at the Debate*, UPSIDE DOWN WORLD, Aug. 31, 2015 [hereinafter Ruiz 2015].

[74] Emily Achtenberg & Rebel Currents, *Why is Evo Morales Reviving Bolivia's Controversial TIPNIS Road?*, NACLA, Aug. 21, 2017.

[75] Amnesty International, *Amnesty International Report 2014/15 – Bolivia*, Feb. 25, 2015, https://www.refworld.org/docid/54f07e14c.html [accessed Aug. 12, 2020].

[76] *Id.*

governmental organizations that have distorted their mission with [local Bolivia organizations] are going to go too.[77]

The Bolivian Forum on the Environment and Development, the League of Environmental Defense, and the Center for Legal Studies and Investigation, all environmental CSOs, which were part of the broader transnational environmental network operating in Bolivia, were similarly accused by high-level officials in the Morales administration of being "enemies"[78] of the state intent on "destabilizing the government," working as "foreign agents," and "meddling" in the government's internal affairs.[79] Those who had received any support from the US Agency for International Development (USAID) were accused of being manipulated by the US Government, and therefore untrustworthy "enemies" of the state.[80] A spokesperson for one of the targeted CSOs (the League of Environmental Defense) described their stigmatization by the Bolivian government in this way:

> We find ourselves essentially gagged and handcuffed when it comes to replying [to], criticizing, or arguing about the government's development policies, which are currently out of control.[81]

The rise of the CSO-led movement to stop the highway project triggered a broader anti-CSO agenda spearheaded by the Morales administration, which focused heavily on environmental and human rights CSOs, especially those with international connections or affiliations. For example, the Center for the Study of Labor and Agrarian Development (CEDLA), the Bolivian Center for Documentation and Information (CEDIB), and the *Tierra* and *Milenio* Foundations, each of which was a well-respected CSO with long histories in the Bolivian context, were accused of "lying and political meddling," being "foreign agents," and promoting a "transnational imperial policy" in an effort to advance the interests of foreign governments and corporations.[82] While at first denying any intention to forcibly shut down any domestic CSOs, the Morales

---

[77] *Bolivia Expels Danish NGO IBIS for Meddling,* GULF TIMES, Dec. 20, 2013, https://www.gulf-times.com/story/375245/Bolivia-expels-Danish-NGO-IBIS-for-meddling.

[78] Fabricant 2019.

[79] Frederico Fuentes, *Bolivia Crisis Deepens Over Disputed Highway,* NGO WATCH, Sept. 11, 2011.

[80] Emily Achtenberg, *Bolivia: Indigenous Groups to March Against TIPNIS Highway,* NACLA, Aug. 12, 2011.

[81] Ellerbeck 2015.

[82] E. Achtenberg & R. Currents, *What's Behind the Bolivian Government's Attack on NGOs?,* NACLA, Sept 3, 2015 [hereinafter Achtenberg & Currents 2015].

administration eventually forced or threatened the closure of many such CSOs, including CEDIB, a Bolivian human rights organization established in 1970 that was openly critical of the government's extractive policies.[83] Despite its long-standing and highly respected place within Bolivian society, CEDIB was similarly framed as a "foreign agent" working to undermine the country's national interests.[84] CEDIB's Director summed up the situation as an all-out attack on many different fundamental rights, with the freedom of association "hit the worst."[85]

While not a CSO, the US Agency for International Development, a US government agency that works closely with and provides significant funding to domestic CSOs all over the world (including in Bolivia), was similarly accused of meddling in the country's internal affairs and forced to leave the country after working there for over half a century.[86] CSOs that had received USAID funding were accused of being manipulated and controlled by the US government, which is sometimes referred to by Bolivian officials as "the Empire."

While the Morales administration used a variety of tactics to impede the ability of CSOs to criticize its development agenda and to constrain the ability to operate autonomously from government control, one of the primary ways it did this was by pushing for the passage of restrictive CSO laws, which were justified as necessary to check their malevolent intent. During Morales' term, four such laws were adopted, including a presidential decree, each of which is described below. Morales was supported in his desire to reign in the independence of CSOs by the legislative branch, which was dominated (at the time each of the four laws was passed) by those on the political left who favored Morales and his development agenda.

The first restrictive CSO law adopted in the Bolivian context was in 2008, two years after Morales came to power. Supreme Regulation No. 29308, or

[83] *Bolivia Expels Danish NGO IBIS for Meddling,* GULF TIMES, Dec. 20, 2013, https://www.gulf-times.com/story/375245/Bolivia-expels-Danish-NGO-IBIS-for-meddling.
[84] David Hill, *Top Bolivian NGO Facing Eviction – Given Just Days to Move Archive,* THE GUARDIAN, Apr. 8, 2017, t https://www.theguardian.com/environment/andes-to-the-amazon/2017/apr/08/top-bolivian-ngo-faces-forced-eviction [hereinafter Hill 2017].
[85] CIVICUS, *Bolivian Government using Law and Force to Cow Civil Society into Silence,* Interview with Marco Antonio Gandarillas, Apr. 5, 2017, available at https://www.civicus.org/index.php/media-resources/news/interviews/2805-bolivian-government-using-law-and-force-to-cow-civil-society-into-silence.
[86] *Bolivian President Evo Morales Expels USAID,* BBC, May 1, 2013, https://www.bbc.com/news/world-latin-america-22371275.

"Regulations for the Mandatory Registry of Public and Private Donations at the Vice Ministry of Public Investment and External Financing (VIPFE)" ("Supreme Regulation"), was adopted on December 11, 2007, and went into effect in January 2008.[87] This regulation imposes significant constraints on the ability of CSOs to accept donations, especially those from foreign sources or multilateral organizations. Under the Supreme Regulation, all donations to CSOs must be registered with VIPFE, a government agency in the executive branch, within thirty days of being donated.[88] If a donation is to be disbursed gradually, the donor must report to VIPFE quarterly until the donation is fully dispersed.[89] Beneficiaries, which include CSOs, are required to report on donations received from multilateral financial organizations, international cooperation agencies, foreign governments, and foreign CSOs. Donations that include "implied political or ideological conditions" are entirely prohibited, as such donations were viewed as a violation of state sovereignty.[90]

Under the 2013 law, *the Law on Legal Entities*,[91] along with a presidential decree, *Decree No. 1597*, issued to regulate this law, all CSOs working in Bolivia, whether foreign or domestic, are required to renew their registration applications, which involves going through a protracted bureaucratic process, revealing all sources of funding, and ensuring that their internal operating statutes 'conform' with the government's national plans and policies.[92] Indeed, a CSO's governing statute must specify the extent to which their activities "take into account the guidelines established in the national plans, the national policies, and the sectorial policies."[93] If a CSO performs any activities different from those specifically listed in its founding statute, its operating permit can be revoked.[94] Revocation, and therefore the dissolution of a CSO, can also occur if

---

[87] Regulations for the Mandatory Registry of Public and Private Donations at the VIPFE, available on ICNL's Digital Legal Library.

[88] Supreme Regulation No. 29308, Art. 2.

[89] *Id.*, Art. 4(c).

[90] ANTONIO PERES VELASCO, THE GLOBAL PHILANTHROPY ENVIRONMENT INDEX: BOLIVIA at 7.

[91] Ley de Otorgación de Personalidades Jurídicas (Law on Legal Entities), Gaceta Oficial, No. 351/2013, signed into law on March 22, 2013, http://www.gacetaoficialdebolivia.gob.bo/ normas/descargarPdf/141719 (accessed July 1, 2015); Reglamento parcial a la Ley de Otorgación de personalidades jurídicas (Regulatory Decree on the Law on Legal Entities), Gaceta Oficial, Decree No. 1597/2013, signed on June 5, 2013, http://www.gacetaoficialdebolivia.gob.bo/ normas/descargarPdf/142134 (accessed July 1, 2015).

[92] Regulatory Decree on the Law on Legal Entities, art. 11(II)(a). *See also Bolivia: Amicus Brief on NGO Regulations*, HUMAN RIGHTS WATCH, Aug. 5, 2015.

[93] Regulatory Decree on the Law on Legal Entities, art. 11(II)(a).

[94] Law on Legal Entities, Art. 14.

it carries out activities that "undermine security or public order," or in cases of "necessity or public interest," all of which are left undefined and therefore vulnerable to government overreach.[95]

The 2013 laws were designed to lessen the autonomy that CSOs have over their own activities and agenda, ensuring that whatever those activities and agendas are, they remain compatible with the priorities and policies of the state. They also established new levels of government control over CSOs by imposing new financial reporting requirements, establishing a more onerous registration renewal process, and requiring CSOs to draft their internal statutes in specific ways. According to an analysis of the 2013 laws by Human Rights Watch:

> Taken together, these provisions give authorities overly broad powers to regulate civil society groups' activities, undermining the right to free association and the ability of human rights defenders to work independently. The presidential decree authorizes officials to dissolve civil society organizations on grounds that invite arbitrary, politically motivated decisions … These vague provisions undermine the right to freedom of association, recognized both in the Constitution and in human rights treaties.[96]

According to journalistic reports published in the aftermath of the 2013 laws' adoption, the new laws created "an atmosphere of fear and self-censorship" among CSOs, as well as a "sense of political vulnerability."[97] Fearful of retaliation by the government, CSOs began to reorient their work toward more apolitical activities and objectives and refrained from any public criticism of government policies.[98]

Another restrictive CSO law passed in 2015, the *Law to make Transparent the Goals and Objectives of the Financial Management of Non-Government Organizations and other Entities that Receive External Resources or Donations*, grants further control and oversight to the government over CSOs' affairs, further diminishing their independence from the state. Under this law, a specially designated minister from the Ministry of Treasure, another executive branch office, is given the authority to oversee all domestic CSO programming and projects that receive foreign funding, which includes projects that have

---

[95] Regulatory Decree on the Law on Legal Entities, art. 19(b).

[96] Human Rights Watch, *Bolivia: Letter to President Evo Morales on Human Rights Legislation*, Dec. 15, 2014, available at https://www.hrw.org/news/2014/12/15/bolivia-letter-president-evo-morales-human-rights-legislation.

[97] Achtenberg & Currents 2015.

[98] Ellerbeck 2015.

received financial assistance from international development agencies or multilateral financial institutions, among others. The Ministry is also tasked with providing work authorizations to those seeking employment within a CSO and certifying where specifically each CSO is permitted to carry out its activities. Without such authorizations and certifications, a CSO cannot sign contracts with public entities, participate in public tenders, open a bank account through the national banking system, request tax exemptions, or receive non-reimbursable external resources.[99] These things constitute significant restraints that most CSOs would find impossible to operate without.

In addition to the stigmatization and "public lynching" campaigns against CSOs by the Morales administration, these laws resulted in an "enormous setback for Bolivian democracy," according to an open letter published by a group of prominent groups of Bolivian leftists who had formerly supported Morales.[100] CSOs, particularly those involved in environmental justice and human rights, were accused of undermining Bolivia's national sovereignty and advancing an imperialist or foreign agenda.[101] The language of national sovereignty was used against those CSOs that threatened to derail President Morales' governing agenda. They were referred to as destabilizing "foreign agents," instigators of coups tainted by "foreign influence," and dangerous anti-nationalists engaged in "eco-imperialism."[102] By harnessing and manipulating the language of national sovereignty and casting certain CSOs as enemies of the state, the Morales administration attempted to undermine the autonomy and independence of the civil society sector, in addition to justifying the passage of restrictive CSO laws.

---

[99] ANTONIO PERES VELASCO, THE GLOBAL PHILANTHROPY ENVIRONMENT INDEX: BOLIVIA at 3.

[100] Open Letter to Vice President García Linera, Aug. 13, 2015, available (in Spanish) at https://rebelion.org/sr-alvaro-garcia-linera-la-critica-intelectual-no-se-combate-a-fuerza-de-censura/.

[101] Achtenberg & Currents 2015 (stating that Morales' Vice President continued to attack the four organizations as "fronts" for geopolitical imperialism, expounding on his thesis … that NGO environmental activism promotes neocolonialism and threatens Bolivian sovereignty."); President Morales has frequently accused activist groups of serving imperialist agenda (stating that "President Morales has frequently accused activist groups of serving imperialist agendas").

[102] Alexandra Ellerbeck & Benjamin Soloway, *Bolivia's Morales Pushes Controversial NIS Highway Forward*, MONGABAY, Aug. 18, 2015.

CASE STUDY #2: INDIA

Like Bolivia, India has adopted four restrictive CSO laws since the turn of the twenty-first century; it has also stigmatized CSOs as "foreign agents," reframed their antagonistic relationship with civil society in national sovereignty terms, and tightened restrictions on CSOs in response to their criticism of government-planned infrastructure projects. Moreover, as in the Bolivian context, many CSOs operating in India have leap-frogged over their national governments to join international movements and networks in an effort to put pressure on the Indian government to adopt or rescind a particular policy (the so-called "Boomerang effect"). Unlike Bolivia, however, three of the four restrictive CSO laws that were adopted by a far right-leaning parliament and Prime Minister. However, the first of the four restrictive CSO laws adopted was under a left-leaning parliament and prime minister, further confirming that the associational counter-revolution is a bi-partisan phenomenon pushed by national leaders from both sides of the political spectrum, despite many claims and assumptions to the contrary.[103]

In fact, the first of the four restrictive CSO laws, which was adopted in 2010 while a left-leaning executive and parliament were in power, is thought to be the most draconian of them all.[104] In its aftermath, India witnessed "an intensifying crackdown on nongovernmental groups," resulting in tens of thousands of CSOs either losing their operating licenses, having their bank accounts frozen, or being forcibly shut down.[105] When Narendra Modi, who is often cited when discussing the closing space trend's spread into India, was elected in 2014, he, in essence, only deepened and furthered a trend that had been set in motion by his left-leaning predecessor.[106]

---

[103] Rohini Mohan, *Narendra Modi's Crackdown on Civil Society in India*, N.Y. TIMES, Jan. 9, 2017 (stating that "illiberal strongmen share a virulent mistrust of civil society. From Vladimir V. Putin's Russia to Recep Tayyip Erdogan's Turkey, illiberal governments regularly use imprisonment, threats and nationalist language to repress nongovernmental organizations. Here in India, Prime Minister Narendra Modi's government is going after their money.")

[104] Sujeet Kumar, *India has been hostile to NGOs for decades, Modi made it worse*, QUARTZ, May 3, 2019 [hereinafter Kumar 2019].

[105] Many articles discuss the crackdown on CSOs following passage of the 2010 FCRA by the government that preceded Modi. *See, e.g.*, Rama Lakshmi, *Activists bristle as India cracks down on foreign funding of NGOs*, WASHINGTON POST, May 19, 2013 (discussing the "intensifying crackdown on nongovernmental groups"); *India Tightens Rules on Foreign Donations to NGOs*, PHILANTHROPY NEWS DIGEST, May 22, 2013.

[106] *Id.*

India, which is home to over three million CSOs, adopted amendments to the 1976 *Foreign Contribution Regulatory Act* (FCRA) in 2010 when the Congress Party, India's leftist party, and then-prime minister Manmohan Singh, a member of the Congress Party, controlled the legislative and executive branches.[107] Under the 2010 amendments, any CSO wishing to receive a foreign donation must first register with the Foreign Contributions Regulations agency, which prohibits CSOs "of a political nature" from accessing any foreign funds whatsoever.[108] CSOs categorized as 'non-political' are similarly prevented from accepting foreign donations if such donations are deemed to be in support of "activities detrimental to the national interest," including matters "connected therewith or incidental" to such activities.[109] Importantly, the Government, on its own determination, gets to decide which CSOs are (and are not) characterized as "political," as well as which activities are "detrimental to the national interest,"[110] and whether the acceptance of a foreign donation is likely "to affect prejudicially ... [the] public interest."[111] Many of the key terms contained within this law– *political nature, national interest, political objectives, public interest, incidental to,* etc. – are left vague or undefined, granting government decision-makers vast discretion in both their definition and designation.[112]

Under the above law, if a CSO wishes to receive foreign funding from a foreign source, no matter whether that source is governmental or private, it must receive specific approval in advance (for a specific amount and from a specifically designated source), and the contribution must then be registered

---

[107] Foreign Contribution (Regulation) Act, No. 42 of 2010, Ministry of Law and Justice, in force from May 11, 2010, available at https://fcraonline.nic.in/home/PDF_Doc/FC-RegulationAct-2010-C.pdf [hereinafter Law No. 42 of 2010].

[108] *Id.*, Chapter II, Section 3(1)(f).

[109] *Id.*, Introduction. *See also* Analysis of International Law, Standards and Principles, Applicable to the Foreign Contributions Regulation Act 2010 and Foreign Contributions Regulation Rules 2011, UN Special Rapporteur on the Rights to Freedom of Peaceful Assembly and of Association, Maina Kiai, UN Human Rights, Office of the High Commissioner, April 20, 2016 [hereinafter Kiai 2016].

[110] *Id.*, Section 5(1).

[111] Law No. 42 of 2010, Section 9(e)(ii).

[112] Kiai 2016, para. 25 (stating that "the FCRA does not provide the necessary precision required for clarity and notice. It lists examples of groups that could be defined as having a 'political nature', but does not provide further definitions or examples for the terms 'political objectives,' 'political activities,' or 'political interests.' This appears to give the government broad discretionary powers that could be applied in an arbitrary and capricious manner.").

with the government.[113] Like the previously described Bolivian law, this process significantly complicates and impedes to the ability of CSOs to obtain funding, especially foreign funding. If permission is sought and granted, a CSO can then receive the foreign donation but only if channeled through a specifically designated and approved Indian bank account.[114] Even then, only CSOs that have been in existence for at least three years and have spent at least one million Indian rupees (approximately USD14,000) on programs and projects with funds *raised in India from Indian sources* are permitted to register to receive a specific foreign contribution.[115] This law shifted significant discretion to the government to determine which CSOs can and cannot receive foreign funding, which for many CSOs operating in India, is essential to their ongoing existence. The ultimate effect of this law has been that only a small percentage of CSOs can legally receive foreign funding, severely truncating the number of CSOs that could otherwise operate in the Indian context and specifically limiting CSOs' ability to join and access the support of TANs.[116]

When Modi came to power in 2014, he continued to actively enforce the new amendments made to the FCRA in addition to pushing for the adoption of new restrictions.[117] Between 2015 and 2018, there was reportedly a 40% decline in foreign funding to CSOs, which for many CSOs meant the end of their organizational existence.[118] Modi repeatedly referred to human rights and environmental CSOs as "anti-national," which carries the malevolent connotation of treasonous in the Indian context.[119] As in Bolivia, in many instances, the government's efforts to restrict CSOs' access to foreign funding emerged in response to transnational non-governmental activism against the government's development agenda, notably including specific infrastructure projects. According to a *New York Times* report, nongovernmental groups in

---

[113] INTERNATIONAL CENTER FOR NOT-FOR-PROFIT LAW, FAQ: INDIA'S FOREIGN CONTRIBUTION REGULATION ACT OF 2010 (Ap. 2018, updated Apr. 2020).

[114] *Id.*

[115] CHARITIES AID FOUNDATION AMERICA, GIVING TO INDIA? FCRA COMPLIANCE AND MORE (2018), available at https://www.cafamerica.org/wp-content/uploads/CAF-America-Giving-to-India.pdf.

[116] *Id.* (stating that "only a small percentage can legally receive foreign funding under India's Foreign Contributions Regulation Act (FCRA).")

[117] *FCRA Licenses of 20,000 NGOs Cancelled,* TIMES OF INDIA, Dec. 27, 2016, available at https://timesofindia.indiatimes.com/india/fcra-licences-of-20000-ngos-cancelled/articleshow/56203438.cms.

[118] Kumar 2019.

[119] Rohini Mohan, *Narendra Modi's Crackdown on Civil Society in India,* N.Y. TIMES, Jan. 9, 2017.

India began to experience trouble and government harassment in 2011–2012 after Prime Minister Singh blamed CSOs from the United States for organizing protests against the Russian-backed project to build India's largest nuclear reactor.[120] In the weeks following these unsubstantiated accusations, the Singh government began restricting the ability of CSOs to access foreign funding, seemingly fearful of the power of this emerging transnational network.[121]

For example, permission to receive foreign donations was revoked from the Indian Social Action Forum (INSAF), a consortium of more than 700 NGOs working throughout India on issues related to indigenous and human rights, after the network expressed their criticism of certain government policies, including its plans to invest in a Russian-backed nuclear power plant.[122] This was a consequential, even existential, decision for the INSAF, which depended at that time on foreign funding for more than 90% of their budget.[123] According to the head of one of the NGOs in the INSAF network:

> The government's action is aimed at curbing our democratic right to dissent and disagree … We dared to challenge the government's new foreign donation rules in the court. We opposed nuclear energy, we campaigned against genetically modified food. We have spoiled the sleep of our prime minister.

A government official who was asked about the decision to revoke INSAF's access to foreign funding responded that when foreign donations are used to criticize Indian policies, "things get complicated, and you never know what the plot is." Instead, he noted, CSOs should use foreign donations only to engage in non-political development work.[124] The Lawyer's Collective, an advocacy group in New Delhi that provides legal assistance to women and other marginalized groups, provides another example. It was similarly prohibited from receiving foreign donations.[125] The revocation of their ability to legally access foreign funding was purported to be in response to their involvement in

---

[120] Rama Lakshmi, *Activists Bristle as India Cracks Down on Foreign Funding of NGOs*, N.Y. TIMES, May 18, 2013 [hereinafter Lakshmi 2013].

[121] *Id.*

[122] *Id.*

[123] *Id.*

[124] *Id.*

[125] *India Tightens Rules of Foreign Donations to NGOs*, PHILANTHROPY NEWS DIGEST, May 22, 2013.

activities that went against the "national interest." [126] These are just two of the many examples that could be cited – by October 2017, reportedly, over 24,000 CSOs had lost their foreign funding licenses in the name of preserving India's national sovereignty or interest.[127] The Lawyers Collective, a group that often represents individuals in cases against the government, the Centre for Promotion of Social Concerns, a human rights organization that often openly criticized government policies, and the Hazards Center, a CSO focused on environmental justice, which would often oppose government development projects, are just three such examples. As in Bolivia, CSOs in India, after leapfrogging over their national counterparts to engage in international alliances and coalitions, and forming into TANs, which then put pressure on the Indian government to adopt or abandon a certain policy proposal, were framed as malevolent actors engaged in undermining India's national interests and sovereignty. This framing was used to push forward, tighten, adopt, and enforce a series of restrictive CSO laws in the Indian context.

CASE STUDY #3: POLAND

With the sole exception of Israel, Poland has adopted the highest number of restrictive CSO laws among the democracies surveyed – six laws in total since 2010, as further discussed in Chapter 5.[128] While one of these laws, *the Law on the National Institute of Freedom*, restricts CSOs' access to foreign funding and is similar to the laws in India and Bolivia discussed above, the other laws pertain more generally to CSOs ability to form, operate, fund themselves, and peacefully assemble. Poland, like Bolivia and India, was classified as a strong democracy during the period under review, 1990 to 2018. While their democracy scores have seen slight declines in recent years, Poland continues to be classified as "free" by Freedom House, the highest label a country can

---

[126] Dezra Shira, *FCRA Compliance in India: 24,000 NGOs Lost their License*, FRONTERA, Oct. 17, 2017.
[127] *Id.*
[128] These include: 2010: Amendments to the Public Benefit and Volunteerism Law [Lifecycle]; 2012: Amendments to the Law on Assemblies [Assembly]; 2016: Anti-Terrorism Law [Counter Terrorism]; 2016: Amendment to the Act on Assemblies [Assembly]; 2017: Bill on Funding for NGOs [Foreign Funding]; 2018: A Bill "on specific solutions related to the organization of sessions of the Conference of the Parties to the United Nations Framework Convention on Climate Change in the Republic of Poland." [Assembly].

receive.[129] Moreover, Poland received the highest score, a 10, by the Polity IV project's Regime Trends Database from 2005 to 2013, when the project ended,[130] and the Economist's Democracy Index has consistently classified Poland as a democracy, albeit a "flawed" one, since 2006.[131]

While four of the six restrictive CSO laws were adopted after President Andrzej Duda, a far-right leaning politician, was elected in 2015, and after the far-right Law and Justice (PiS) party acquired their majority position in Poland's legislature, the first two restrictive laws were adopted by the centrist Civic Platform party and under the watch of centrist President Bronislaw Komorowski (a member of Civic Platform). The restrictions imposed on civil society in Poland in recent years are often automatically blamed on the PiS party and President Duda, which in many cases is a fair representation.[132] However, this fails to take into account that the narrowing of civil society's autonomy in Poland, as in India, began in the years before the far-right party rose to power. Similar to Bolivia and India, actors on both sides of the political divide, not just those on the far right (as is often assumed), have participated in the associational counter-revolution, suggesting that governmental actors of all varieties and partisan affiliations are feeling threatened by the rising influence and transnational tendencies of CSOs.

A law adopted in 2010 (under the centrist president and parliament) involved amending the *Public Benefit and Volunteerism Law of 2003*,[133] a law celebrated by human rights activists when originally adopted as "a long-awaited law that will enable Polish NGOs to develop closer working relationships with the public administration and provide new opportunities for the nonprofit sector to diversify its resource base."[134] It was considered an "NGO sector Constitution," intended to regulate the relationship between the public sector and Poland's

---

[129] Freedom House, Freedom in the World, Poland, 2020 available at https://freedomhouse. org/country/poland/freedom-world/2020. You can access all previous years that scores have been given from this page.

[130] *Polity IV Country Regime Trends, 1946–2013*, available at http://www.systemicpeace.org/polity/polity4x.htm.

[131] THE ECONOMIST INTELLIGENCE UNIT, DEMOCRACY INDEX 2019, A YEAR OF DEMOCRATIC SETBACKS AND POPULAR PROTEST, see Table 3 (at p.19).

[132] *See, e.g., Poland's New Front: A Government's War Against Civil Society*, HUMAN RIGHTS FIRST, Aug. 2017.

[133] Original Law: Law on Public Benefit and Volunteerism, Apr. 24, 2003, available at https://www.legislationline.org/documents/id/4594.

[134] International Center for Not-for-Profit Law, *Poland adopts new law on Public Benefit Activity and Volunteerism*, May 9, 2003.

civil society and ensure that the latter had a robust array of enforceable rights.[135] However, the 2010 amendments incorporated new restrictions into this otherwise progressive CSO law, which made it much harder for CSOs to claim the benefits and rights contained within the law. The new restrictions made it much more onerous, for example, for a CSO to obtain and maintain public benefit status, which bestows various tax benefits. Under the 2010 amendments, a CSO now has to go through a burdensome process to obtain this status by demonstrating how their activities continuously benefited the public for two full years in advance of their application (for public benefit status). They also have to create and fund a specifically designated employee whose job is to monitor and document the CSO's public benefit activities. As such, a CSO wishing to apply for public benefit status can't be a new organization. It must be at least two years old and have enough revenue to continually engage in public benefit activities and hire an employee specifically tasked with tracking such activities. Further, the 2010 amendments restrict public benefit organizations from engaging in any type of commercial activities and severely limit the amount of funding that each CSO can receive from the commercial sector, thereby placing a variety of new obstacles on their ability to access funding, including domestic funding.[136]

   The second law, which was also adopted under a centrist government, was a set of amendments to the *Law on Public Assemblies*, which went into effect in October 2012.[137] These amendments imposed significant new restrictions on the ability of CSOs to organize and hold public demonstrations. The leader of a public demonstration, under the new amendments, now has to receive prior approval by the municipality where the demonstration will take place; to receive such approval, the leader must submit detailed personal information, specific details on the expected protest, and a personal photo.[138] If permission is granted, the municipality then grants the leader a special ID that the leader must carry at all times during the demonstration, which is authorized only for a specific time, place, number of participants, and route.[139] The amendments empower the government to send a representative to oversee the demonstration where more than 500 people are involved and disperse the

---

[135] *Id.*

[136] *Id.*

[137] Amendments to the Law on Assemblies, Oct. 9, 2012, unofficial translation available at https://www.legislationline.org/download/id/4827/file/Law_amending_%20Law%20on%20 assemblies1990_2012_en.pdf.

[138] *Id.*, Art. 3(b)(1).

[139] *Id.*, Art. 1(3).

demonstration under unspecified conditions.[140] Criminal sanctions for violations were also included in the new amendments.[141]

Additional amendments to this law, imposing even tighter restrictions on the ability of CSOs to organize public demonstrations, were adopted roughly four years later, in December 2016, after the PiS party gained control of the Polish Parliament and President Duda was elected. Unlike the earlier amendments, these caught the attention of human rights advocates. Human Rights Watch, for example, referred to the 2016 amendments as "excessive and unwarranted limitations on the right to free assembly," without mentioning the earlier restrictions from 2012.[142] The 2016 amendments followed on the heels of widespread opposition to a proposed abortion bill, which, if adopted, would have criminalized virtually all abortions performed in Poland, including in instances of rape or incest. This bill was strongly supported by the PiS party and the Catholic Church. Human rights and watchdog organizations throughout Poland joined with foreign CSOs and international pro-choice advocates around the globe to launch a massive worldwide mobilization effort to derail the bill.[143] Protests were staged in cities throughout the world, in addition to strikes, letter-writing campaigns, and demonstrations. The enormous response, especially the mass demonstrations held in the streets of cities throughout Poland, the so-called "black protests" (named for the all-black clothing worn by protesters), took the government by surprise (see picture below). According to the Minister of Science and Higher Education, Jarosław Gowin, the protests "caused us [the government] to think and taught us humility."[144] According to one activist who participated in the demonstrations, "[t]he protest was bigger than anyone expected. People were astonished ... Warsaw was swarming with women in black. It was amazing to feel the energy and the anger, the emotional intensity was incredible."[145]

---

[140] *Id.*, Art. 8(1).

[141] *Id.*, Chapter 2a.

[142] Human Rights Watch, *Eroding Checks and Balances: Rule of Law and Human Rights Under Attack in Poland*, Oct. 24, 2017 [hereinafter *Eroding Check and Balances* 2017].

[143] *Polish Government to Back Down on Full Abortion Bill*, DEUTSCHE WELLE, May 10, 2016, available at https://www.dw.com/en/polish-government-to-back-down-on-full-abortion-ban/a-35965442.

[144] Christian Davies, *Poland's Abortion Ban Proposal Near Collapse after Mass Protests*, THE GUARDIAN, Oct. 5, 2016, available at https://www.theguardian.com/world/2016/oct/05/polish-government-performs-u-turn-on-total-abortion-ban.

[145] *Id.*

Figure 4.1: "Poland's Abortion Ban Proposal Near Collapse after Mass Protests".

Picture from: Christian Davies, "Poland's Abortion Ban Proposal Near Collapse after Mass Protests," *the Guardian*, October 5, 2016, available at https://www.theguardian.com/world/2016/oct/05/polish-government-performs-u-turn-on-total-abortion-ban.

These anti-abortion bill demonstrations were backed by international activists and CSOs from around the world as well as the EU.[146] Ultimately, the pressure both domestically and internationally was so intense that the bill was withdrawn.[147] However, in the aftermath of this event, the new restrictive amendments to *the Law on Public Assemblies* were proposed and adopted.[148]

The new amendments created a new category of assembly, so-called "regular" or "cyclical assemblies," which are defined as assemblies devoted to patriotic, religious or historic events occurring on a cyclical basis. This definition essentially ensures that assemblies favorable to the state's agenda are given priority over all other assemblies, including spontaneous assemblies and counter-demonstrations, which can easily be characterized as unpatriotic and wouldn't normally quality as religious, historic, or cyclical. Previously, the law gave priority to the first organizer to file a request, irrespective of the

---

[146] *Black Monday: Polish Women Strike against Abortion Ban*, BBC NEWS, Oct. 3, 2016, available at https://www.bbc.com/news/world-europe-37540139.
[147] *Id.*
[148] *Eroding Check and Balances* 2017.

substantive or recurrent nature of the demonstration. [149] However, under the new law, the government can prohibit one group from protesting or assembling if it interferes with a 'regularly occurring assembly,' most of which are organized by either the state itself or the Church.[150] Hundreds of CSOs appealed to the president to veto the law, arguing that it violated their constitutional and international human right to freedom of assembly.[151] Nevertheless, the law came into force in April 2017.

Another restrictive CSO law was adopted in October of 2017, impacting CSOs' ability to access domestic and foreign funding. *The Law on the National Institute of Freedom* creates a new government agency, the National Center for Civil Society Development, which is overseen by the Prime Minister's office. This new agency is empowered to control and oversee the distribution of all public funding (including public funding from foreign sources) to CSOs, including funds from the European Union and the so-called Norway grants, the largest sources of funding for CSOs operating in Central and Eastern Europe.[152] Prior to this law, public funding allocation determinations for CSOs were made by a diverse array of actors from various executive branch ministries working in close consultation with local governments and CSOs, "a system that facilitated distribution of resources to multiple beneficiaries."[153] However, the new law centralized this critical decision-making process into the hands of an individual appointed by the Prime Minister's office, cutting out all other voices in the funding allocation process. According to the Helsinki Foundation for Human Rights, an international human rights organization headquartered in Warsaw, this law "represented a step backward" for civil society and "created a systemic danger for the operation and independent development of NGOs in Poland."[154] In a statement condemning the passage of this law, the Helsinki Foundation characterized the new law in this way:

---

[149] Front Line Defenders, *Polish Parliament approves restrictive amendments to the Law on Assemblies*, Dec. 6, 2016, available at https://www.frontlinedefenders.org/en/statement-report/polish-parliament-approves-restrictive-amendments-law-assemblies.

[150] *Id.*

[151] Human Rights House Foundation, *Poland must Drop Restrictive Amendments to the Law on Assemblies*, Dec. 1, 2016, available at https://humanrightshouse.org/articles/poland-must-drop-restrictive-amendments-to-law-on-assemblies/.

[152] Melissa Hooper, *Polish Prime Minister Signs Restrictive "Anti-NGO Law"*, HUMAN RIGHTS FIRST, Oct. 16, 2017.

[153] *Eroding Checks and Balances* 2017.

[154] *Poland's Rightwing Government Takes Control of NGO Funding*, AFP, Sept. 15, 2017.

In our opinion, the adoption of the Act on the National Freedom Institute- Centre for the Development of Civil Society will result in a dramatic restriction of civic freedoms, in spite of the Act's title ... Awarding the Institute the sole power to allocate budgetary funds to social projects and organisations means that the control over this part of the public sphere is given to state political authorities rather than the people. This remains in conflict with the constitutional principle of subsidiarity and support for [an] open society.[155]

The final, or most recent, restrictive CSO law to be adopted in Poland during the period reviewed was *the Law on Specific Solutions Related to the Organization of Sessions of the Conference of the Parties to the United Nations Framework Convention on Climate Change in the Republic of Poland*, which was signed into law by President Duda in January 2018.[156] This law was adopted by the PiS-led Polish parliament in the lead-up to the 24th annual Conference of the Parties to the UN Framework Convention on Climate Change (COP24), which was held in Katowice, Poland, at the end of November in 2018. It prohibited all spontaneous demonstrations during the entirety of the UN climate talks and dramatically expanded the surveillance powers of the police and secret service agencies to collect and use the personal data of activists and organizations without their consent and, in general, without the usual privacy safeguards in place.[157] This law effectively outlawed the ability of large-scale human rights defenders and environmentalists, including transnational activist networks, from gathering and protesting during COP24.[158] This law was

---

[155] National Freedom Institute Act: Helsinki Committee in Poland issues statement, the Helsinki Foundation for Human Rights, Oct. 2, 2017.

[156] *The Bill on specific solutions related to the organization of sessions of the Conference of the Parties to the United Nations Framework Convention on Climate Change in the Republic of Poland*, adopted on Jan. 10, 2018, and signed by the President on Jan. 29, 2018 (the original copy of the bill is attached to this letter). See COP24 Digital Protection Advice Bulletin, Front Line Defenders, Nov. 25, 2018, available at https://www.frontlinedefenders.org/en/statement-report/cop24-digital-protection-advice-bulletin.

[157] Joint Statement issued by the Special Rapporteur on the issue of human rights obligations relating to the enjoyment of a safe, clean, healthy and sustainable environment; the Special Rapporteur on the right to privacy; the Special Rapporteur on the promotion and protection of the right to freedom of opinion and expression; the Special Rapporteur on the rights to freedom of peaceful assembly and of association and the Special Rapporteur on the situation of human rights defenders, Apr. 23, 2018, available at https://www.ohchr.org/Documents/Issues/Opinion/Legislation/OL_POL_23.04.18.pdf.

[158] *Environmentalists prevented from attending COP24*, AMNESTY INTERNATIONAL, Dec. 11, 2018, available at https://www.business-humanrights.org/en/poland-civil-society-

justified, as with all the other laws discussed, as necessary to eliminate the "threat to [Poland's] national sovereignty" posed by such activism.[159] As before, CSOs were publicly accused of threatening the state's interests and independence, and accordingly, framed as antagonistic and malicious actors in need of restraint and increased oversight. As in Bolivia and India, this law had a chilling effect on CSO-led activism both before and during COP24. According to Amnesty International, this law placed "undue pressure on activists and human rights defenders" and had a "chilling effect" on potential participants. Many activists from the Global South required travel visas to attend, electing not to participate at all.[160]

The restrictive CSO laws adopted in Poland, as in India and Bolivia, were not adopted in isolation but were part of a broader campaign to weaken TANs, lessen or eliminate the sting of the boomerang effect, and prevent CSOs from leap-frogging over the state to gain international allies in support of their cause. In Poland, this campaign has been particularly intense and sweeping, coupled as it was with an effort to weaken the independence of both the judiciary, including the Supreme Court, and the media.[161] Though it goes beyond the scope of this book, it is worth noting that the passage of restrictive CSO laws is often embedded within a broader campaign to undermine other key democratic institutions, such as the media and the judiciary, as has been seen in recent years in Hungary, Poland and elsewhere.

CONCLUSION

Bolivia, India, and Poland exemplify how democratic states have come to view CSOs as threats to their national sovereignty over the course of the twenty-first century. Similar framing of CSOs as antagonistic to the state's sovereignty and national interests has appeared in many other democratic states as well: in

---

raises-concerns-around-restrictions-on-protests-as-cop-24-climate-negotiations-kick-off#c180531.

[159] *Id.*

[160] Kate Wheeling, *Over a dozen climate activists denied entry to Poland amid crackdown*, PACIFIC STANDARD, Dec. 8, 2018, available at https://psmag.com/environment/climate-activists-denied-entry-to-poland-for-cop24.

[161] Cas Mudde, *Poland's rightwing populist win should be a wake-up call for democrats worldwide*, THE GUARDIAN, Oct. 21, 2019.

Canada,[162] Australia,[163] the United States,[164] the UK,[165] and Kenya,[166] among many others. States make these claims by emphasizing CSO's foreign connections: their receipt of foreign funds, their members in TANs, their use of the boomerangs, and their attempt to leap-frog over their national governments to locate and gain international allies for their cause. This perception and these foreign connections and strategies appear to be driving the world's strongest democratic states to impose additional new restrictions on CSOs' ability to form, operate, access funding, and assemble. The language of national sovereignty has come to define the framing and treatment of CSOs in many democratic states, and restrictive CSO laws are justified as necessary for the sake of preserving and protecting the nation's independence. Language that, in the past, was only employed to describe other state actors is not routinely being used to describe non-state actors, specifically CSOs.[167]

---

[162] Jacqueline Van de Velde, *The Foreign Agent Problem: An International Legal Solution to Domestic Restrictions on NGOs*, 40 CARDOZO L. REV. (2019).

[163] Dennis Shanahan, *Activists "Must Come Clean on Foreign Funds"*, AUSTRALIAN, Oct. 26, 2016.

[164] Adam Federman, *Revealed: US Listed Climate Activist Group as "Extremists" Alongside Mass Killers*, THE GUARDIAN, Jan. 13, 2020.

[165] Vikram Dodd & Jamie Grierson, *Non-Violent Groups on UK Counter-Terror List Threaten Legal Action*, THE GUARDIAN, Jan. 22, 2020.

[166] *"They Just Want to Silence Us": Abuses against Environmental Activists at Kenya's Coast Region*, HUMAN RIGHTS WATCH, Dec. 17, 2018, available at https://www.hrw.org/report/2018/12/17/they-just-want-silence-us/abuses-against-environmental-activists-kenyas-coast#.

[167] Miriam Matejova et al., *The Politics of Repressing Environmentalists as Agents of Foreign Influence*, 72 AUST. J. INT'L AFF. 145–62, 146 (2018) [hereinafter Matejova et al. 2018].

CHAPTER 5:

MAPPING THE SPREAD OF RESTRICTIVE CSO LAWS IN THE WORLD'S STRONGEST DEMOCRATIC STATES

Human rights organisations and campaign groups are facing their biggest crackdown in a generation as a wave of countries pass restrictive laws and curtail activity … This global wave of restrictions has a rapidity and breadth to its spread we've not seen before, that arguably represents a seismic shift and closing down of human rights space not seen in a generation.[1]

This chapter maps and documents the spread of restrictive CSO laws in the world's strongest democratic states for a nearly thirty-year period, from 1990 to 2018. It documents how many such laws have appeared, what types, and the intensity with which each democratic state has participated in this trend. And finally, this chapter fills a gap in the existing literature, which often suggests but without offering further confirmation or empirical proof, that the closing space trend, or the associational counter-revolution, has spread into democratic states. Before fully exploring the findings, a few key definitions are in order.

KEY DEFINITIONS

STRONG DEMOCRATIC STATE. The research presented below, and in this book, is narrowed to the world's most well-established, historically entrenched, fully consolidated democracies in the world, which are referred to throughout as "strong democratic states." This elite category includes some states that are arguably starting to fall outside the parameters of this definition, such as Hungary and Poland, whose democratic credentials have come into serious question in recent years.[2] The Regime Trends Dataset, which is part of the Polity

---

[1] Harriet Sherwood, "Human Rights Groups Face Global Crackdown 'Not Seen in a Generation,'" *the Guardian*, Aug. 2015.

[2] Note, however, that the Polity V Project, which I depended up for my democracy scores, continues to rate Hungary and Poland as "full" democracies, which means they have received

V project overseen by the Center for Systemic Peace, was used to identify the strongest democracies in the world.[3] This is a highly regarded and often relied upon database, especially among political scientists. Based on Polity's twenty-one point scale, which ranges from −10 to +10, a "democratic" state is one that receives a score of six or higher; a perfect ten corresponds to "full" democracy.[4] The Polity scheme consists of six component measures designed to capture the key qualities that comprise a democratic system of governance, which include the method of executive recruitment (how the executive comes to power), constraints on executive authority, and political competition.[5] Usefully, neither the autonomy of the civil society sector nor respect for the freedom of association are specifically included in Polity's definition of democracy, minimizing the potential for spurious findings. Polity's user manual explicitly states, "we do not include coded data on civil liberties," which includes the freedom to form into associations.[6] One or both typically feature in other democracy measures, such as the one established by Freedom House.[7]

The Polity IV Regime Trends dataset includes all "major, independent states in the global system," defined as states having a population greater than 500,000; this includes 167 nations. For each of these 167 states, an "annual polity" score is given for the years spanning 1800–2017, allowing one to clearly identify whether a particular country was a "strong democracy" in the years leading up to (and following) the adoption of a particular CSO law. The review presented below was confined to the period spanning 1990–2018, which includes the decade known as the associational revolution, or civil society's "golden age," as well as the period generally referred to as the closing space or associational counter-revolution when CSOs were targeted by many states

---

the highest score, a 10. Hungary has received a 10 since 1990, and Poland since 1992. *See* Freedom House, "Freedom in the World 2019," 2019, available at https://freedomhouse.org/report/freedom-world/freedom-world-2019; Monty Marshall, "Polity IV Project: User Manual." Polity IV Project, Center for Systemic Peace, Oct. 24, 2018. http://www.systemicpeace.org/inscr/p4manualv2016.pdf (last accessed July 2019) [hereinafter Marshall 2018].

[3] Polity IV Project, *Regime Trends 2018*, available at http://systemicpeace.org/polity/polity4.htm (last accessed June 6, 2019).

[4] I exclude laws passed by "democratic" states during times of martial law or in the aftermath of coups, such as occurred in Turkey and Thailand in recent years (despite maintaining their democracy status according to Polity).

[5] Marshall 2018.

[6] *Id.* at 14.

[7] Freedom House, *Freedom in the World Report 2018: Methodology*, available at https://freedomhouse.org/report/methodology-freedom-world-2018 (last accessed June 6, 2019).

throughout the world.[8] In order to narrow in on the world's leading democracies, I identified all countries that obtained a score of at least 9 (so either a 9 or a 10, the two highest scores) on Polity's regime trends scale for at least five consecutive years between 1990 and 2018. While Polity labels a country as "democratic" if it obtains a score of six or higher, the goal of this project was to focus on the least likely class of states to participate in a trend that results in the lessening of CSOs' autonomy. This was determined to be not just those states that fulfill the minimum requirements of a democracy (those obtaining a score of 6, 7 or 8), but those that robustly fulfilled all of these requirements (those obtaining a 9 or a 10). I did not, however, isolate this review only to those scores who obtained a perfect 10, as this would have limited the number of cases substantially to only a small handful of states. This list of "strong democratic states" came to fifty-nine countries (see Figure 5.1).

For each of the "strong democratic states," I carefully researched and documented their CSO legal frameworks, collecting all relevant CSO laws (proposed, adopted and withdrawn/rejected) that I was able to locate, including laws that appeared permissive, restrictive and neutral on their face. Locating civil society laws is not a simple or straightforward process as there is no single source that gathers all such laws in one location. The key sources include the International Center for Not-for-Profit Law's Civic Freedom Monitor,[9] as well as their extensive online library,[10] USAID's CSO Sustainability Index,[11] Annual country reports from the US State Department Bureau of

---

[8] Lester Salamon, *The Rise of the Nonprofit Sector*, 73 FOREIGN AFF. 109–22 (1994); Jessica T. Mathews, *Power Shift*, 76 FOREIGN AFF. 50–66 (1997); Rutzen 2015.

[9] The International Center for Not-for-Profit Law's Civic Freedom Monitor is available at http://www.icnl.org/research/monitor/. This database contains detailed reports on 51 countries, which focus on their civil society legal and regulatory framework and, in many cases, includes brief commentary on whether such laws violate human rights norms. Reports are frequently updated.

[10] The International Center for Not-for-Profit Law's Online Library, available at http://www.icnl.org/research/library/ol/. This extensive e-library contains access to the text of many CSO laws, as well as reports pertaining to civil society-related developments in individual countries. It contains 3884 resources from 206 countries and territories in 62 languages.

[11] USAID's CSO Sustainability Index, available at https://www.usaid.gov/europe-eurasia-civil-society. The CSO Sustainability Index assesses progress in the development of nonprofit organizations and CSOs in 29 countries across Central and Eastern Europe and Eurasia. The index reports on the strength and overall viability of civil society organizations in each country it covers, and has a specific section focused on the country's civil society "legal environment." It includes detailed discussion of any new or existing legislation impacting the civil society sector. For a detailed review of their

Democracy, Human Rights and Labor,[12] the World Movement for Democracy's Defending Civil Society Project,[13] Civicus,[14] Human Rights Watch reports,[15] and freedom house country reports.[16] Each of these sources, in different ways and to varying degrees, collect data on CSO-related legislation and/or the status of the freedom of association in each country I reviewed (see Appendix 6 for additional details). Some, such as ICNL, helpfully provide commentary on each law as well. Each of the above sources was scoured for each of the 59 countries under review in an effort to locate all relevant CSO laws, with the hoped-for result that as accurate a picture as possible could be presented below on the CSO legal landscape for each.

---

methodology, go to https://www.usaid.gov/what-we-do/democracy-human-rights-and-governance/cso-sustainability-index-methodology.

[12] Annual country reports from the US State Department Bureau of Democracy, Human Rights and Labor, available at https://www.state.gov/j/drl/rls/hrrpt/humanrightsreport/index.htm#wrapper. Includes reports on nearly 200 countries and territories worldwide, including all member states of the United Nations and any country receiving U.S. foreign assistance. Each report assesses whether the country under review has respected the freedom of association, and typically includes discussion of the adoption of any legislation infringing on certain core human rights which underlie the existence and operations of CSOs, such as the freedom of association, assembly and expression. Reports are published annually.

[13] The World Movement for Democracy's Defending Civil Society Project, available at https://www.movedemocracy.org/. Since 2007, the Defending Civil Society project has assisted activists and CSOs seeking to reform repressive laws targeting civil society. As such, they frequently report on the existence of such laws in their "News & Alerts" page located here: https://www.movedemocracy.org/news. They also provide useful resources in evaluating whether laws are restrictive or in violation of human rights norms in their "Defending Civil Society Toolkit", available here: http://prod.defendingcivilsociety.org/en/index.php/home.

[14] CIVICUS: World Alliance for Citizen Participation, available here https://www.civicus.org/. CIVICUS, an organization dedicated to strengthening civil society around the globe, publishes a variety of reports, including their useful State of Civil Society annual report, which discusses the state of civil society around the globe, with many details from individual countries. They also produce a variety of other resources and publications that provide useful context on the legal and regulatory environments for civil society actors in many countries around the world. Annual reports began in 2010 and can be accessed here: http://www.civicus.org/index.php/media-center/reports-publications/annual-reports.

[15] Human Rights Watch's country reports are available at https://www.hrw.org/ and Human Rights Watch World Reports (https://www.hrw.org/world-report/2017); both include annual updates on country's human rights status, and include discussions of legislation related to the freedom of association.

[16] Freedom house reports are available at https://freedomhouse.org/reports. Freedom house reports annually on each of the world's 193 states, as well as a variety of territories.

RESTRICTIVE CSO LAW. After all relevant CSO laws were located, each law had to be evaluated in order to determine whether it could be characterized as a "restrictive CSO law."

To make this determination, each law was subjected to an analysis under international human rights law, which establishes the principles and parameters pertaining to the permissibility of laws that derogate from the freedom of association. The right for CSOs to form and operate free from government restrictions is rooted in the freedom of association, a fundamental human right enshrined in a variety of international legal instruments, including: Article 20 of the *Universal Declaration of Human Rights,* Article 22 of the ICCPR, Article 24 of *The Arab Charter on Human Rights,* Article 10 of the *African Charter on Human and Peoples' Rights,* Article 16 of the *American Convention on Human Rights,* and Article 11 of the *European Convention on Human rights,* among others.[17] According to the ICCPR, a foundational international human rights treaty ratified by 167 countries around the world:

> Everyone shall have the right to freedom of association with others ... No restrictions may be placed on the exercise of this right other than those which are prescribed by law and which are necessary in a democratic society in the interests of national security or public safety, public order (ordre public), the protection of public health or morals or the protection of the rights and freedoms of others.[18]

According to international human rights law, any legal restrictions on the freedom to associate are presumptively impermissible unless the restriction fulfills three strict conditions, namely that the restriction is: (1) prescribed by law; (2) considered necessary in a democratic society; and (3) adopted in furtherance of one of four permissible justifications, which include: national security/public safety; public order; protection of public health or morals; or protection of others' rights and freedoms. The freedom of association has been further interpreted by international human rights courts and attorneys as requiring states to issue "convincing and compelling reasons" any time a restriction, however small, is placed on the right to associate, and that the

---

[17] This right is also recognized in various International Labor Organization conventions, as well as the founding charters and constitutions of nations around the world, such as Article 2 of the Canadian Charter of Rights and Freedoms which identifies the right to association as a "fundamental freedom".

[18] International Covenant on Civil and Political Rights (ICCPR) (Dec. 16, 1966). For the full text of the ICCPR go to: http://www.cirp.org/library/ethics/UN-covenant/ [https://perma.cc/SL8 M-ZE98]. For information about the ICCPR go to: http://cil.nus.edu.sg/1966/1966-international-covenant-on-civil-and-political-rights-iccpr/

restriction is strictly "proportionate to the legitimate aim pursued."[19] Moreover, in determining whether a restriction is permissible, "it is important to consider whether or not there are less intrusive means available to accomplish the desired end."[20] Theoretically, every restriction placed on the freedom of association by a state actor, which includes any new law or regulation that imposes a new requirement or that subtracts from their previous level of autonomy, should first go through this legal analysis in order to determine its permissibility under international law.

Figure 5.1: The three categories of legal restrictions imposed on CSOs – Barriers to Lifecycle, Funding, and Assembly – and the specific restrictions that comprise each of these categories. Adapted from Glasius et al. 2020.

Barriers to Lifecycle	Barriers to Funding (Foreign & Domestic)	Barriers to Assembly
New burdensome registration requirements.	Prior government approval required for foreign or domestic funding.	Restrictions on CSOs engaging in political activities.
No opportunity to contest a denied registration application.	Requiring foreign donations or funds to be channeled through the government, or deposited in a government approved bank.	Special restrictions on foreign-funded CSOs engaging in political activities.
Special restrictions on registration of foreign-funded CSOs.	Prohibition on access to foreign or domestic funding.	Prohibition on CSOs engaging in political activities.
Lengthy and expensive registration requirements, including no specific time limits on issuing registration decisions.	Prohibition on foreign or domestic funding to certain types of CSOs.	Restrictions on the ability of CSOs to engage in public demonstrations.
	Prohibition on the use of foreign funding for certain activities (typically, those labeled as "political").	Prohibition on CSOs ability to engage in public demonstrations.

Guidance from human rights case law, as well as recent IR scholarship on illiberal norm diffusion, was also helpful in specifically identifying when a law should be labeled as "restrictive."[21] Individual laws were reviewed and labeled

---

[19] Sidiropoulos v. Greece, 4 Eur. Ct. H.R. 500 at 40 (1998).

[20] *Id.* at 24–25.

[21] Marlies Glasius et al., *Illiberal Norm Diffusion: How Do Governments Learn to Restrict Nongovernmental Organizations?*, 64 INT'L STUD. Q. 453–68 [hereinafter Glasius et. al.

as "restrictive" only where a *new* restriction was placed on the CSO sector (or one sector of CSOs), a restriction that didn't previously exist, or if the law required CSOs to reduce their previous level of operational, financial and/or legal autonomy in some meaningful way. More specifically, laws were labeled as "restrictive" when they fell into one of three categories; namely, the law imposed a (1) barrier to a CSO's lifecycle, which includes its formation, operations and/or dissolution; (2) barrier to a CSO's ability to access funding, both foreign and domestic; and (3) barriers to a CSO's ability to participate in an assembly. The specific ways these categories were broken down are enumerated in Figure 5.1 below.[22]

Once located using the process outlined above, each law was carefully evaluated for whether it fell into one of the above categories, and more specifically, whether it matched one of the specific restrictions enumerated within each category. See Appendix 7 for a complete listing of all of the laws that were located; each one is categorized as being a barrier to "Lifecycle," "Domestic Funding, "Foreign Funding," or "Assembly" law. Lifecycle laws, which are the primary laws governing the existence of CSOs, include laws outlining how a CSO can form, and once formed, how it should operate, perform its activities, and when necessary, dissolve. Lifecycle laws also typically outline a CSO's reporting and auditing obligations, penalties for noncompliance, and scope of permissible (and impermissible) activities. Assembly laws include laws impacting the ability of CSOs to hold public demonstrations and events, including protests and rallies. Funding laws govern how and under what conditions a CSO can receive funding, whether foreign or domestic, and how they can access other sources of support, such as through fundraising, philanthropy, and donations. Because foreign funding laws are often treated as separate and distinct within the literature on CSOs, and because they raise different concerns and are often justified in different ways, funding laws were labeled as either "foreign" or "domestic."

By broadly defining 'restrictive CSO legislation', I overcome a key criticism of the existing literature on the closing space phenomenon, namely that it narrowly focuses on only one type of law – foreign funding laws – to the exclusion of all others. Focusing on only one specific type of law offers only a small and potentially misleading snapshot of the broader legal environment for

---

2020]; Darin Christensen & Jeremy M. Weinstein, *Defunding Dissent: Restrictions on Aid to NGOs*, 24 J. DEMOCRACY 77–91 (2013).

[22] This list was adapted from Glasius et. al. 2020, which was based on a prior list first established by Christensen and Weinstein. It is also drawn from international human rights law case law and authoritative interpretations (see discussion above).

CSOs, which in reality are shaped and affected by a multitude of different types of laws.[23] Despite that most of the literature and reporting on the closing space trend focuses on foreign funding laws, a recent study published in 2018 found that foreign funding laws constitute only 28% of the legal restrictions impacting CSOs adopted in recent years.[24] In contrast, the more foundational "lifecycle" laws account for roughly 47% of such laws, and another 25% impact the ability of CSO's to exercise their right to freedom of assembly, so-called "assembly laws."[25] As presented in the empirical results presented below, a similar breakdown in the types of restrictive CSO laws being passed by the world's strongest democratic states was found, with foreign funding laws constituting only a minority of the restrictive laws being adopted.

I not only include formal "laws" in my review, policy pronouncements, executive orders, and other official decrees that carry *the force* of law are included as well. As such, my definition of "law" is wider in scope than formal legislation adopted by a legislative branch according to the typical legislative rules. For example, a restrictive policy framework adopted in 2012 in Slovakia, a "full democracy" according to Polity, directly led to the de-registration of over 4000 "noncompliant" NGOs. This policy framework, which directly addresses and impacts CSOs without the need for any further legislation, has the effect of law, and thus, was treated as equivalent to a "restrictive CSO law" in my analysis. For a policy to be included, however, the impact on CSOs had to be obvious and direct, as in the previous example; in other words, it had to address CSOs directly *and* directly affect their behavior or organizational existence without the need for further implementing legislation. For example, an official announcement of a policy that asserts a need for greater oversight over the civil society sector, but does not require or trigger any specific actions in furtherance of that announcement, would not go far enough to be included as equivalent to a "law" in the empirical results revealed below.

In most cases, whether a pronouncement carries the force of law or not is obvious because its legal status is recognized in the law (or in case law, often constitutional case law) as legally binding.[26] For example, Spain issues legally

---

[23] *E.g.*, Darin Christensen & Jeremy M. Weinstein, *Defunding Dissent: Restrictions on Aid to NGOs*, 24 J. DEMOCRACY 77–91 (2013); Dupuy et al., *Hands off my Regime!*; Dupuy & Prakash, Why Restrictive NGO Foreign Funding Laws Reduce Voter Turnout in Africa's National Elections, *Nonprofit and Voluntary Sector Quarterly*, Jan. 6, 2020.
[24] International Center for Not-for-Profit Law 2018 at 10.
[25] *Id.*
[26] For example, in the US context, the Supreme Court has interpreted the President's Article II powers as including the authority to issue legally binding executive orders. *See*

binding royal decrees, which are authorized in Article 86 of their Constitution; the US issues legally binding executive orders, which have been interpreted by the US Supreme Court as inherent in Article 2 of the US Constitution.[27]

Only federal/national level laws were examined for this project; state and local level laws were excluded. The latter, which can also significantly impact CSOs, potentially opens the door to a different and more parochial set of motivating factors not always relevant to, or just different from, those experienced by national governments, which face heightened international audience costs and different domestic pressures than those experienced by non-federal officials who are accountable to smaller constituencies. To be sure, this meant excluding certain relevant laws from this book's scope of analysis. Examples include the spate of recent laws proposed and adopted in US states that impose new restrictions on CSOs' protest activities[28] and the similar string of restrictive protest measures adopted in certain Australian states.[29] Yet, scoping the project in this way was necessary for both practical and conceptual reasons: searching for all sub-federal laws is an infeasible project for one researcher working alone, and conceptually, as stated above, my sense is that different factors contribute to the passage of sub-federal and federal laws. Moreover, because I was conservative when choosing which laws went into my database for analysis, it can safely be said that, if anything, I understate my ultimate conclusion (that strong democratic states, like their authoritarian counterparts, are narrowing the autonomy of their CSO sectors by adopting restrictive CSO legislation).

Civil Society Organization (CSO). As defined in Chapter 1, a "CSO" is a non-governmental, not-for-profit organization formed voluntarily by individuals to pursue shared concerns or interests. International or transnational CSOs, terms that are used synonymously, include CSOs that perform their work or activities in more than one state. This inclusive definition includes a wide variety of organizations; it is broader and more encompassing than the more typically referenced "NGOs," which are in fact only one type of CSO. The definition of CSO utilized in this book does, however, exclude government-created NGOs (GONGOs) and terrorist organizations and other criminal syndicates, which, while non-governmental, have crime as one of their primary

---

Myers v. United States, 272 US 52 (1926). Additionally, certain acts of Congress delegate to the President the authority to issue a legally binding executive order.

[27] *E.g.,* Myers v. United States, 272 US 52 (1926).

[28] International Center for Not for Profit Law, *Protest Law Tracker,* 2019, available at http://www.icnl.org/usprotestlawtracker/.

[29] Matt Ford, *The New Legislation Targeting Protesters,* The Atlantic, Feb. 28, 2017; Kristen Alexander, *Australian State Bans Right to Protest, Daily Beast,* Mar. 13, 2014.

goals. CSOs, as defined herein, can have almost any goal with the exception of profit-making or crime. However, the media and political parties, which some consider aspects of civil society, are also excluded from the definition of CSO. Different and more restrictive rules can and should apply to both of these categories of organizations. In democratic states, at least, the media is typically regulated under its own set of laws and regulations that take into account the unique and critical role that it plays throughout the country and its widespread accessibility to a broad swath of the citizenry, including children. And in many democracies, CSOs are specifically prohibited from campaigning, supporting a political candidate, or otherwise getting involved with political parties, especially CSOs categorized as public benefit organizations or charities.[30] As one key example of how the rules differ between CSOs and political parties, most countries around the world prohibit political parties from accessing foreign donations.[31] This is generally accepted and not viewed as restrictive or controversial;[32] in contrast, there is extensive criticism and widespread condemnation of imposing foreign funding bans on CSOs.[33]

While a multitude of definitions have been proposed for "civil society organizations," the definition used in this book focuses on the three most common features that unite them.[34] A CSO must be non-governmental (not formed or operated by or on behalf of a government entity), non-profit (their primary purpose for forming and existing is not profit-making), and voluntary

---

[30] In the United States, for example, a charitable organization categorized by the IRS as a 501(c)(3), is prohibited from contributing a substantial part of their activities to carrying on propaganda or otherwise attempting to influence legislation, and they are prohibited from becoming involved in political campaigns for public office. In England, Wales, Ireland, and Canada, a charitable organization is prohibited from forming for the primary purpose of engaging in political activities and can never support a political party or candidate. In most of these countries, non-charitable CSOs can, however, participate in political activities. *See NGOs in the Political Realm*, 12 INT'L J. NOT-FOR-PROFIT L. (Nov 2009).

[31] See Is there a ban on donations from foreign interests to political parties?, International Institute for Democracy and Electoral Assistance (IDEA), list of countries available at https://www.idea.int/data-tools/question-view/527 (last accessed Aug. 2020) [hereinafter IDEA 2020]; A compilation of political party statutes, National Democratic Institute, 2011, available at https://www.ndi.org/sites/default/files/Political-Parties-Statutes-ENG.pdf.

[32] IDEA 2020.

[33] *E.g., Global assault on NGOs reaches crisis point as new laws curb vital human rights work*, AMNESTY INTERNATIONAL, Feb. 21, 2018.

[34] U.S. State Department, *Non-Governmental Organizations (NGOs) in the United States*, Jan. 2017; Ferguson 2012 at 15–16; Wolff & Poppe 2015 at 5; KECK & SIKKINK 1999, at 92; WORLD MOVEMENT FOR DEMOCRACY AND ICNL, DEFENDING CIVIL SOCIETY REPORT (2nd ed. 2012), n.1.

(the organization was founded by individuals who, on their own accord and through no compulsion or government-imposed mandate, effectuated its creation in order to pursue shared interests or concerns). Some definitions include an additional element having to do with pursuing a "public benefit" or a "public good."[35] However, the definition used herein does not include this element; instead, it includes organizations formed for any lawful purpose, whether characterized as a "public benefit" or not.

Temporal Scope: 1990–2018. The search for restrictive CSO laws was confined to the time period from 1990–2018. 1990 roughly corresponds to the start of the "associational revolution," when CSOs proliferated globally, established themselves as legitimate non-state actors, and began to wield significant influence over the course of international and domestic affairs.[36] It also roughly corresponds with the end of the third wave of democracy. Starting the search in 1990 allows for variation and temporal patterns to appear, including key moments of particularly intense legislative activity. This time frame also encompasses certain key events in international politics that potentially could have influenced the passage of restrictive CSO laws, as has been suggested in various reports on the closing space trend. These include the 9/11 attacks, the color revolutions that swept Eastern Europe in the early 2000s, the Arab Spring that erupted throughout the Middle East in the years after 2010, or the passage of certain high-profile restrictive CSO laws elsewhere, such as India's 2010 restrictive foreign funding or Russia's 2012 foreign agents law.

FINDINGS: THE SPREAD OF RESTRICTIVE CSO LAWS IN STRONG DEMOCRATIC STATES

The CSO legal frameworks for each of the world's strongest democracies, a list of 59 states, were located and examined for the period spanning 1990–2018. A total of 86 adopted restrictive CSO laws were discovered after a lengthy and meticulous search using the process described above. Additionally, 10 proposed and 13 withdrawn or rejected restrictive CSO laws were discovered. All are listed (and categorized) in Appendix 7.

Among the states that adopted a restrictive CSO law, nearly 67% (22 of 33) have adopted two or more restrictive CSOs laws, and over a third (36%, or 12 of 33) have adopted three or more (see Figure 5.2).

---

[35] Dan Cardinali, *The Adaptive Challenge of Restoring Trust in Civil Society*, STANFORD SOC. INNOVATION REV., June 2018.
[36] Salamon 1994; Jessica T. Mathews, *Power Shift*, 76 FOREIGN AFF. 50–66 (1997).

Figure 5.2:No. of Restrictive CSO Laws Adopted.

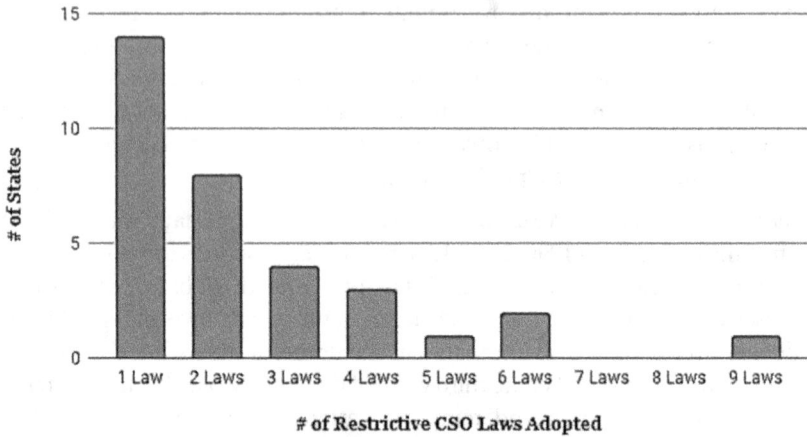

# of Restrictive CSO Laws Adopted

One state, Israel, has adopted nine such laws, while both Australia and Poland have adopted six, and France five. Bolivia, Croatia, and India have enacted four; and Hungary, New Zealand, Spain, the United Kingdom, and the US closely follow: each has adopted three (see Figure 5.3).

Figure 5.3: Adopters of Multiple Restrictive CSO Laws.

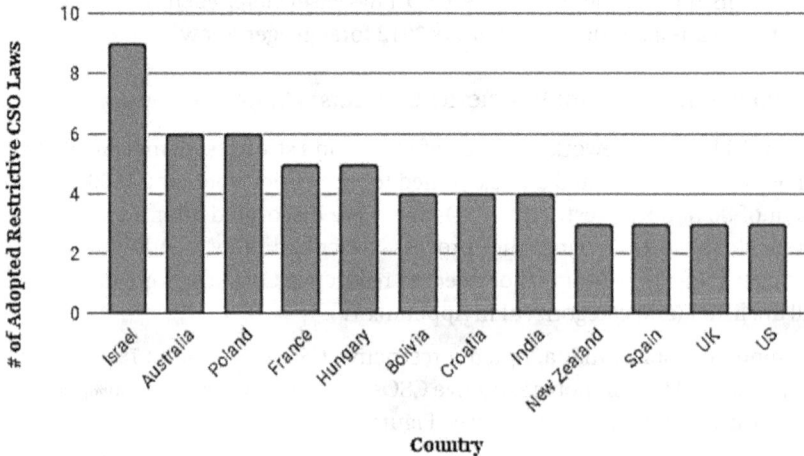

Country

Such patterns suggest that restrictive CSO laws are often adopted in clusters within a single state, with the passage of one law often leading to the passage of additional restrictions. In Hungary and India, for example, and in certain non-democracies, such as Russia and Ethiopia, a series of CSO restrictions were adopted over the course of several years, with the later laws often increasing the level of restrictiveness or stiffening the penalties associated with the earlier law. In India, new legal restrictions on CSOs' ability to access foreign funding were adopted in 2010; these restrictions were tightened further in 2015 following the adoption of new amendments to the Foreign Contribution (Regulation) Act.[37] In Hungary, a string of restrictive CSO laws have been adopted in recent years as part of Prime Minister Victor Orban's broader campaign to create an "illiberal democracy."[38] A string of three restrictive CSO laws were adopted in 2018, which were colloquially referred to as the "Stop Soros Laws," referring to the philanthropist George Soros, whose Open Society Foundations and Central European University were based in Hungary (until forced out in late 2018).[39] These laws, which came on the heels of an earlier 2017 restrictive CSO law, were part of a broader campaign by the Orban government to eliminate any source of opposition or challenge to his agenda, which targeted the judiciary and the media, in addition to the non-governmental sector.[40] And in Israel, their restrictive CSO laws were clustered as well – three were adopted in consecutive order in 2011, and the remaining six were adopted between 2015 and 2018, typically in clusters of two. Many of these laws were part of a broader campaign by the Netanyahu government to eliminate foreign influence in Israeli politics, as well as criticism of the government's agenda or government institutions, notably including the IDF.[41]

Of the adopted 86 restrictive CSO laws, 58 of them (or 67%), the vast majority, involve lifecycle or framework CSO laws, which as defined above are the primary laws governing the existence, operations, domestic funding, and dissolution of CSOs. An additional 15 laws restrict CSOs' ability to access foreign resources, while only four of the adopted laws pertain to CSOs' access to domestic funding. An additional ten laws involve CSOs' ability to participate in assemblies or public demonstrations (see Figure 5.4). These findings suggest that governments are targeting CSOs in a more robust and comprehensive way than is often assumed. They are not only restricting their ability to access

---

[37] Amendments to the Foreign Contribution (Regulation) Act were made in 2010 and 2015. *See* Sujeet Kumar, *India has been hostile to NGOs for decades. Modi made it worse,* QUARTZ, May 3, 2019.

[38] *Hungarian PM sees shift to illiberal Christian democracy in 2019 European vote,* REUTERS, July 28, 2018 (reporting by Krisztina Than & Sandor Peto; editing by Mark Heinrich).

[39] *E.g.,* Marton Dunai, *Hungary approves "Stop Soros' Law", defying EU, rights groups,* REUTERS, June 20, 2018; Susan Adams, *Why Hungary forced George Soros-backed Central European University to leave the country,* FORBES, Dec. 4, 2018.

[40] *E.g.,* Zselyke Csaky, *Dropping the Democratic Façade,* NATIONS IN TRANSIT 2020 (2020); Yasmeen Serhan, *The EU Watches as Hungary Kills Democracy,* THE ATLANTIC, Apr. 2, 2020.

[41] Peter Beaumont, *Israel passes law to force NGOs to reveal foreign funding,* THE GUARDIAN, July 12, 2016; Maayan Lubell, *Israel passes law to ban groups critical of state, military from schools,* REUTERS, July 17, 2018.

foreign funding – indeed, only 17% of democratic states have adopted laws with this intent – but more often, they are restricting or complicating their ability to form, register, and carry out their daily operations. Moreover, while some blame the spread of CSO legal restrictions on the increase in protest activity around the globe, these findings suggest that only a small number of the adopted laws (less than 11%) target CSOs' ability to participate in and lead demonstrations.

Figure 5.4: Types of Restrictive CSO Laws Adopted in Strong Democratic States, 1990-2018.

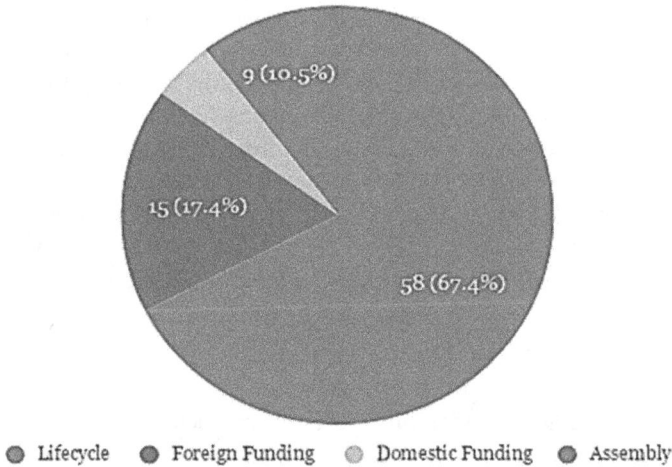

    ⬤ Lifecycle   ⬤ Foreign Funding   ◉ Domestic Funding   ⬤ Assembly

In terms of timing, the trend line is very clear and consistent: the proposal and passage of restrictive CSO laws in strong democratic states is a recent phenomenon; it's not just a twenty-first-century trend, but an even more recent (roughly) post-2010 trend (see Figure 5.5). The vast majority of the restrictive CSO laws adopted, 62 of the 86 adopted laws (or 72%), were passed from 2013 to 2018; and all 11 of the current proposals were proposed in 2017 or later, with the exception of one proposed in 2016. 2016 and 2017 saw the highest number of adoptions and proposals: 15 separate laws were adopted each year, and 8 were proposed (and remain proposals) in the two years combined. Tracing the temporal arc of proposed and adopted restrictive CSO laws, it appears that the associational counter-revolution was accelerating and gaining momentum in strong democratic states at least until 2017, as other reports on the closing space trend have similarly asserted with respect to non-democratic states.[42] My findings also confirm that the 1990s were indeed a "golden age" for CSOs in

---

[42] International Center for Not-for-Profit Law 2018; Rutzen 2015.

democratic states. There were very few new legislative restrictions – only three (3%) – placed on CSOs in the entirety of that decade.

Figure 5.5: # of Restrictive CSO Laws Adopted Each Year Since 1990.

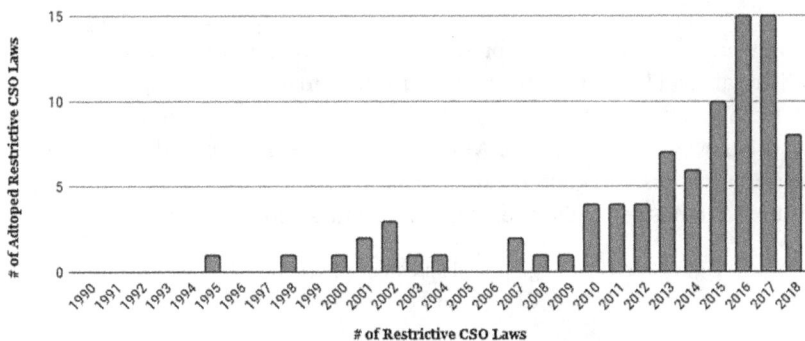

# of Restrictive CSO Laws

The trend line revealed in Figure 5.5 also confirms the relative newness and recent momentum behind the spread of restrictive CSO laws into democratic countries. However, the sudden decline in 2018 perhaps suggests that this trend has peaked or reached saturation point. However, the downturn in adoption rates in 2018 does not necessarily suggest anything about the reversal of this trend (or the resurrection of the associational revolution). Instead, it suggests that this trend is now entrenched and that the passage of additional new laws is no longer viewed as necessary.

In terms of geographic spread, all regions and continents of the world have been impacted by the spread of restrictive CSO laws in recent years, as previous reports confirm.[43] And democracies are no exception, as this book now confirms. Among the world's strongest democratic countries, European countries adopted the highest number of restrictive CSO laws: 22 of the 33 democracies from Europe, or two-thirds, have adopted a restrictive CSO law since 1990. All combined, the number of restrictive CSO laws adopted in Europe total 46, over 50% of the total laws. The fewest restrictive CSO laws were passed in African democracies; only two of the six African democracies, or one-third, have adopted a restrictive CSO law. Falling in the middle between these two were Asian countries – four (of seven) Asian democracies adopted a combined 15 restrictive CSO laws (17% of the total) – and Latin American democracies – five of the nine Latin American states adopted nine such laws (10%). The two countries from North America, the US and Canada, have both

---

[43] *E.g.*, ICNL, Effective Donor Responses to the Challenge of Closing Civic Space (May 19, 2018) at 9–10, available at https://www.icnl.org/post/report/effective-donor-responses.

adopted restrictive CSO laws (eight in total). And finally, the only country from the Middle East to qualify as a "strong democratic state," Israel, has the highest passage rate of any of the countries under review, having adopted nine restrictive CSO laws (see Figures 5.6 and 5.7). The broad geographical scope of this phenomenon further confirms that this trend is not isolated to one region or only one part of the world but has spread throughout the globe. While the individual details of the laws gathered differ, many of them have a similar intent: to narrow the autonomy of their CSO sectors and/or to impose additional layers of government oversight. While more intense and pronounced in certain areas than others, this genuinely global trend may have started in authoritarian contexts but has certainly spread into the world's democratic states as well.

Figure 5.6: The Geographical Spread of Restrictive CSO Laws in the World's Strongest Democratic States.

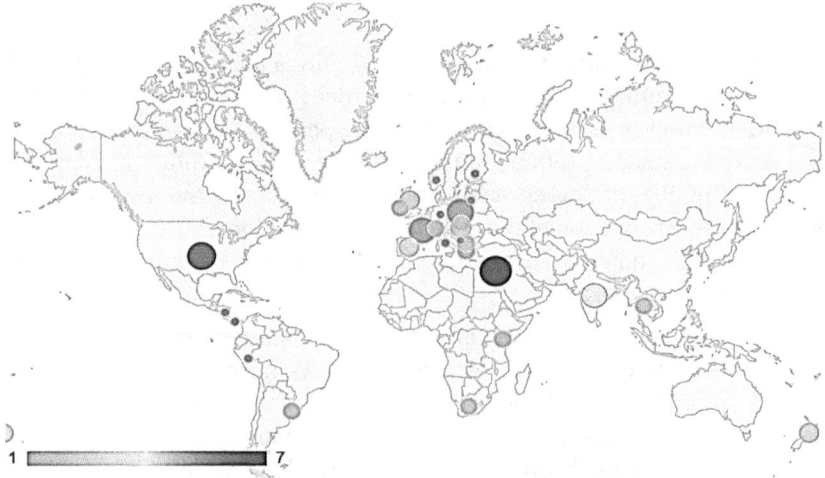

Figure 5.7: No. of States in each Region to adopt a Restrictive CSO Law.

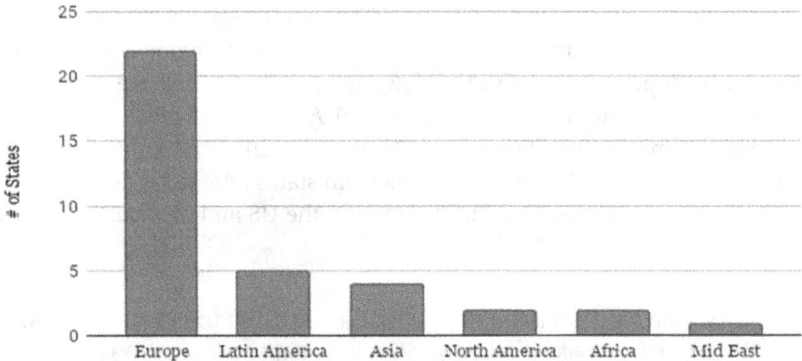

28 of the 59 states that I reviewed are members of the Organisation for Economic Co-operation and Development (OECD), an intergovernmental organization focused on stimulating economic progress and world trade founded in 1961 composed of 35 member states. Many consider the members of the OECD to be among the world's wealthiest, strongest and most developed democracies.[44] Yet, 21 of the 28 OECD states to qualify as strong democratic states, nearly 60% of total OECD countries (and 71% of the OECD countries I examined), have adopted at least one restrictive CSO law. Among the remaining 32 states that are not members of the OECD, only 15 of these states, nearly 47%, have adopted at least one restrictive CSO law, making the "top tier" OECD democracies (in my case selection) even more likely than the "lower tier" group to adopt a restrictive CSO law. My findings cast doubt on existing studies that tend to assume that this elite club of states has uniformly strong democratic checks and balances in place, including permissive CSO legal frameworks.[45]

Also contradicting commonly held assumptions, various countries that are typically cited as (or assumed to be) the highest performers with respect to the freedom of association and respect for human rights more generally, are also restrictive CSO law adopters. A recent survey found Norway, Sweden, Switzerland, Latvia, Estonia and Slovenia to be among the top 10% of states in terms of their respect and protection for the freedoms of association and assembly. [46] More specifically, Denmark, Norway, Sweden, Finland, Germany, Switzerland, Ireland, Belgium, Greece and Slovenia were among the very top performers on a measurement of Civil Society Participation.[47] These "top performers" consistently appear in other civil society indexes and human rights rankings as well.[48] Yet, most of these highly regarded European countries have adopted at least one law imposing new restrictions on CSOs since the turn of the twenty-first century – and most often, in or after 2015. Only three of the

---

[44] The reason why not all OECD states appear in my list of 59 strong democratic states is likely due to the fact that OECD membership is voluntary and because it's focused on countries with strong economies. My rubric was entirely focused on regime type or political system (democracy) and nothing more, unlike the OECD, which abides by a different membership criteria.

[45] Elizabeth Bloodgood et al., *National Styles of NGO Regulation*, 43 NON-PROFIT & VOLUNTARY SECTOR Q. (Feb. 2013).

[46] Annika Silva-Leander & Joseph Noonan, *Is the Space for Civil Society Really Shrinking?*, INTERNATIONAL IDEA, July 17, 2018.

[47] *Id.*

[48] *E.g.*, CIVICUS 2019, 2017.

above-mentioned states have *not* imposed any new legal restrictions on their civil society sectors: Sweden, Slovenia, and Estonia.[49]

CONCLUSION

Each of the "strong democratic countries" included in the above analysis has ratified the International Covenant on Civil and Political Rights (ICCPR), which codifies the freedom of association and is considered binding international law. Nearly all are also signatories to a regional human rights treaty that similarly protects this right, and with rare exceptions, such as in Australia, each nation reviewed recognizes the rights to association and assembly in their national constitution.[50] Each of the countries reviewed is a signatory of the key human rights treaty codifying the freedom of association, the International Covenant on Civil and Political Rights, which constitutes binding international law. Adding further confirmation to recent research on human rights treaty adoption, treaty ratification does not, on its own, appear to influence a state's willingness to infringe on rights and freedoms contained in that treaty.[51]

The findings presented in this chapter confirm that the associational counter-revolution is not isolated to countries with authoritarian governance systems, countries known for egregious human rights violations against civil society actors, or countries with weak economies or less than fully developed status, as was previously assumed.[52] These findings also confirm that this trend does not implicate only one type of law, namely foreign funding laws, or one category of CSO (human rights and other advocacy organizations), but instead, a broader array of laws and CSOs. Most importantly, the research presented above supports the idea that the closing space trend is a truly global phenomenon, one that transcends geography, GDP, regime type, development status, and most importantly, one that is not confined only to repressive, non-democratic regimes with histories of overt persecution and vocal condemnation of civil

---

[49] Note that I did not include Latvia in my review of "strong democratic states."

[50] The US is another exception. The right to association, though not explicitly in the US Constitution (unlike most other states in the world), was recognized as implicit in the US Constitution by the US Supreme Court in the case of Roberts v. United States Jaycees, 468 US 609 (1984). See the official UN ratification table for the ICCPR here: http://indicators.ohchr.org/.

[51] DeMattee 2019; Hathaway 2002. Ph.D. Candidate Anthony DeMattee found, in a recent study, that ratification of human rights treaties does not prevent the adoption of laws infringing on the freedom of association without constitutional rules specifically making treaties equivalent to ordinary legislation, meaning that they become automatically binding upon ratification.

[52] Bakke et al. 2018; Dupuy & Prakash 2017; Dupuy et al. 2015.

society actors.[53] Indeed, well over half (58%) of the strong democratic countries reviewed have adopted at least one restrictive CSO law in the last two decades. When proposed laws are added to this list, this total comes to over 63% of all "strong democratic states."

These findings confirm a routinely alleged claim but, at least to my knowledge, has not been empirically confirmed until now. The research and activist communities can now assert, with empirical proof to back their claim, that the closing space phenomenon has indeed spread into democratic states, including the world's strongest democratic states. It's too early to ascertain whether the trend lines presented above will continue in the coming years and if the remaining twenty-five strong democracies that haven't imposed a restrictive CSO law since 1990 will so do in the near term. However, what is clear is that the rate at which such laws are being adopted and proposed in democratic states (63% to date) is keeping pace with, or according to some estimates, even rising above the percentages seen in less democratic states.[54]

---

[53] Chrystie F. Swiney, *Undemocratic Civil Society Laws Are Appearing in Democracies*, OPENGLOBALRIGHTS, Mar. 28, 2019; Chrystie F. Swiney, *Laws Are Chipping Away at Democracy Around the World*, THE CONVERSATION, Apr. 2, 2019.
[54] Dupuy et al. 2016; Christensen & Weinstein 2013; Rutzen 2015.

CHAPTER 6:

IMPLICATIONS OF THE ASSOCIATIONAL

COUNTER-REVOLUTION

In democratic countries, the knowledge of how to form associations is the mother of all knowledge since the success of all the others depends on it.

Alexis de Tocqueville, Democracy in America (1835)

This chapter assesses the primary implications, or consequences, of the associational counter-revolution's spread into the world's democratic states. It asks and answers the question: why does this counter-revolution even matter? The answer, in brief, is that the associational counter-revolution matters because democracy matters. As CSOs continue to face the imposition of additional restrictions (legal and otherwise) on their ability to operate autonomously from government control, the very thing that makes them unique and impactful, democracy, will continue to decay. The global democratic decay thesis, while not uniformly agreed upon, is a well-documented phenomenon that closely tracks the evolution of the associational counter-revolution. Given that an independent civil society sector is essential to any well-functioning democracy, when the autonomy of CSOs declines, so too does the strength of democracy.[1] This important, indeed essential, connection between the spread of restrictive CSO laws and global democratic decay is explored below.

THE CONNECTION BETWEEN CSOs' AUTONOMY AND DEMOCRACY

It is well established that an independent civil society sector and active civic engagement are prerequisites for a well-functioning democracy.[2] Scholars and democracy theorists, including perhaps the most renowned of them all, Alexis de Tocqueville, have long observed that where democracy flourishes, so too does an autonomous civil society sector; the two always, by necessity, coexist.[3] In Tocqueville's attempt to uncover the sources of America's success at creating

---

[1] ALEXIS DE TOCQUEVILLE, DEMOCRACY IN AMERICA (1840) [hereinafter TOCQUEVILLE 1840]; ROBERT PUTNAM, MAKING DEMOCRACY WORK: CIVIC TRADITIONS IN MODERN ITALY (1993).
[2] *Id.*
[3] TOCQUEVILLE 1840.

a vibrant democracy, he pointed first and foremost to one thing: America's unmatched network of civil society organizations (CSOs), what he referred to as "civic associations." According to Tocqueville, nothing is "more deserving of our attention" than understanding the "art" of civic associations, which he referred to as the "mother of science," the foundation upon which "the progress of all the rest depends."[4] For Tocqueville, independent civic associations were, and are, the source of democracy's strength, the spark that leads to its existence, and the fuel that keeps it going. Without a robust and diversified network of nongovernmental civic associations, democracy, in Tocqueville's view, will fall prey to "the despotism of faction," "the arbitrary power of a prince," or "the most galling tyranny."[5] In other words, CSOs are both an essential precursor to democracy's emergence *and* an essential ingredient for its continuation.

While perhaps no one has ever spoken with as much elegance about the necessary linkage between CSOs' autonomy and democracy as Tocqueville, other highly regarded theorists and political figures have spoken with equal conviction on this topic. Robert Dahl, for example, considered by many the father of modern political science whose widely cited definition of democracy (what he referred to as "polyarchy") established him as a towering voice on the topic, designated the freedom of association a key institutional requisite for any electoral democracy. Without this critical freedom, which allows individuals to voluntarily coalesce into groups that are disconnected from the government, elections risk becoming mere charades and democracy, an empty shell.[6] For Dahl, one of the "procedural minimum" requirements for any country to qualify as a democracy includes the right of citizens "to form relatively independent associations or organizations," a claim made by numerous other democracy scholars.[7] In later publications, Dahl became even more insistent on the need for CSOs to have "associational autonomy," which he viewed as essential to a well-functioning democracy.[8] Without the right of civic associations to operate free from government interference or control, they are unable to perform their core role, which they alone are uniquely poised to do – to hold elected officials accountable and to operate as independent watchdogs over the political system.

---

[4] *Id.*, Vol. 1 at 195.

[5] *Id.*

[6] ROBERT DAHL, POLYARCHY (1971) [hereinafter DAHL 1971].

[7] *E.g.*, Philippe C. Schmitter & Terry Lynn Karl, *What Democracy Is ... and Is Not*, 2 J. DEMOCRACY 75–88, at 81 (1991) [hereinafter Schmitter & Karl 1991].

[8] ROBERT DAHL, DEMOCRACY AND ITS CRITICS (1989) [hereinafter DAHL 1989].

In his well-known best seller *Bowling Alone*, American political scientist Robert Putnam similarly connects the robustness of a state's civil society sector with the strength of that state's democracy.[9] Focusing on the US context specifically, he connects the sharp decrease in the number of American civic associations over the years with declines in American democracy, a connection made more broadly by British historian Niall Ferguson, who contends that history's greatest nations were built on the backs of civil society associations, and conversely, that the downfall of these nations can be explained by the diminishment of those associations.[10] The literature on democratic transitions, coming from a very different vantage point and typically looking at developing countries, similarly confirms the powerful role played by civil society in the emergence of any new democracy.[11] This extensive body of literature reveals that a mobilized civil society sector is often the "critical actor" in a country's "breakthrough to democracy."[12] Moreover, empirical studies by those who have studied democratic deconsolidation have also made connections between the strength of a democracy and the autonomy of its civil society sector. In a study examining the state of democracy worldwide from 1971 to 2017, the authors found, following an extensive empirical review, that in countries where democratic institutions were deconsolidating, the freedom of association was both weak and restricted by the state.[13] Certain economists have reached similar conclusions using very different tools and findings. MIT-based economists Daron Acemoglu and James Robinson, in their 2012 book *Why Nations Fail*, marshal an extraordinary volume of historical evidence from medieval to modern times. It makes an institutionalist argument that the rise and fall of nations is determined by whether a nation has a network of "inclusive institutions" in place to ensure that the state is accurately taking into account the opinions of its citizens.[14]

---

[9] ROBERT PUTNAM, BOWLING ALONE: THE COLLAPSE AND REVIVAL OF AMERICAN COMMUNITY (2000).

[10] NIALL FERGUSON, THE GREAT DEGENERATION: HOW INSTITUTIONS DECAY AND ECONOMIES DIE (2010).

[11] *E.g.*, Mehran Kamrava & Frank O. Mora, *Civil Society and Democratisation in Comparative Perspective: Latin America and the Middle East*, 19 THIRD WORLD Q. 893–915 (Dec. 1998); Nancy Bermeo, *What the Democratization Literature Says – or Doesn't Say – About Postwar Democratization*, 9 GLOBAL GOVERNANCE 159–77 (2003); Monica Threlfall, *Reassessing the Role of Civil Society Organizations in the Transition to Democracy in Spain*, 15 DEMOCRATIZATION 930–951 (2008).

[12] *E.g.*, Michael Bernhard & Ekrem Karakoc, *Civil Society and the Legacies of Dictatorship*, 59 WORLD POL. 539–67, at 542 (2007).

[13] Anna Lührmann et al., *State of the World 2017: Autocratization and Exclusion?*, 25 *Democratization* 1321–40 (2018).

[14] DARON ACEMOGLU & JAMES ROBINSON, WHY NATIONS FAILS: THE ORIGINS OF POWER, PROSPERITY AND POVERTY (2012).

Democracy theorists conclude that the presence of an autonomous civil society sector is what makes elections the most visible and, some argue, among the most essential elements of a democracy, meaningful.[15] In states where elections are held, but civil society is weak, which some refer to as an "illiberal democracy," elected officials with authoritarian leanings tend to entrench themselves in power and rule autocratically, such as in Russia, Malaysia and Cambodia.[16] Similarly, but conversely, Fareed Zakaria, whose eclectic ideas make him difficult to categorize, describes civil society organizations as "essential" to the "maintenance of a liberal democracy."[17]

The ability to form a non-governmental group of whatever variety, based on the wishes, concerns or shared ideals of its members, is, like free speech, a right that should generally be permitted irrespective of the substantive content or focus of any individual group. So long as the group doesn't engage in criminal activity and are otherwise law-abiding, they should, according to human rights activists and scholars, be permitted to operate no matter their mission or cause. Analogizing once again to free speech, while the right to associate is not and should not be unlimited,[18] allowing individuals to coalesce on the basis of shared goals, no matter those goals, is essential because allowing otherwise could be a slippery slope toward government censorship.[19] Just as many individuals, particularly in the American context, would be uncomfortable with the idea of the government determining the content of their public expressions, so too, are there legitimate concerns about the government deciding which

---

[15] DAHL 1989; Schmitter & Karl 1991.

[16] Fareed Zakaria, *The Rise of Illiberal Democracy*, 76 FOREIGN AFF. 22–43 (Nov.–Dec. 1997).

[17] Michael N. Barnett & Martha Finnemore, *The Politics, Power, and Pathologies of International Organizations*, 53 INT'L ORG. 699–732 (1999); Sean Illing, *Fareed Zakaria Made a Scary Prediction about Democracy in 1997 – and It's Coming True*, VOX, Jan. 18, 2017.

[18] In the US context, where the right to free speech is considered to be the most protected in the world, there are still exceptions. Individuals are not permitted to incited actions that would harm others (Schenck v. United States, 249 U.S. 47(1919)), to make or distribute obscene materials (Roth v. United States, 354 U.S. 476 (1957)), to burn draft cards as an anti-war protest (United States v. O'Brien, 391 U.S. 367 (1968)), and a variety of other exceptions. As with free speech, the right to associate and form into groups is not unlimited, it can properly be constrained in a variety of contexts, which tend to parallel those areas where speech can appropriately be restricted.

[19] Note that there are opponents, including liberal opponents, to the view that speech should be generally permitted no matter its substance. *See, e.g.,* Nathan J. Robinson, *Thinking Strategically about Freed Speech and Violence*, CURRENT AFF., Aug. 20, 2017. Robinson, like others, argues that free speech when allowed unrestrained only increases the likelihood of violence. Some argue, for example, that the Antifa movement in the US, due to its radicalized anti-right language, should be legally restricted, at least when it passes a certain threshold.

CSOs should and should not be permitted to exist, receive funding, or shut down. Moreover, like free speech, allowing individuals to form into groups for whatever reason provides them with a non-violent way to vent and express their views, which, if contained or repressed, could simmer and then explode into acts of violence.

Most importantly of all perhaps, allowing groups to form for any purpose (absent violence or criminality) is an expression of democracy in its purest sense of the term: it allows citizens to express and enact their personal views, no matter those views, in order to shape their own polity in the ways they wish. CSOs create a bridge between citizens and their elected officials; they operate as a middle-man of sorts, transmitting concerns and messages louder and with greater impact than any individual could ever hope to do on their own. As such, when their autonomy to form and operate is constrained, civil society is not able to perform its democracy promoting and maintaining role, arguably its most critical function.

THE STATE OF GLOBAL DEMOCRACY

Recent research suggests that democracy is on the wane around the globe, a phenomenon variously referred to as democratic backsliding,[20] democratic deconsolidation,[21] democratic decay,[22] and the "global democratic recession."[23] For thirteen straight years in a row, Freedom House, an independent watchdog organization that measures and reports on the state of democracy around the world, has catalogued declines in global freedoms in its 2019 report, with established democracies dominating the list of countries reflecting significant setbacks.[24] Countries labeled "free" accounted for a larger share of the declines than at any time in the past decade, and nearly one-quarter of the countries experiencing declines were in Europe. This new reality stands in stark

---

[20] *E.g.*, Aziz Huq & Tom Ginsburg, *How to Lose a Constitutional Democracy*, 65 UCLA L. REV. 78–170 (2018).

[21] Roberto Stefan Foa & Yascha Mounk, *The Danger of Deconsolidation: The Democratic Disconnect*, 27 J. DEMOCRACY 5–17 (2016).

[22] See the Dem-Dec website (short for "democratic decay"), an excellent resource for examining the topic of Democratic Decay, created by Dr. Tom Gerald Daly, available at https://www.democratic-decay.org/.

[23] Larry Diamond, *Facing up to the Democratic Recession*, 26 J. DEMOCRACY 141–55 (Jan. 2015); hear a recent interview with Larry Diamond talking about the "global democratic recession" on NPR, on Aug. 3, 2017, during All Things Considered, available here: http://www.npr.org/2017/08/03/541432445/decline-in-democracy-spreads-across-the-globe-as-authoritarian-leaders-rise.

[24] Freedom House 2019.

juxtaposition to earlier times; from 1975 to 2005, for example, Freedom House recorded nearly 30 years of constant gains.[25] The Economist's Democracy Index, while a bit more optimistic than Freedom House, found evidence of ongoing and deepening disillusionment with democracy and dwindling numbers of people living under some form of genuine democratic governance. Indeed, it found that only 4.5% of the human population now lives in what qualifies as a "full democracy."[26] Though disputed by some,[27] these findings are supported by a growing body of scholars and policy analysts focused on democratic decay.[28]

THE ASSOCIATIONAL COUNTER-REVOLUTION & GLOBAL DEMOCRATIC DECAY

Multiple scholars who support the democratic decay thesis have decried the lack of conceptual tools necessary for identifying the "early warning signs" that such decay is underway, while others have focused on our lack of understanding of "the series of discrete and interconnected events and actions that often proceed undetected" toward democratic deconsolidation.[29] At least one such scholar has pointed to the adoption of "ever–more expansive laws empowering the state to maintain law and order" as one such early warning sign.[30] But this linkage has, to my knowledge, never been confirmed or specifically traced to the passage of restrictive CSO laws. The research presented in this book reveals a close parallel between these two trends, suggesting that one profound implication of the associational counter-revolution is democratic decay.

These two global trends – the associational counter-revolution and democratic decay – have unfolded seemingly in tandem. However, they are typically examined separately by two different communities of experts and scholars, seemingly unbeknownst to one another. While the associational

---

[25] Mark Goldberg, *When Soft Power Salutes Despots*, THE AMERICAN PROSPECT, Nov. 14, 2017.

[26] The United States, as just one example, is no longer characterized as a "full democracy." It was downgraded from its status as a "full" to a "flawed" democracy for the first time in the Index's history in 2016. The *EIU Democracy Index 2018, World Democracy Report*, available at https://www.eiu.com/topic/democracy-index.

[27] Nancy Bermeo, *On Democratic Backsliding*, 27 J. *Democracy* 5–19 (2016); Levitsky & Way 2015.

[28] *E.g.*, Tom Daly, *Democratic Decay in "Keystone Democracies": The Real Threat to Global Constitutionalism?*, I-CONNECT BLOG, May 10, 2017.

[29] Horowitz & Macdonald 2017; Daly 2017; Asli Bali, *Electoral Authoritarianism Revisited*, I-CONNECT BLOG, Nov. 1, 2017.

[30] Michael Horowitz & Julia Macdonald, *Will Killer Robots Be Banned? Lessons from Past Civil Society Campaigns*, LAWFARE, Nov. 5, 2017.

counter-revolution is mostly tracked and examined by policy activists and human rights attorneys,[31] global democratic decay is largely tracked by political scientists.[32] Moreover, while trackers of the closing space phenomenon have largely failed to examine how this trend is spreading into democracies and interacting with the democratic decay thesis, the academics studying democratic decay have largely failed to notice the role and relevance of the closing space phenomenon in those countries experiencing democratic backsliding. These two consequential global trends, being closely tracked by two separate communities looking through two very different sets of lenses, have been studied largely in isolation and without reference to the other.

This is perplexing given that both trends seem, at first glance, to share many identifying traits. In addition to following a similar temporal trajectory, both are global in scope, appearing in all geographical regions of the world; both have been gaining momentum since approximately 2005; many of the same states have been implicated, including established, consolidated democracies; both are incremental, state-led, and being done largely under the veneer of legality (through the passage of laws that impinge on key democratic rights, such as the freedom of association); both seem to involve a growing preoccupation by states with national sovereignty and national security at the expense of all other concerns, notably including human rights concerns; and finally, both require closer empirical examination.

As previously stated, the temporal trajectory of the democratic decay trend closely parallels the associational counter-revolution: after an initial golden age in the 1990s following the end of the Cold War, democratic progress began to plateau following the turn of the century, exhibiting signs of a fragility and reversal by 2006,[33] and elicit warnings from increasingly concerned democracy observers by 2015.[34] As with the closing space global trend, warnings about the deteriorating plight of global democracy have grown increasingly urgent in

---

[31] Examples include: ICNL and CIVICUS, both international non-profit organizations, which operate much like think tanks, and focus on the closing space trend in all its dimensions and varities.

[32] Tom Daly, *Democratic Decay in "Keystone Democracies": The Real Threat to Global Constitutionalism?*, I-CONNECT BLOG, May 10, 2017; Roberto Stefan Foa & Yascha Mounk, *The Danger of Deconsolidation: The Democratic Disconnect*, 27 J. DEMOCRACY 5–17 (2016).

[33] Larry Diamond, *Facing up to the Democratic Recession*, 26 J. DEMOCRACY 141–55, at 144 (Jan. 2015) (stating that: "The world has been in a mild but protracted democratic recession since about 2006").

A number of restrictive CSO laws began to be passed in 2005–2006, and their number has increased since then.

[34] *See* Mark F. Plattner, *Is Democracy in Decline?*, 26 J. DEMOCRACY 5–10 (2015) (citing Freedom House reports).

recent years. Since 2015, a number of academic journals and policy publications have devoted entire issues to examining democratic decay,[35] numerous books have been written on the subject,[36] and radio programs and podcasts have assessed whether democracy has reached its "breaking point?"[37]

SHRINKING SPACES FOR CSOS IN STRONG DEMOCRATIC STATES

While none of the 59 "strong democratic states" that formed the focus of this book can be characterized as being fully "closed" to an autonomous civil society sector, my research strongly suggests that the trajectory is toward a narrowing or shrinking of autonomous spaces for CSOs to operate. As Figure 6.1 reveals, the vast majority of the nearly sixty democratic countries whose civil society legal frameworks were reviewed have been characterized by CIVICUS, a leading global civil society watchdog organization, as having a "narrowed," "obstructed," or "repressed" environment for civil society.[38]

Figure 6.1: CIVICUS Ratings on the Environment forCSOs in the World's Strongest Democratic States.

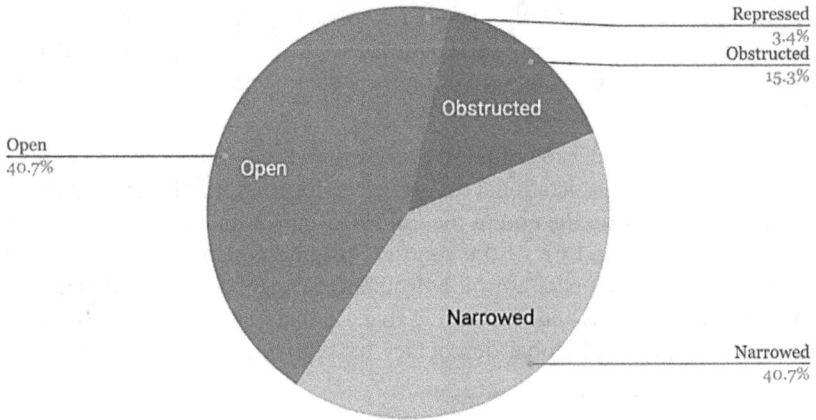

Repressed
3.4%
Obstructed
15.3%
Open
40.7%
Narrowed
40.7%

---

[35] For example, the 25th Anniversary edition of *The Journal of Democracy* was devoted to the question of "Is Democracy in Decline?": see 26 J. DEMOCRACY 5–10 (2015). Similarly, *The Economist* devoted its March 2014 edition to the question: "What's Gone Wrong with Democracy?"

[36] LARRY DIAMOND & MARK PLATTNER, DEMOCRACY IN DECLINE? (2015).

[37] *Has Democracy Reached its Breaking Point,* CNN, Apr. 26, 2017 (interviewing and quoting Arch Puddington, Distinguished Fellow of Democracy Studies at Freedom House).

[38] These ratings were drawn from the CIVICUS Monitor, which is available at https://monitor. civicus.org/. Its methodology is explained here: https://monitor.civicus.org/about/; and the different ratings ("open," "narrowed," etc.) are described here: https://monitor.civicus.org/ Ratings/.

Indeed, 35 of the 59 democratic states examined, nearly 60%, no longer have an "open" and fully enabling environment for CSOs to operate. In nine of the democracies examined, their enabling environment for CSOs is categorized as "obstructed," and in two (Nicaragua and Thailand), the environment for CSOs is defined as "repressed" (see Figure 6.2). The number of countries with civil society sectors defined as "open" (24) is equivalent to those with environments rated as "narrowed," a startling reality given that this is limited only to the world's strongest democratic states (see Appendix 8 for the complete list).

Figure 6.2: No. of the World's Strongest Democratic States to receive each of CIVICUS' Ratings for CSO Environment. Source: The CIVICUS Monitor, available at https://monitor.civicus.org/.

CIVICUS Rating	# of Democracies
Open	24
Narrowed	24
Obstructed	9
Repressed	2
Total	**59**

For democracy to remain strong, indeed for it to even continue functioning at a minimum, an independent civil society is necessary, and for civil society to be independent, we have to understand not only the domestic factors that might lead to its lack of independence but whether global forces or trends are also contributing to this outcome. In countries without autonomous civil society sectors, the individuals in power, whether elected or there by fiat, tend to enact their personal agendas and not those of the individuals they are in power to represent. Thus begins the cyclical, chicken-in-egg process: the lack of a robust civil society sector leads to the deterioration of democracy, and the further deterioration of democracy leads to the further weakening of, and the narrowing of spaces for, civil society. Without civil society, democracy cannot exist; without democracy, civil society cannot emerge and, even if they succeed in emerging, hold the elected leaders to account in any meaningful way.

CONSEQUENCES OF RESTRICTIVE CSO LAWS ON CSOS

What precisely is the connection between restrictive CSO laws, CSOs themselves and democracy? Restrictive CSO laws impact CSOs' ability to operate, effectively hold states to account, and in some cases, survive. If CSOs can't operate autonomously from the government, they cannot effectively hold elected leaders to account, and if restrictions become too onerous, small and under-funded CSOs will choose not to register or to dissolve. Restrictive CSO laws can also chill associational activity, stigmatize the civil society sector, and deter minority and disadvantaged communities, who are often already fearful of antagonizing state actors from forming into groups.[39]

Though less is known about the effects of restrictive CSO laws in democratic states, one can assess the impact of such laws in non-democratic contexts, which have been more thoroughly examined. In these less democratic contexts, the effects of such laws have been dire. In Ethiopia, for example, domestic human rights CSOs all but vanished in the years following the passage of an extremely restrictive CSO law, the Charities and Societies Proclamation of 2009.[40] In Azerbaijan, following the passage of a series of restrictive CSO regulations in 2013–2014, which imposed additional administrative barriers and burdens on CSOs and their funders, most independent advocacy CSOs scaled-down, discontinued their work, or left the country altogether.[41]

In Russia, following the passage of the Foreign Agents Law in 2012, which requires CSOs that receive any foreign donations and are engaged in vaguely defined "political activities" be labeled as "foreign agents," a label akin to foreign espionage in the Russian context, has led many CSOs, particularly those engaged in human rights and government accountability, to self-censor, limit their scope of activities, or voluntarily dissolve.[42] Recent reports suggest that over a third of Russia's CSOs have stopped operating, with many choosing to voluntarily dissolve rather than face the stigma associated with the 'foreign agent' label or the costs associated with challenging the label in court.[43]

In Bangladesh, recent reports suggest that in the wake of the 2016 Foreign Donations (Voluntary Activities) Regulation Bill's passage, a restrictive CSO law that places tight constraints on CSOs' ability to receive foreign funds, many CSOs, particularly smaller ones, have been forced to shut down due to insufficient funding, while the registration rates of new CSOs have dramatically

---

[39] BEN HAYES, THE IMPACT OF INTERNATIONAL COUNTER-TERRORISM ON CIVIL SOCIETY ORGANIZATIONS: UNDERSTANDING THE ROLE OF THE FINANCIAL ACTION TASK FORCE (Analysis 68, Apr. 2017). The *International Journal for Not-for-Profit Law* devoted one whole issue (Vol. 11, No. 4 (Aug. 2009)) to understanding the effects of Restrictions on Foreign Funding on CSOs; available at http://www.icnl.org/research/journal/vol11iss4/vol11iss4.pdf.
[40] Dupuy et al. 2015.
[41] Durna Safarova, *Azerbaijan: Suffocation of NGOs Raises Questions About Donor Strategy*, EURASIANET, Oct. 10, 2017.
[42] COUNCIL OF EUROPE, THE SHRINKING SPACE FOR HUMAN RIGHTS ORGANISATIONS (Apr. 2017).
[43] Charles Digges, *"Foreign Agent" Law Has Put 33 Percent of Russia's NGOs out of Business*, BELLONA, Oct. 20, 2015; Alexei Kozlov, *Russia's "Foreign Agents" Law Is Bankrupting Campaigners and Activists*, OPENDEMOCRACY, Nov. 9, 2017.

declined.[44] These are just a few of the many examples. And these examples are not irrelevant to democratic states; multiple reports have suggested linkages or similarities between restrictive CSO laws passed in India, Hungary and elsewhere with Russia's foreign agent law.[45]

Though we know less about the impact of restrictive CSO laws in democratic states, as previously stated, an emerging body of empirical evidence does suggest that such laws are having similar, even if less egregious, consequences. In India, for example, recent reports confirm that more than 24,000 CSOs lost their operating licenses following the adoption of new, more restrictive amendments to the Foreign Contributions Regulation Act in 2010 and 2011.[46] The new amendments prohibit any organizations of "a political nature" from receiving external assistance and grant the government broad authority in prohibiting any CSO from receiving foreign contributions when deemed "detrimental to the national interest."[47] In Turkey, which is perhaps an unfair example because of the current political context, a series of executive decrees following the failed coup in 2016 granted the government broad authority to dissolve and control the actions of CSOs. Under these decrees, more than 1,400 CSOs have been involuntarily shut down by government orders.[48]

And in the US in 2017, a policy was adopted requiring foreign CSOs that provide health care services to women and children to first sign a pledge promising not to perform any abortion-related activities, including those that involve educational opportunities or counseling, in order to receive any amount of US health aid.[49] This requirement has had a significant chilling effect on many NGOs that provide healthcare to impoverished families around the world and are dependent, for their existence, on US foreign aid.[50] According to

---

[44] Islam Shariful, *Screws Tighten on NGOs*, DHAKA TRIBUNE BLOG, Oct. 26, 2017.

[45] Yasmeen Serhan, *Hungary's Anti-Foreign NGO Law*, THE ATLANTIC, June 13, 2017; *Foreign Funding of NGOs: Donors: Keep Out*, THE ECONOMIST, Sept. 14, 2014.

[46] Melissa Cyrill & Adam Pitman, *FCRA Compliance in India: How 24,000 NGOs Lost Their License*, INDIA BRIEFING NEWS, Sept. 28, 2017.

[47] Wolff & Poppe 2015; Chaudhry 2016 at 62–63.

[48] William Armstrong, *Interview: Max Hoffman on Turkish Civil Society under Siege*, HÜRRIYET DAILY NEWS, 2017.

[49] Human Rights Watch. 2018. "Trump's 'Mexico City Policy' or 'Global Gag Rule.'" Questions and Answers. Human Rights Watch. Under the expanded Mexico City Policy, described as the "global gag rule" passed by previous republican administrations but this time "on steroids," adopted by President Trump in January of 2017, foreign CSOs wishing to receive any amount of global US health funding, must first sign a pledge promising to not engage in any abortion-related activities whatsoever, including counseling or education

[50] VANESSA RIOS, CRISIS IN CARE: YEAR TWO IMPACT OF TRUMP'S GLOBAL GAG RULE (2019).

one affected NGO, this policy, which not only implicates sexual and reproductive health services, including abortion, but also affects the provision of nutrition and maternal health services and the ability to reach a sub-sector of women who are victims of gender-based violence, is "literally killing women."[51] A study by the Kaiser Family Foundation found that at least 1,275 foreign NGOs and nearly 500 US NGOs have been negatively impacted, and specifically, their speech and activities curtailed, by this US policy.[52] Needless to say, the law can and does have very real consequences for CSOs and their ability to operate, flourish and even survive.

A BELLWETHER FOR DEMOCRATIC DECAY?

While future research needs to narrow in on the specific effects of restrictive CSO laws in democratic states, including their impact on the state of democracy itself, the findings presented in this book offer the possibility of identifying an early warning sign that democratic decay is underway. Future research building upon the findings presented herein by both legal scholars and political scientists is necessary to create a more accurate rubric for determining when and under what circumstances democratic decay is likely to occur. Additional research into the precise connection between the passage of restrictive CSO laws and democratic decay is needed to better understand, and therefore prevent, the further unraveling of the post-Cold war optimism in the power of democracy and the associational revolution.

WHAT IS AT STAKE?

Needless to say, the stakes of this research are high. Many tend to forget that democracy continues to be an experiment and a tenuous one at that. Democracy is, to be sure, a historic anomaly in all of recorded political history. Dictatorships, empires, aristocracies, tribes, monarchies, and oligarchies: these – not democracy – are the governance structures that have (with a few notable, narrow and brief exceptions) defined global politics since the rise of

---

[51] Amy Lieberman, *Two Years in, Report Finds "Global Gag Rule" Cuts Access to Health Care*, DEVEX, June 5, 2019.
[52] KELLIE MOSS & JENNIFER KATES, HOW MANY FOREIGN NGOS ARE SUBJECT TO THE EXPANDED MEXICO CITY POLICY? (2017). In addition to the expanded Mexico City Policy, thirty-five US states have proposed or adopted 100 laws imposing new restrictions on individuals' and CSOs' ability to protest in the past three years. See the *US Protest Law Tracker, International Center for Not-for-Profit*, available at http://www.icnl.org/usprotestlaw tracker/ (last accessed June 6, 2019).

humanity.[53] Democracy is the exception. Only in recent decades, the 1970s and 1980s, could one even talk about democracy as a common form of governance seen in more than a small handful of states. Indeed, until the early twentieth century, one could count on two hands the total number of democracies in the world (see Figure 6.3).

Figure 6.3: A graph of the number of democratic states from 1800–2003, from the Polity IV Project. Source: The Polity IV Project, available at http://www.systemicpeace.org/polity/polity4.htm. The y axis is the number of nations scoring an 8 or higher on the combined Polity score.

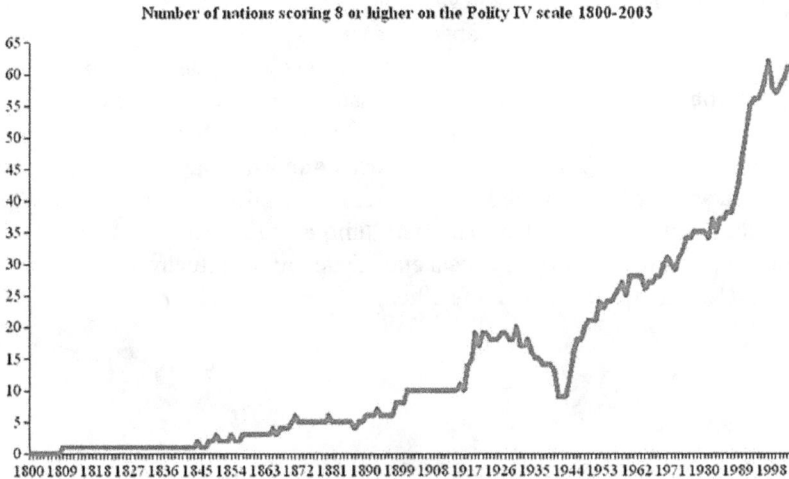

Number of nations scoring 8 or higher on the Polity IV scale 1800-2003

Recent research from the United States, historically one of the world's strongest and most emblematic democracies, suggests that while rhetorical support for democracy remains strong among older populations, younger voters, including millennials, are increasingly skeptical of democracy's potential. Recent surveys reveal that only about 30% of Americans born in the 1980s believe that it is "essential" to live in a democracy, a figure that jumps to 75% among those born in the 1930s.[54] Other surveys show that when voters in the US are confronted with a choice between commitment to foundational democratic principles or

---

[53] The ancient Greeks in the 4th and 5th centuries BCE and the early Romans in the 6th century both experimented with democracy, but neither experiment lasted. Grecian democracy lasted for less than 200 years; and Roman democracy for about 250 years.
[54] Roberto Stefan Foa & Yascha Mounk, *The Danger of Deconsolidation: The Democratic Disconnect*, 27 J. DEMOCRACY 5–17 (2016).

partisanship, the latter often prevails.[55] Similarly, only 2% of European millennials place democracy among their top five most important social values; and polls conducted in Australia, New Zealand, Sweden, and Britain report similar findings.[56]

Some have suggested that we are witnessing the gradual demise of the modern experiment with democracy.[57] Other historical experiments with democracy lasted for roughly two centuries – ancient Greek democracy lasted for roughly 200 years, and the Romans constructed a democratic polity that lasted roughly two and a half centuries. [58] Perhaps our current version of democracy, which is roughly 230 years old, is also in its final gasps. Plato, one of the earliest thinkers to speculate on the virtues of democracy, predicted that allowing people to govern themselves would eventually lead the masses to support the rule of tyrants,[59] a prediction also made by Abraham Lincoln[60] and Alexis de Tocqueville in their own times.[61] Regardless, what can be said with certainty is that an independent civil society and the ongoing existence of democracy are inextricably linked. One cannot exist without the other, at least not in any genuine form. They can both limp along for some time while the other remains dormant or in a weakened state, but eventually, the demise of one will lead to the downfall of the other.

---

[55] Mattew Graham & Milan W. Svolik, *Democracy in America? Partisanship, Polarization and the Robustness of Support for Democracy in the United States*, 114 Am. Pol. Sci. Rev. 392 (2020).

[56] Christian Rapp, *Young Europe 2017: The Youth Study of TUI Foundation*, TUI FOUNDATION, May 4, 2019, Hannover/Berlin, available at https://www.tui-stiftung.de/en/media/young-europe-2017-the-youth-study-of-tui-foundation/.

[57] Fareed Zakaria, *The Rise of Illiberal Democracy*, 76 FOREIGN AFF. 22–43 (Nov.–Dec. 1997).

[58] Joseph Stromberg, *The Real Birth of American Democracy*, SMITHSONIAN, Sept. 20, 2011.

[59] Lawrence Torcello, *Why Tyranny could be the Inevitable outcome of Democracy*, THE CONVERSATION, Nov. 11, 2019, available at http://theconversation.com/why-tyranny-could-be-the-inevitable-outcome-of-democracy-126158.

[60] Philip Gourevitch, *Abraham Lincoln Warned us About Donald Trump*, THE NEW YORKER, Mar. 15, 2016.

[61] Arthur Milikh, *Alexis de Tocqueville Predicted the Tyranny of the Majority in Our Modern World*, THE DAILY SIGNAL, July 29, 2015.

CHAPTER 7:

CONCLUSION

A time may come when the anomalies and irregularities are so glaring that an alternative theory, better able to take account of these realities, will come to dominate the field [of international relations].

Hedly Bull, The Anarchical Society 274 (1977)

Global democracy is not the only thing at stake with respect to the associational counter-revolution. So too is the very nature of the current international order, which is premised (as Chapter 2 detailed) on the foundational idea that states, and states alone, are the only relevant units within the international system.[1] Yet, the fact that states of all types, from all regions of the world, now feel compelled to push back against rising non-state actors, CSOs, suggests that the global balance of power, and with it, the Westphalian system, is in the process of transformation. This concluding chapter examines the implications of the associational counter-revolution on the changing nature of international relations in the twenty-first century and beyond.

THE SOCIETY OF ASSOCIATIONS

Scholar of International Relations and International Law Professor Anthony Arend, in his book *Legal Rules and International Society*, published just before the turn of the new century, speculates on the changing nature of the global order. While not willing to concede, as others have radically dared, that the Westphalian system is in a precarious state of imminent collapse or headed toward extinction, he nevertheless agrees that change is afoot. Asking what the international order of the future will look like, Arend responds:

> As the international system continues to change, I believe that what we may begin to observe is the development of a "society of associations" … [This society] would be composed of a variety of international actors. States may exist, but they would exist alongside several different types of nonstate actors. As common interests, common values, common

---

[1] KENNETH WALTZ, THEORY OF INTERNATIONAL POLITICS (1979) [hereinafter WALTZ 1979].

rules, and common institutions would begin to develop among these different types of associations, a society would develop among them.[2]

This new "society of associations," according to Arend, will be "messy" – the units will be dissimilar (rather than monolithic and categorically identical, as the Westphalian order prescribes); it will include both state *and* non-state actors, as well as national, sub-national, and transnational actors, notably including nongovernmental organizations, or CSOs.[3] Arend describes the raft of new non-state actors that have become active in international politics as "important actors" in their own right within "the international arena." They have "political structures and political leaders" and now command both "authority and loyalty," things that used to characterize states uniquely.[4] Moreover, they no longer operate as mere appendages of states, which historically served as the (exclusive) representatives of their people, CSOs, and subnational governments at the international level.

THE GLOBAL DIFFUSION OF POWER

The diffusion of power to non-state actors at the global level was foreseen by certain prescient theorists in the latter part of the twentieth century. IR scholar Hedley Bull, for example, was one of the first to suggest that the international system would slowly migrate back into a "neomedieval" system comprised of both state and non-state actors who operate within overlapping circles of authority and jurisdiction (as was seen in medieval times).[5] According to this provocative thesis, "it is conceivable that the sovereign states might disappear and be replaced not by a world government but by a modern and secular equivalent of the kind of universal political organization that existed in Western Christendom in the Middle Ages."[6] During medieval times, according to Bull, sovereignty was non-existent, at least as we understand that concept today. Writing in the late 1970s, long before CSOs' "golden age," the invention of the internet, the rise of powerful transnational networks,[7] and the awareness that our most urgent and existential challenges – climate change, infectious

---

[2] ANTHONY AREND, LEGAL RULES AND INTERNATIONAL SOCIETY 196 (1999).

[3] *Id.* at 8.

[4] *Id.* at 171.

[5] HEDLEY BULL, THE ANARCHICAL STATE: A STUDY OF ORDER IN WORLD POLITICS (1977) [hereinafter BULL 1977].

[6] *Id.* at 254.

[7] Michele Acuto and others have written extensively about the rise of city networks. *E.g,* M. Acuto et al., *City Diplomacy: Towards More Strategic Networking?*, 8 GLOBAL POLICY 14–22 (2017).

pandemics, migration, and pervasive inequality – require global, rather than national, solutions, Bull predicted that a fundamental shift would transpire in the global order within the next century. This shift, Bull predicted, would involve the replacement of national sovereignty as the overarching ordering principle of international politics with a more amorphous principle that makes room for multiple, overlapping authorities. More specifically, Bull predicted that five trends would signal that this shift was underway and that "a secular reincarnation of the system of overlapping or segmented authority that characterized medieval Christendom" was upon us.[8] These trends include: the regional integration of states, the rise of loyalties attached to non-sovereign territorial entities, the restoration of private international violence, the technological unification of the world, and most importantly, for the purposes of this book, the rise of transnational non-governmental organizations. Without exception, each one of these trends, by the turn of the twenty-first century, had become a reality, and these realities are even more apparent today.

Since Bull's time, other international relations scholars, including Bruce Cronin, Joseph Lepgold, and while a bit more skeptical, Anthony Arend (cited above), among others, have similarly predicted either a return to, or the dawning of, a new epoch in global politics where the state no longer occupies the exclusive, or even dominant, seat of power. Instead, the state is viewed as being simply one among a heterogenous array of actors that embody varying, and in some cases overlapping, levels of authority.[9] While the nation-state form remains intact, change is indeed afoot, as these and other scholars have predicted. This change, in my view, is directly linked to the rise and proliferation of non-state actors, notably including CSOs, which have triggered states to engage in behaviors that attempt to re-balance the global balance of power in their favor.

While the diffusion of global power to non-state actors is no longer a revolutionary or even a bold idea, it decisively is both – conceptually revolutionary and bold – when juxtaposed with the canons and foundational ideals of the modern international political and legal order. The international order crafted after World War II (WWII), which was created exclusively by and for states, and the infrastructure that was built up to support it, is myopically oriented around the belief that the nation-state is the pinnacle and exclusive

---

[8] BULL 1977 at 264.

[9] Bruce Cronin & Joseph Lepgold, A New Medievalism? Conflicting International Authorities and Competing Localities in the Twenty-First Century, unpublished paper presented at the conference on "The Changing Nature of Sovereignty in the New World Order," Center for International Affairs, Harvard University, April 1995, cited in ANTHONY AREND, LEGAL RULES AND INTERNATIONAL SOCIETY (1999).

actor on the international stage. The entire conceptual and physical infrastructure built up to conduct international relations in the post-WWII era – notably including the international legal system and the network of intergovernmental organizations, including the United Nations and its influential seven-member Security Council – were not only designed exclusively by and for states. They are premised on the idea that states, and states alone, are the central representatives in the global political arena.

TOWARDS A NEW THEORY OF INTERNATIONAL POLITICS

Waltz himself conceded that "theories ... may not last" and will and should, with time, be replaced by better ones.[10] By "better," Waltz was referring to the explanatory power of a theory. The usefulness and explanatory relevance of Waltz's balance of power theory, which, as the previous chapter discussed, is, in reality, an ancient theory that can be traced back to ancient Greek and Roman times, still seems to hold explanatory power at the systemic, international level. However, Waltz's broader theory of international politics is starting to show significant signs of outdatedness primarily because of its ongoing myopic fixation on states, and more specifically, the world's most powerful states – with power measured in terms of their traditional "hard" power resources (military might and economic strength).[11] For Waltz, the only relevant "unit" within the international political system is the state, and the only form of "power" that matters is military and economic strength. These core propositions can, and extensively have been, challenged on numerous fronts, notably including his overly narrow conceptualization of the relevant units operating with the international sphere and the nature of power, or the ability to coerce others to do what you want, in today's world.[12] This chapter hopes to add to this chorus of criticism by adding new insights and empirical data to the claim that it's time for an updated version of Waltz's theory of international politics, which, in my view, continues to hold explanatory power and to offer many valuable

---

[10] Waltz 1979 at 6, 9.

[11] *Id.*

[12] *E.g.*, Helen Milner, *The Assumption of Anarchy in IR: A Critique, in* NEOREALISM AND NEOLIBERALISM 143–69 (David A. Baldwin ed., 1993); Colin Elman, *Horses for Courses: Why Not Neorealist Theories of Foreign Policy?*, 6 SECURITY STUD. 7–53 (1996); William Wohlforth, *The Stability of a Unipolar World*, 24 INT'L SECURITY 5–41 (Summer 1999); Stephen Brooks & William Wohlforth, *Hard Times for Soft Balancing*, 30 INT'L SECURITY 72–108 (Summer 2005); John Vasquez, *Realist Paradigm and Degenerative versus Progressive Research Programs: An Appraisal of Neotraditional Research on Waltz's Balancing Proposition*, 91 AM. POL. SCI. REV. 899–912 (Dec. 1997); REALISM AND THE BALANCING OF POWER (John Vasquez & Colin Elman eds., 2002).

contributions to our understanding of international politics, but is nevertheless in desperate need of updating.

To begin with the operative units at the international level, the previous chapters revealed the ways in which civil society organizations (CSOs) have risen up in unprecedented new ways over the past several decades to become formidable actors in global politics.[13] As I have argued in previous chapters, their rise has been so profound and consequential that states have begun counter-balancing their influence in a whole variety of ways, only one of which has been the focus of this research; the adoption of restrictive CSO laws. However, states of all varieties have used a variety of tools and methods, some legal, others extralegal, and others illegal, to contain the spread and influence of the autonomous non-governmental sector, especially at the international level. Democracies, and specifically the world's strongest democracies, were narrowly focused on as they represent the least likely candidates to engage in this type of behavior. While they have tended to target CSOs using the legal systems and through the passage of legislation, rather than through acts of harassment, violence, and other unlawful means, their overall goal to reduce the independence and autonomy of CSOs has been broadly the same. States throughout the world appear to have awoken to the new reality that confronts them, namely that states are no longer the only relevant actor – or "unit" in the words of Waltz – in town. States no longer channel all of their time and attention into counter-balancing the hard power of other states, but they are now engaged in counter-balancing against non-state actors too.

And this brings us to the highly contested concept of power. While the balance of power theory continues to prove useful in explaining and predicting the behaviors of the units that comprise the international order, even when one expands the concept of "units" as I have done, the concept of "power" also needs tweaking and expanding in order to maintain its relevance in the modern world. As a brief reminder, theories are not meant to be mirrors of reality; that is not their purpose. Instead, theories are explanatory devices used to help make sense of, and ideally to predict and exert some level of control over, complex phenomena whose causes are not directly observable.[14] Applying balance of power theory to the closing space phenomenon, specifically its spread into democratic states, exemplifies this distinction perfectly. While the balance of power theory cannot describe or foretell the global rise and spread of restrictive legislation against a particular transnational actor, it can, however,

---

[13] A similar analysis could be written about other non-state actors, such as terrorists or corporations, but I have chosen to focus specifically on CSOs, which itself is a vast and broad category.

[14] WALTZ 1979.

be useful in *explaining* this phenomenon, in helping us make sense of it and, therefore, to predict whether and to what extent it can be expected to continue. But this theory only makes sense and is useful if the concept of power – like the concept of "unit" – is expanded and re-interpreted anew.

CSOS & SOFT POWER

CSOs' influence, assertiveness, and ability to shape outcomes at the international level have been escalating over the past three decades. This is true despite the fact that they do not command militaries, possess weapons, or have access to the powerful tools and rights inherent to sovereignty, all the things we tend to think of when we think of "power" at the international level. Yet CSOs nevertheless have the ability to exercise influence over others, and specifically, the ability to get other actors to do something that they otherwise would not do, which is a traditional definition for power.[15] CSOs' "power" is largely reflected in their ability to attract people, money, goods, and causes from around the world, a concept known as "soft power."

Soft power is the ability to achieve objectives, often foreign policy objectives, through attraction and persuasion, rather than force or coercion.[16] According to Joseph Nye, who coined the term "soft power" in 1990, in the highly digitized and interconnected world, we currently inhabit, where power is more diffuse, and our common challenges are often interdependent, "victory often depends not on whose army wins, but on whose story wins."[17] And CSOs are especially adept at telling "stories," or rather, at reframing the argument so that a state (or other non-state) actor is forced into changing their behavior through the sheer force of argumentation. Examples of this include CSOs' efforts to end Apartheid in South Africa;[18] the CSO-led movement to ban wars of aggression, landmines, and nuclear weapons within international law;[19] and the civil society-led global

---

[15] This classic definition of "power" was formulated by renowned political scientist Robert Dahl. *See* Robert Dahl, *The Concept of Power*, 2 BEHAV. SCI. 201, 201–15 (1957).

[16] JONATHAN MCCLORY, THE SOFT POWER 30: A GLOBAL RANKING OF SOFT POWER 12 (2018), https://softpower30.com/wp-content/uploads/2018/07/The-Soft-Power-30-Report-2018.pdf.

[17] Joseph Nye, *The Information Revolution and Soft Power*, 113 CURRENT HIST. 19, 20 (2014) (citing John Arquilla).

[18] Audie Klotz, *Transnational Activism and Global Transformations: The Anti-Apartheid and Abolitionist Experiences*, 8 EUR. J. INT'L REL. 49–76 (2002).

[19] HATHAWAY & SHAPIRO 2017; Richard Price, *Reversing the Gun Sights: Transnational Civil Society Targets Land Mines*, 52 INT'L ORG. 613–44 (1998); Matthew Bolton, *A Brief Guide to the New Nuclear Weapons Ban Treaty*, JUST SECURITY, July 14, 2017.

campaign to raise awareness of violence against women, with the most recent manifestation of this being the #MeToo Movement.[20]

Professor Nye, like Waltz and most political scientists, applied his innovative new term of "soft power" only to states and employed it only for the purpose of explaining state behavior, reflecting the state-centric "conceptual jail" that continues to imprison the field of international relations.[21] Yet, soft power is especially, perhaps uniquely, useful in explaining the rising influence of non-state actors, such CSOs, within international politics in recent years. Indeed, the things that Nye identifies as comprising a nation's "soft power" – their favorability toward foreign countries, foreigners, and tourists; the number of higher education institutions, embassies, museums, and cultural organizations; technological and digital sophistication; access to creative industries and entertainment; and the ability to facilitate foreign exchanges, among others – resonate with the types of services, causes, and programs offered by CSOs.[22] The same things that give states increased soft power give CSOs soft power, which in recent decades CSOs have become particularly adept at acquiring and utilizing to serve their ends. One way in which they have done this is by utilizing soft law techniques and tools, another term that needs to be introduced and incorporated into an updated theory of international politics.

CSOs & Soft Law

Soft law is directly connected to, and in correlation with, soft power: as one increases, so too does the other. This is why, in part, states continued for so long to maintain their exclusive grip over international politics. Under traditional black letter international law, which is designed to deal with state behavior with very few exceptions,[23] is effectively blind to the existence of CSOs. Indeed, reference to "civil society" is entirely absent from the traditional sources of international law, which include treaties (which are defined as international agreements concluded between "states"), customary international law (which is based on "state practice", and general principles of law recognized by

---

[20] Sophie Gilbert, *The Movement of #MeToo*, THE ATLANTIC, Oct. 16, 2017; Mala Htun & S. Laurel Weldon, *The Civic Origins of Progressive Policy Change: Combating Violence against Women in Global Perspective, 1975–2005*, 106 AM. POL. SCI. REV. 548–69 (2012). What I mean here is an enormous success in bringing visibility and awareness to the issue of sexual assault and violence against women, not unfortunately, in solving the problem.

[21] JOSEPH NYE, BOUND TO LEAD: THE CHANGING NATURE OF AMERICAN POWER (1990).

[22] McCLORY, *supra* note 253, at 31–33.

[23] The exceptions primarily include international human rights law and international criminal law, both of which deal with the actions or treatment of individuals.

"civilized nations."[24] Needless to say, under the traditional canons of international law, civil society activists and groups cannot form treaties,[25] contribute to the formation of customary international law, or contribute to the formation of "general principles of law."[26] Nor can they obtain legal standing in the International Court of Justice and most other international courts or tribunals.[27] And while "non-governmental organizations" is mentioned once in the entirety of the UN Charter, the term "civil society" is entirely missing, which stands in stark contrast to the terms "state" and "nation," which appear over forty times.[28] Moreover, under international law, CSOs lack legal personality, which means they do not have rights, duties, or recognition under the law.[29] Therefore they cannot be held liable for international legal violations[30] or become full, independent members of state-based international organizations, including the UN (or any of its primary organs), whose exclusive membership includes only "peace loving *states*."[31]

The Vienna Convention on the Law of Treaties, the key international instrument governing the creation and enforcement of international treaties

---

[24] *See* UN Charter and ICJ Statute, *supra* note 8, art. 38(1), (defining traditional sources of international law as treaties, custom, general principles of law, the decisions of lower courts, and scholarly writings).

[25] *See* Vienna Convention on the Law of Treaties art. 2, May 23, 1969, 1155 U.N.T.S. 331, 8 I.L.M. 679 (1969) (defining a treaty as an "international agreement concluded between States").

[26] *See generally* Daniel Bodansky, *The Concept of Customary International Law*, 16 MICH. J. INT'L L. 667, 670 (1995) (stating that customary international law is determined by examining state practice and *opinio juris*).

[27] *See generally* UN Charter and ICJ Statute, *supra* note 8, art. 34(1).

[28] *See* UN Charter and ICJ Statute, *supra* note 8. Note that the Preamble to the UN Charter does mention that the representative governments drafting the Charter met in the "City" of San Francisco. This is not a substantive inclusion of the word "city," so I did not include it.

[29] RICHARD PUGH ET AL., INTERNATIONAL LAW: CASES AND MATERIALS 248 (4th ed. 2001); Blank, *The City and the World*, *supra* note 23, at 892.

[30] *See* RESTATEMENT (THIRD) FOREIGN RELATIONS LAW OF THE UNITED STATES § 207(c) (AM. LAW INST. 1987). International law is governed by a broad rule concerning "state responsibility" for all violations of IL committed within its territory, whether committed by the federal government or not. The state is responsible for the acts of all of its "officials or its organs," which has been implied to include all sub-national authorities. This means that virtually all actions of cities are treated as if they were the actions of the state. *Id.*

[31] UN Charter and ICJ Statute, *supra* note 8, art. 4(1). *See also* UNITED NATIONS, About UN Membership, http://www.un.org/en/sections/member-states/about-un-membership/index.html (last visited Jan. 12, 2020) (noting that non-state actors, including civil society organizations and the Holy See, can serve as observers in certain international organizations, such as the United Nations).

(the primary source of IL), explicitly defines treaties as international agreements formed between *states*.[32] This foundational convention makes no mention whatsoever of any other entity bearing this critical law-making authority; it applies to states (and organizations composed of states) alone.[33] The omission of non-state actors, and CSOs specifically, in the canons and study of international law is also reflected in the syllabi for international law courses; a non-exhaustive but extensive online search of such syllabi found virtually no mentions of the role of CSOs within international law.[34]

The foundational principle of international law is the same foundational principle of modern international relations: states are the highest and exclusive authority, the Leviathan, over their territories.[35] With rare exceptions, international law treats states as the makers and shapers of its content and the gatekeepers of implementation and enforcement.[36] As political scientist James Rosenau and others have argued, the state centrism that infects the fields of both international relations and international law is a "conceptual jail" that prevents us from noticing the rise of other non-state actors in international affairs.[37]

As with power, CSOs have acquired "softer" versions of the law in order to get around the many formal barriers and hurdles to their acquisition of hard law, as described above. Soft law describes those quasi-legal instruments that are neither strictly binding nor completely lacking in legal significance, such as declarations, guidelines, protocols, principles, policy declarations, codes of

---

[32] Vienna Convention on the Law of Treaties, *supra* note 28, art. 2(1)(a).

[33] *Id.* art. 1 ("The present Convention applies to treaties between States."). *See also id.* art. 7 (affirming that representatives of states belonging to international organizations can also conclude treaties). This is an application of the *expressio unius est exclusio alterius* canon. By including organizations of states, convention participants showed they considered (or had the opportunity to consider) other viable non-state actors and rejected them.

[34] Needless to say, there are hundreds, if not thousands, of international law courses nation-wide and globally, each of which is accompanied by a syllabus. I reviewed roughly fifty syllabi that I located through a simple online search. This is admittedly an anecdotal approach, but it is nevertheless reflective, in my opinion, of the lack of focus on cities in international law courses.

[35] *See* THOMAS HOBBES, LEVIATHAN: OR THE MATTER, FORME AND POWER OF A COMMONWEALTH, ECCLESIASTICAL AND CIVIL (1886).

[36] Implementation and enforcement tasks are arguably shifting to allow for other actors to be involved. *See generally* Oomen & Baumgärtel, *supra* note 1, at 626.

[37] *See* Chan, *supra* note 1, at 138 (citing JAMES ROSENAU, ALONG THE DOMESTIC-FOREIGN FRONTIER: EXPLORING GOVERNANCE IN A TURBULENT WORLD 15–17 (1997); JAMES ROSENAU, DISTANT PROXIMITIES: DYNAMICS BEYOND GLOBALIZATION 410 (2003) ("[w]hat is domestic is also foreign and what is foreign is also domestic").

conduct, communications, and the like.[38] They are not enforceable in the traditional ways but, nevertheless, can have a decisive impact and influence over state behavior. UN General Assembly Resolutions are a classic example of international soft law (as made by nation-states); they are legally significant and can and often do influence state behavior but are not legally binding or enforceable in a court of law.[39] In contrast, hard law, in the international context, includes binding legal agreements, with the classic example being an international treaty.[40]

Hard law includes responsibilities and rights that are legally enforceable by authorized courts or tribunals, backed by a police or military force, and that impose real consequences (typically including fines, imprisonment, or obligatory corrective action).[41] Soft law, on the other hand, which includes non-enforceable standards and norms, relies on the force of persuasion, reputation, and cooption (the same mechanisms through which soft power is exercised) to induce voluntary compliance.[42] Though soft law has been criticized as "vague," "uncompelling," and "weak," one powerful fact cannot be uncontested: it is often followed.[43] According to a leading international law textbook, "states do in fact respect and rely on 'soft law' norms," just as they comply with many hard law norms even when they know that enforcement is extremely unlikely.[44] In many cases, and especially at the international level, soft law norms transform or crystallize into hard law; this is how much of customary international law is formed. Much of international environmental law, for example, started out as 'soft law' norms, but, as time went on, global actors decided to embody those norms in formal international treaties, such as the Paris Climate Agreement.[45]

---

[38] Gregory Shaffer & Mark Pollack, *Hard vs Soft Law: Alternatives, Complements, and Antagonists in International Governance*, 94 MINN. L. REV. 706 (2010); Bryan Druzin, *Why Does Soft Law Have Any Power Anyway?*, 7 ASIAN J. INT'L L. 361 (2017).

[39] Stephen M. Schwebel, *The Effect of Resolutions of the U.N. General Assembly on Customary International Law*, 73 AM. SOC'Y INT'L L. PROC. 301 (1979).

[40] Vienna Convention on the Law of Treaties, May 23, 1969, 1155 U.N.T.S. 331, 8 I.L.M. 679 (1969).

[41] Shaffer & Pollack, *supra* note 260, at 724.

[42] Druzin, *supra* note 260, at 366–70.

[43] Prosper Weil, *Towards Relative Normativity in International Law*. 77 AM. J. INT'L L. 413, 414 (1983).

[44] PUGH ET AL., *supra* note 32, at 34.

[45] *Id.*

The hard versus soft law dichotomy,[46] when combined with the hard versus soft power distinction, can help to explain the rise of CSOs internationally in recent years despite their ongoing powerlessness from a formal international legal and political perspective. Hard and soft power are disconnected; one can exist without the other. For example, while North Korea's hard power is high, it is lacking entirely in soft power; it has little to no ability to change other states' behavior through the power of attraction to its values or policy objectives. Similarly, while America has traditionally been strong on both soft and hard power, some (including Joseph Nye himself) argue that in the Trump era, its soft power has plummeted.[47] While CSOs remain powerless from a hard power and hard law perspective, as briefly outlined below, they have increasingly high levels of soft power, which they are using to adopt soft law instruments, which increases their level of soft power – and so the cycle goes.

UPDATING THE LEXICON OF INTERNATIONAL RELATIONS & INTERNATIONAL LAW

The myopic fixation on states is built into the core vocabulary associated with the international political and legal world order – the United *Nations* (the successor to the League of *Nations*), inter*nation*al law, inter*national* organizations, inter*nation*al relations, inter*national* diplomacy – making it difficult to even talk about global politics without employing the word "nation." Yet, the international arena is no longer the exclusive playground of states but instead a crowded arena buzzing with a variety of non-state actors, some of which are governmental, some of which are private, and some of which defy both those categories. This arena can no longer accurately be characterized as "international" or as governed exclusively by "international law" or the traditional rules of "international relations." Broader and more inclusive terms are now necessary when talking about what is occurring in international politics. According to Professor Janne Nijman, who advocates for using the

---

[46] Note that this distinction is contested by some scholars. Legal positivists tend to deny the very concept of "soft" law since law, by definition, is "binding" in their view. For example, Jan Klabbers, a legal positivist, contends that law cannot be "more or less binding" and that the concept of soft law is logically flawed. *See* Jan Klabbers, *The Redundancy of Soft Law*, 65 NORDIC J. INT'L L. 167, 168–81 (1996) (advocating retention of the "traditional binary conception of law"). Professor Prosper Weil makes a slightly different argument when he claims that the proliferation of "soft law" weakens the international legal system by blurring the line between law and nonlaw. *See* Weil, *supra* note 265, at 414–15.

[47] Joseph Nye, *Donald Trump and the Decline of US Soft Power*, PROJECT SYNDICATE (Feb. 6, 2018), https://www.project-syndicate.org/commentary/trump-american-soft-power-decline-by-joseph-s--nye-2018-02.

term 'global' rather than international, "we are facing a moment of foreign policy transformation: We are shifting from an international to a global society," in which non-state actors are "rising as key foreign policy actor[s]."[48] Global society, global governance, global relations, global law, global actors: these terms better reflect our international empirical reality. To remain aligned with empirical realities, international lawyers and scholars of international relations should start incorporating these terms into their vocabulary, and a simple way to start is by replacing "international" with "global."

We could refer to this lexical and paradigm shift perhaps as the "globalization" of international relations or simply as "global relations." By focusing on the "global" dimensions of international relations, and by eliminating (where possible and where unnecessary) our exclusive reliance on the terms "nation" and "state," my hope is that this would open the field up to a more accurate understanding of global politics. All of the questions asked by international relations and international legal scholars – who are the relevant actors, what influence are they exerting, what tools and techniques are they using to coerce others into behaving in certain ways, and what levers of power do they hold – must continue to be asked, but with a broader array of "units" and with a broader conceptualization of "power" in mind. Only then will we have a more complete picture of global – not international! – relations.

Under our current conceptual framework – a world order built on the idea that states are the sole international actors that matter and that hard power and hard law are the determinants of international influence – CSOs naturally appear powerless. Yet, when new concepts are embraced, and new terminology is employed, the status of CSOs looks entirely different. CSOs embody increased levels of soft power, which they've acquired in part by increasing their arsenal of soft legal tools. They are forming into powerful large-scale networks, allying with well-connected international organizations, gaining seats on UN decision-making bodies, successfully lobbying for inclusion in multilateral agendas, mirroring state-based coalitions and events, and adopting their own body of global laws, which they use to hold each other accountable.[49] They are participating in global, not international, politics, alongside an array of other

---

[48] Janne Nijman, *Renaissance of the City as Global Actor: The Role of Foreign Policy and International Law Practices in the Construction of Cities as Global Actors, in* THE TRANSFORMATION OF FOREIGN POLICY: DRAWING AND MANAGING BOUNDARIES FROM ANTIQUITY TO THE PRESENT 209, 236 (Andreas Fahrmeir et al. eds., 2016).

[49] Chrystie Swiney, *The Urbanization Of International Law & International Relations: The Rising Soft Power & Soft Law Of Cities In Global Governance*, 41 MICH. INT'L L.J. 227 (June 2020) [hereinafter Swiney 2020].

non-state actors, and their voices, opinions, and needs are being heard. It is time to break out of the state-centric "conceptual jail" that has defined international relations and law since at least the post-WWII era and to see global (not international) politics for what it is: a complex domain of states and non-state actors cooperating and competing together to shape global (not international) policies and to participate in global (not international) governance.[50]

FUTURE RESEARCH

As legal scholar Anne-Marie Slaughter declared nearly fifteen years ago, a "new world order" is emerging in which non-state actors, notably including CSOs, are taking on more influential and assertive roles on the world stage.[51] The nation-state, according to Slaughter, has begun to disaggregate into sub-component parts, which are now rising up, pushing ahead, and in many cases, leaping over the world's historic Leviathans to join forces with other non-state actors to stake out their own policy positions at the global level.[52] While we tend to focus on globalization and digitization as the key trends of the twenty-first century, those trends are primarily realized through the overarching trend of our times – the global diffusion of power to non-state actors.

New concepts, paradigms, and conceptual frameworks are needed to understand this new reality. Old terms, such as international relations, international law, and international organizations, which carry the word "nation" within them, are starting to sound out-of-touch and anachronistic in an era when global governance involves a multitude of actors involved in a variety of activities traditionally performed only by states. The concepts of soft law, soft power, global law, and global relations, while just a start, will put us on the path of better understanding how CSOs and other non-state actors can

---

[50] ROSENAU, *supra* note 42, at 15–17; *see e.g.*, Chan, *supra* note 1, at 138.

[51] *See generally* Slaughter, *supra* note 17. Note that while cities do not feature in Slaughter's argument that a new world order has arisen (instead, she focuses primarily on non-governmental sub-state actors), her theory of the "disaggregated state" – and the rise of sub-national actors at the international level – maps perfectly onto the rise of cities, which seems to coincide with the rise in influence of non-governmental actors. *See id.*, at 325. For an analysis of Slaughter's argument, see Frug & Barron, *supra* note 14, at 23–24. According to Frug and Barron, "cities are involved in the very kinds of networks that Slaughter describes." *Id.* at 24.

[52] *See* Chan, *supra* note 1, at 2; Charles Hermann, *Book Note*, 85 AM. POL. SCI. REV. 1081 (1991) (reviewing JAMES ROSENAU, TURBULENCE IN WORLD POLITICS: A THEORY OF CHANGE AND CONTINUITY (1990)). *See generally* SOFIE BOUTELIGIER, CITIES, NETWORKS, AND GLOBAL ENVIRONMENTAL GOVERNANCE: SPACES OF INNOVATION, PLACES OF LEADERSHIP (2012); Oomen & Baumgärtel, *supra* note 1, at 608.

remain both formally powerless under the current international legal regime; yet informally influential, and increasingly so, in a global political arena defined by a diffusion of actors and power. CSOs, through their use of soft law instruments, savvy strategies, and influential alliances, are acquiring more and more soft power in the global sphere. All of which is allowing them to contribute not only to the implementation and enforcement of global agendas and international law but to contribute to their very formation.

The rising influence of CSOs, and other non-state actors, is naturally causing states to push back, or in the words of Kenneth Waltz, to recalibrate the global balance of power in their decisive power. These realities must be understood, studied, mapped, and explained, as this book makes a partial attempt to do. In addition, a new lexicon that better maps onto our new empirical realities and that incorporates all relevant actors, both state and non-state, in both national and global politics, is needed. Expanding our state-and-nation-centric language will, I hope, expand our paradigms, concepts and minds so that we can better describe, explain and predict global affairs, the very goal of the field of international relations.

Future research is needed to continue where this book leaves off. It's imperative not only to expand and re-think the language that we use to understand international relations and to better assess the implications of the associational counter-revolution on the state of global democracy, but more specifically, to understand the full impact of specific types of laws on specific types of CSOs. It is critical not only to map the adoption dates and rates, and various typologies of these laws, as was done in Chapter 5 but also to track the ongoing *effects* of these laws on particular sectors of civil society. Will they lead to the demise of entire categories of CSOs, as has occurred in Ethiopia with respect to human rights CSOs?[53] Moreover, additional research is needed into the specific ways in which CSOs are adapting and responding to the new wave of legal and extralegal restrictions being placed on them by an increasing number of states.[54] Finally, researchers from the fields of international relations and law must collaborate and engage in interdisciplinary research to fully explore the full scope of challenges, problems, and opportunities afforded by the associational counter-revolution in the decades ahead.

---

[53] Kendra E. Dupuy et al., *Who Survived? Ethiopia's Regulatory Crackdown on Foreign-Funded NGOs*, 22 REV. INT'L POL. ECON. 419–56 (2014).
[54] Julia Oram & Deborah Doane, *NGOs Are Adapting to the Closing Space When They Must Push Back*, OPEN GLOBAL RIGHTS, Dec. 19, 2017.

CONCLUSION

This book offers a novel explanation for why well over half the world's strongest democratic states, like so many states throughout the world, have adopted laws restricting the autonomy of their civil society sectors. The explanation offered operates at the international rather than the domestic level of analysis and tells a different story than the one most commonly told, which focuses on the rise of illiberal regimes in the years following the turn of the new century. The explanation offered is based on notions of national sovereignty and balance of power theory, as articulated by Kenneth Waltz, and the story begins not at the turn of the twenty-first century but after the Second World War, when the modern international legal and political order was installed. The modern world order, which institutionalized, prioritized, and emphasized the principles of national sovereignty and territorial integrity above and beyond all others, views threats to these principles, no matter the source, as threatening. As the balance of power theory predicts, states will engage in balancing behaviors not only when they feel that their competitive advantage is threatened by another state but when they feel that their national sovereignty is being undermined.[55] While the balance of power theory, and indeed all of international relations theory, is focused on explaining the relations among and between states, this theory can also be used to explain the antagonistic relationship between states and CSOs over the past two decades.

By narrowing in on the least likely set of actors to participate in this trend (the world's strongest democratic states), the hope is ultimately to explain why so many states, whatever their governance structure, have been engaging in broadly similar activities (notably, lessening CSOs' level of autonomy through the passage of restrictive CSO laws) over the past two decades.[56] The theory proposed is that CSOs' exponential rise during the associational revolution triggered states to take notice of their rising influence and assertiveness in both national and international politics. In an effort to maintain their place of primacy and exclusivity in the international order, States are now pushing back and engaging in traditional balancing behaviors to counter the rising influence of CSOs and the broad transnational networks they are forming with foreign CSOs, or TANs. States are doing this by casting CSOs as foreign actors or agents, by labeling their activities as maliciously intent on undermining their national sovereignty and territorial integrity, and in general, by casting them as enemies

---

[55] K. WALTZ, THEORY OF INTERNATIONAL POLITICS (2010).
[56] Andrew Bennett & Colin Elman, Case Study Methods in the International Relations Subfield, 40 COMP. POL. STUD. 170–95 at 170 (Feb. 2007); Jason Seawright & John Gerring, *Case Selection Techniques in Case Study Research: A Menu of Qualitative and Quantitative Options*, 61 POL. RES. Q. 294–308 (June 2008); JOHN GERRING, CASE STUDY RESEARCH (2007).

of the state. In this way, states are utilizing the conceptual underpinnings of the modern international order to prevent the further rise of CSOs.

This topic matters because democracy matters and democracy can only exist where an independent civil society exists. Only time will tell whether the associational counter-revolution is a lasting global trend or just a temporary blip in the still short history of democracy's modern existence. While the historical records do not yield an optimistic forecast concerning the endurance of democracy, they do, however, display an unyielding desire on the part of individuals to voluntarily associate, to form into groups and coalitions on the basis of a shared concern or cause, independent of the government or the market.[57] This human desire to associate is so widely accepted that it has become a widely recognized international human right, codified in various human rights treaties and the majority of state constitutions. This right has come under attack by the spread of restrictive CSO laws appearing in countries across the world, including those who have historically supported it most robustly. Tracking and understanding what compelled the passage of these laws is the first step to ensuring that the freedom of association is protected, and protecting the freedom and association is essential if democracy is to defy the dismal prediction of history.

---

[57] Boris DeWiel, *A Conceptual History of Civil Society: From Greek Beginnings to the End of Marx*, 6 PAST IMPERFECT 3–42, at 7 (1997) (discussing records from 5 BCE, kept by the sophists, discussing the existence of civil society groups).

Appendices

* Data was collected using the Database of Political Institutions, published by the World Bank, available at https://datacatalog.worldbank.org/dataset/wps22 83-database-political-institutions.

Hyper-nationalist = Right (for political orientation) + Nationalist (yes)

Democratic Country	Year a Restrictive CSO Law was Adopted	Political Orientation	Nationalist	Hyper-nationalist
*Australia (4)	2016	Right	No	No
Australia	2015	Right	No	No
Australia	2014	Right	No	No
Australia	2013	Left	No	No
*Austria (1)	2015	Left	No	No
*Belgium (1)	2002	Right	Yes	Yes
Bolivia (4)	2013	Left	No	No
Bolivia	2013	Left	No	No
Bolivia	2008	Left	No	No
Bolivia	2007	Left	No	No
Bulgaria (1)	2016	Right	No	No
*Canada (2)	2015	Right	No	No
Canada	2013	Right	No	No
Croatia (4)	2016	Right	Yes	Yes
Croatia	2015	Center	No	No
Croatia	2014	Center	No	No
Croatia	1995	Right	Yes	Yes
*Denmark (1)	2017	Left	No	No
*Finland (1)	2015	Right	No	No
France (5)	2017	Left	No	No
France	2017	Left	No	No
France	2016	Left	No	No
France	2015	Left	No	No
France	2010	Right	No	No
*Germany (1)	2017	Right	No	No
Greece (2)	2013	Right	No	No
Greece	2016	Left	No	No
*Hungary (5)	2011	Right	Yes**	Yes

Hungary	2017	Right	Yes**	Yes
Hungary	2018	Right	Yes**	Yes
Hungary	2018	Right	Yes**	Yes
Hungary	2018	Right	Yes**	Yes
India (4)	2010	Left	No	No
India	2015	Right	No	No
India	2016	Right	No	No
India	2017	Right	No	No
*Ireland (2)	2001	Center	No	No
Ireland	2009	Center	No	No
*Israel (7)	2011	Right	No	No
Israel	2011	Right	No	No
Israel	2011	Right	No	No
Israel	2015	Right	No	No
Israel	2016	Right	No	No
Israel	2017	Right	No	No
Israel	2018	Right	No	No
*Italy (1)	2017	Center-Left	No	No
Kenya (2) (NR)	2014	Right*	No*	No
Kenya	2016	Right*	No*	No
*Lithuania (1)(NR)	2014	Center	No	No
*Luxembourg				
Macedonia (2)	2016	Right	Yes	Yes
Macedonia	2016	Right	Yes	Yes
Montenegro (1)	2012	Center	No	No
*New Zealand	2002	Left	No	No
New Zealand	2007	Left	No	No
New Zealand	2017	Right	No	No
Nicaragua (1)	2015	Left	No	No
*Norway (1)	2017	Left	No	No
Panama (1)	2017	Right	Yes	Yes
Peru (1)	2002	Center	No	No
*Poland (5)	2010	Right	No	No
Poland	2012	Center	No	No
Poland	2016	Right	No	No
Poland	2016	Right	No	No
Poland	2017	Right	No	No
*Slovakia	2014	Left	No	No
Slovakia	2016	Left	No	No
South Africa (2)	2012	Left	No	No

South Africa	2017	Left	No	No
*Spain	2013	Right	No	No
Spain	2014	Right	No	No
Spain	2015	Right	No	No
Thailand (2)	1998	Right	No	No
Thailand	2000	Right	No	No
*United Kingdom	2010	Left	No	No
United Kingdom	2014	Right	No	No
United Kingdom	2016	Right	No	No
*United States (6)	2001	Right	No	No
United States	2003	Right	No	No
United States	2009	Left	No	No
United States	2011	Left	No	No
United States	2015	Left	No	No
United States	2017	Right	Yes**	Yes
*Uruguay (2)	2004	Right	No	No
Uruguay	2010	Left	No	No

APPENDIX 2: POLITICAL ORIENTATION OF THE DOMINANT PARTY IN THE LEGISLATIVE BRANCH AT THE TIME OF RESTRICTIVE CSO ADOPTION

*Data was collected using the Database of Political Institutions, published by the World Bank, available at https://datacatalog.worldbank.org/dataset/wps22 83-database-political-institutions.

Each "Democratic Country" was ranked as democratic in the year that a restrictive CSO law was adopted. See the definition of "strong democratic state" in Chapter 5.

Democratic Country	Adopted	Political Orientation	Nationalist	Hyper-nationalist
Albania				
*Australia (4)	2016	Right	No	
Australia	2015	Right	No	
Australia	2014	Right	No	
Australia	2013	Left	No	
*Austria (1)	2015	Left	No	
*Belgium (1)	2002	Right	Yes	Yes
Bolivia (4)	2013	Left	No	
Bolivia	2013	Left	No	
Bolivia	2008	Left	No	
Bolivia	2007	Left	No	
Bulgaria (1)	2016	Right	No	
*Canada (2)	2015	Right	No	
Canada	2013	Right	No	
*Cape Verde				
*Chile				
Comoros				
*Costa Rica				
Croatia (4)	2016	Right	Yes* (I question this label, DPI's label, for the Croatian Democratic Union	Yes
Croatia	2015	Left	No	
Croatia	2014	Left	No	
Croatia	1995	Right	Yes* (I question this label, but it is how DPI labeled them)	Yes
*Cyprus				
*Czech Republic				

*Denmark (1)	2017	Right	No	
Ecuador				
Estonia				
*Finland (1)	2015	Right	No	
France (5)	2017	Left	No	
France	2017	Left	No	
France	2016	Left		
France	2015	Left		
France	2010	Right		
*Germany (1)	2017	Right	No	
Greece (2)	2013	Left	No	
Greece	2016	Right	No	
*Hungary (5)	2011	Right	Yes* (DPI said "no" for nationalist, but I disagree)	Yes
Hungary	2017	Right	Yes* (DPI said "no" for nationalist, but I disagree)	
Hungary	2018	Right	Yes* (DPI said "no" for nationalist, but I disagree)	Yes
Hungary	2018	Right	Yes* (DPI said "no" for nationalist, but I disagree)	Yes
Hungary	2018	Right	Yes* (DPI said "no" for nationalist, but I disagree)	Yes
*Iceland				
India (4)	2010	Left	No	
India	2015	Right	No	
India	2016	Right	No	
India	2017	Right	Yes*	I disagree with the DPI's classification of the BJP party as not nationalist. Most other sources consider it nationalist. For example, Foreign Policy and experts writing on civil society laws. See article in Foreign Policy by Ronald Krebs and James Ron here: http://foreignpolicy.co m/2018/06/07/democr acies-need-a-little-help-from-their-friends/.

*Ireland (2)	2001	Centrist	No	
Ireland	2009	Centrist	No	
*Israel (7)	2011	Right	No	
Israel	2011	Right	No	
Israel	2011	Right	No	
Israel	2015	Right	No	
Israel	2016	Right	No	
Israel	2017	Right	No	
Israel	2018	Right	No	
*Italy (1)	2017	Center-Left	No	
Jamaica				
*Japan				
Kenya (2) (NR)	2014	Right	No (unclear)	
Kenya	2016	Right	No (unclear)	
*Lithuania (1)(NR)	2014	Left	No	
*Luxembourg				
Macedonia (2)	2016	Right	Yes	Yes
Macedonia	2016	Right	Yes	Yes
Madagascar				
*Mauritius				
Moldova				
*Mongolia				
Montenegro (1)	2012	Center-Left	No	
*Netherlands				
*New Zealand	2002	Left	No	
New Zealand	2007	Left	No	
New Zealand	2017	Right	No	
Nicaragua (1)	2015	Left	No	
*Norway (1)	2017	Right	No	
Panama (1)	2017	Center-Left	No	
Peru (1)	2002	Center	No	
*Poland (5)	2010	Center-Right	No	
Poland	2012	Center Right	No	
Poland	2016	Right	Yes	Yes
Poland	2016	Right	Yes	Yes
Poland	2017	Right	Yes	Yes
*Portugal				
Romania				
*Slovakia	2014	Left	No	

Slovakia	2016	Left	No		
*Slovenia					
South Africa (2)	2012	Left	No		
South Africa	2017	Left	No		
*Spain	2013	Right	No		
Spain	2014	Right	No		
Spain	2015	Right	No		
*Sweden					
*Switzerland	2012	Right	Yes	Yes	
Switzerland	2016	Right	Yes	Yes	
*Taiwan					
Thailand (2)	1998	Right	No		
Thailand	2000	Right	No		
*Trinidad & Tobago					
*United Kingdom	2010	Left	No		
United Kingdom	2014	Right	No		
United Kingdom	2016	Right	No		
*United States (6)	2001	Right	No		
United States	2003	Right	No		
United States	2009	Left	No		
United States	2011	Left	No		
United States	2015	Left	No		
United States	2017	Right	No		
*Uruguay (2)	2004	Left	No		
Uruguay	2010	Left	No		

APPENDIX 3: NUMBER OF PROTESTS IN THE WORLD'S STRONGEST DEMOCRATIC STATES FROM 1990–2018

*Data was Drawn from three sources: GDELT (available at https://www.gdelt project.org/), The Mass Mobilization Project (available at https://massmobilization. github.io/index.html) and the Economist Intelligence Unit, Democracy on the Edge Report from 2015 (available at https://www.eiu.com/public/topical_report. aspx?campaignid=Democracyontheedge).

*For more detailed information, see my full Data set here: https://docs.google. com/spreadsheets/d/1_3O7sw6u7DarLMB4ds0OWHlabwc0pWkBP1mzPcicF 00/edit?usp=sharing .

Each "Democratic Country" was ranked as democratic in the year that a restrictive CSO law was adopted. See the definition of "strong democratic state" in Chapter 5.

Democratic Country	Restrictive CSO Laws Adopted	No Restrictive CSO Law	Protest Proceeded Passage of Law?
Albania	*47 protests b/t 1990–2017	No	
*Australia (6)	June 2018		
	June 2018		
	February 2016		
	No Specific Month 2015		
	May 2014		
	Dec 2013		
*Austria (1)	February 2015		13 protests b/t 1990–2017
*Belgium (1)	May 2002		Yes, but only one (only 31 protests total b/t 1990–2017)
Bolivia (4)	June 2013		Yes: 7
Bolivia	June 2013		Yes: 7
Bolivia	Jan 2008		Yes: 6
Bolivia	Oct 2007		
Bulgaria (1)	July 2016		Yes: 119 protests b/t 1990–2017; 16 from 2010–2017)
*Canada (2)	June 2015		No
Canada	June 2013		Yes
*Cape Verde		No	*2 protests between 1990–2017!

*Chile		No	*146 Protests between 1990 and 2017; protests occurred in every year except for 2017; 31 protests since 2010. Many large-scale.
Comoros		No	*51 protests b/t 1990–2017; 4 b/t 2010–2017
*Costa Rica		No	*B/t 1990–2017, 36 protests total (most relatively small); Between 2009–2017, only 2 protests. And the two that occurred were relatively small – 200 and 50 participants respectively, the smaller one lasted nearly two weeks, but was very specific (taxi drivers protesting against uber), the other, while broader in purpose (over broader economic grievances/ economic policies), only lasted one day.
Croatia (4)	Feb 2016		No (15 protests b/t 1990–2017; 6 between 2010–2017)
Croatia	Nov 2015		Yes
Croatia	June 2014		Yes
Croatia	June 1995		
*Cyprus		No	*120 protests b/w 1990–2017; 21 from 2010–2017; 78 protests b/t 2010–2017
*Czech Republic		No	*B/t 1990–2017, 19 protests, many large-scale, variety of grievances, mostly over labor and economic issues
*Denmark (1)	Dec 2017	No	No (9 protests between 1990–2017; 1 protest b/t 2010–2017
Ecuador		No	*148 protests b/t 1990–2017; 16 from 2010–2017; a mix of large and small.
Estonia		No	*47 protests b/t 1990–2017; 3 b/t 2010–2017
*Finland (1)	June 2015		No (11 protests b/t 1990–2017; 6 b/t 2010–2017)
France (5)	Nov 2017		Yes (460 Protests between 1990–2017!; 121 b/t 2010–2017)
France	Oct 2017		Yes (460 Protests between 1990–2017!; 121 b/t 2010–2017)
France	Nov 2016		Yes (460 Protests between 1990–2017!; 121 b/t 2010–2017))
France	Nov 2015		Yes (460 Protests between 1990–2017!; 121 b/t 2010–2017)
France	Feb 2010		Yes (460 Protests between 1990–2017!; 121 b/t 2010–2017)
*Germany (1)	June 2017		Yes (290 protests between 1990–2017; 155 b/t 2010–2017)
Greece (2)	Dec 2013		Yes (297 protests b/t 1990–2017; 172 b/t 2010–2017)
Greece	Jan 2016		Yes (297 protests b/t 1990–2017; 172 b/t 2010–2017)
*Hungary (3)	Dec 2011		Yes (54 protests b/t 1990–2017)
Hungary	June 2017		Yes (54 protests b/t 1990–2017)

Hungary	June 2018		Yes (54 protests b/t 1990–2017; 19 b/t 2010–2017)
*Iceland		No	
India (4)	Sept 2010		Yes (173 protests b/t 1990–2017; 67 protests b/t 2010–2017)
India	Dec 2015		Yes*(173 protests b/t 1990–2017; 67 protests b/t 2010–2017)
India	July 2016		Yes (173 protests b/t 1990–2017; 67 protests b/t 2010–2017)
India	Oct 2017		Yes (173 protests b/t 1990–2017; 67 protests b/t 2010–2017)
*Ireland (2)	Oct 2001		Yes, but only 2 small ones
Ireland	Feb 2009		
*Israel (7)	March 2011		
Israel	March 2011		Yes
Israel	July 2011		Yes
Israel	July 2016		Yes
Israel	Aug 2016		
Israel	March 2017		
Israel	Jan 2018		
*Italy (1)	July 2017		Yes (145 protests b/t 1990–2017; 40 protests b/t 2010–2017)
Jamaica		No	
*Japan		No	*58 protests b/t 1990–2017; 9 protests between 2010–2017
Kenya (2) (NR)	Dec 2014		Yes (333 protests b/t 1990–2017; 257 b/t 2010–2017)
Kenya	June 2016		Yes (333 protests b/t 1990–2017; 257 b/t 2010–2017)
*Lithuania (1)(NR)	July 2014		Yes (33 protests b/t 1990–2017; 3 b/t 2010–2017)
*Luxembourg		No	*Only 3 protests between 1990–2017, none between 2010–2017
Macedonia	Dec 2016		Yes (71 protests b/w 1991–2017; 28 b/t 2010–2017)
Madagascar		No	*59 protests b/t 1990–2017; 9 protests between 2010–2017
*Mauritius		No	*13 protests b/t 1990–2017; 2 from 2010–2017
Moldova			*102 protests b/t 1990–2017; 34 b/t 2010–2017
*Mongolia		No	
Montenegro			9 b/t 2006–2017 (data only available from these dates)
*Netherlands		No	*Only 10 protests between 1990–2017, most small, but one large scale one in 1997; 6 b/t 2010–2017
*New Zealand (3)	Oct 2002		

New Zealand	Nov 2007		
New Zealand	Dec 2017		
Nicaragua (1)	Dec 2015		Yes
*Norway (1)	Dec 2017		No (6 protests since 1990–2017; 1 since 2010–2017)
Panama (1)	March 2017		Yes
Peru (1)	April 2002		Yes
*Poland (5)	Jan 2010		Yes (105 protests b/t 1990–2017; 21 b/t 2010–2017)
Poland	June 2012		Yes (105 protests b/t 1990–2017; 21 b/t 2010–2017)
Poland	Jun 2016		Yes (105 protests b/t 1990–2017; 21 b/t 2010–2017)
Poland	Dec 2016		Yes (105 protests b/t 1990–2017; 21 b/t 2010–2017)
Poland	Oct 2017		Yes (105 protests b/t 1990–2017; 21 b/t 2010–2017)
Poland	Jan 2018		Yes (105 protests b/t 1990–2017; 21 b/t 2010–2017)
*Portugal		No	
Romania		No	*198 protests b/t 1990–2017; 49 protests b/t 2010–2017
*Slovakia	March 2013		Yes (27 protests b/t 1990–2017)
Slovakia	Nov 2016		Yes (27 protests b/t 1990–2017)
*Slovenia		No	*20 protests b/t 1990–2017; 9 b/t 2010–2017, many large-scale
South Africa (2)	July 2012		Yes
South Africa	April 2017		
*Spain	? 2013		Yes (114 protests b/t 1990–2018; 51 protests b/t 2010–2017)
Spain	May 5, 2014		Yes (114 protests b/t 1990–2018; 51 protests b/t 2010–2017)
Spain	March 2015		Yes (114 protests b/t 1990–2018; 51 protests b/t 2010–2017)
*Sweden		No	*9 protests b/t 1990–2017; 5 protests b/t 2010–2017
*Switzerland	March 2012		
Switzerland	February 2016		Only 4 protests b/t 1990–2017
*Taiwan		No	*137 protests b/t 1990–2017
Thailand (2)	? 1998		234 protests b/t 1990–2017; 82 b/t 2010–2017
Thailand	? 2000		234 protests b/t 1990–2017; 82 b/t 2010–2017
*Trinidad & Tobago		No	

*United Kingdom	Dec 2010		Yes (b/t 1990–2017, there were 509 protests.
United Kingdom	Jan 2014		Yes
United Kingdom	March 2016		Yes
*United States (6)	Oct 2001		
United States	2003		
United States	2009 (proposed in 2007)		Yes
United States	Jan 2015		Yes*
United States	Jan 2017		Yes
Uruguay	March 2017		Yes

APPENDIX 4: NUMBER OF TERRORIST ATTACKS IN THE WORLD'S STRONGEST DEMOCRATIC STATES IN THE TWO YEARS PRECEDING PASSAGE OF A RESTRICTIVE CSO LAW

*Data from the Global Database of Terrorism (GDT) based out of the University of Maryland's Department of Criminology and Criminal Justice (available at https://www.start.umd.edu/data-tools/global-terrorism-database-gtd)

*For access to my full dataset pertaining to terrorism, go to: https://docs. google.com/spreadsheets/d/1gE9ZdpETJ5GIvVeV80otra6_6vc5hguLvcJKpjU WJjM/edit?usp=sharing.

Each "Democratic Country" was ranked as democratic in the year that a restrictive CSO law was adopted. See the definition of "strong democratic state" in Chapter 5.

Democratic Country	Year of CSO Law Adoption	Terrorist Incidents in the 2 years prior to the law's passage
Albania		79
Australia (6)	2018	13
Australia	2018	13
*Australia	2016	31
Australia	2015	23
Australia	2014	9
Australia	2013	1
*Austria (1)	2015	1
*Belgium (1)	2002	3
Bolivia (4)	2013	1
Bolivia	2013	1
Bolivia	2008	3
Bolivia	2007	4
Bulgaria (1)	2016	4
*Canada (2)	2015	12
Canada	2013	7
Cape Verde		
Chile		548
Comoros		5
Costa Rica		9
Croatia (4)	2016	0
Croatia	2015	2
Croatia	2014	2
Croatia	1995	5

Cyprus		74
Czech Republic		32
*Denmark (1)	2017	5
Ecuador		104
Estonia		16
*Finland (1)	2015	9
France (5)	2017	64
France	2017	64
France	2016	77
France	2015	69
France	2010	25
*Germany (1)	2017	136
Greece (2)	2013	87
Greece	2016	88
*Hungary (5)	2011	1
Hungary	2017	1
Hungary	2018	0
Hungary	2018	0
Hungary	2018	0
*Iceland		2
India (4)	2010	1864
India	2015	2438
India	2016	2769
India	2017	2875
*Ireland (2)	2001	5
Ireland	2009	6
*Israel (9)	2011	101
Israel	2011	101
Israel	2011	101
Israel	2015	388
Israel	2016	401
Israel	2017	140
Israel	2017	140
Israel	2018	2933
Israel	2018	2933
*Italy (1)	2017	24
Jamaica		23
Japan		237

Kenya (2) (NR)	2014	275
Kenya	2016	251
*Lithuania (1)(NR)	2014	8
Luxembourg		3
Macedonia (2)	2016	7
Macedonia	2016	7
Madagascar		27
Mauritius		0
Moldova		21
Mongolia		
Montenegro (1)	2012	0
*Netherlands		68
*New Zealand (3)	2002	1
New Zealand	2007	1
New Zealand	2017	2
Nicaragua (1)	2015	3
*Norway (1)	2017	1
Panama (1)	2017	1
Peru (1)	2002	8
*Poland (6)	2010	1
Poland	2012	1
Poland	2016	2
Poland	2016	2
Poland	2017	3
Poland	2018	3
Portugal		7
Romania		3
*Slovakia	2014	0
Slovakia	2016	1
Slovakia	2013	0
Slovenia		6
South Africa (2)	2012	975
South Africa	2017	61
*Spain (3)	2013	6
Spain	2014	10
Spain	2015	10
Sweden		117
*Switzerland	2012	3

Switzerland	2016	1
Taiwan		48
Thailand (2)	1998	43
Thailand	2000	12
Trinidad & Tobago		17
*United Kingdom (3)	2010	119
United Kingdom	2014	295
United Kingdom	2016	322
*United States (3)	2001	123
United States	2003	107
United States	2017	167
*Uruguay (2)	2004	1
Uruguay	2010	2

APPENDIX 5: NUMBER OF NEIGHBORS (TO THE WORLD'S STRONGEST DEMOCRATIC STATES) TO ADOPT A RESTRICTIVE CSO LAW IN THE TWO YEARS PRIOR TO A RESTRICTIVE CSO LAW'S PASSAGE

*Neighbors include States that Geographically Border the Democratic State Under Review (listed in the first Column); where the latter is an Island, it includes the Geographically closest States.

*For access to the full Dataset on neighborhood effects, go to: https://docs. google.com/spreadsheets/d/1INsnWb9k3YwTNgmP9re5bvBILukIqBSu_9Ine_ 0ckQ8/edit?usp=sharing.

Democratic Country	# of Neighbors	Immediate Neighbor Passed a Restrictive CSO Law?	Immediate Neighbor passed a Restrictive CSO Law?	OECD	Adopted
Albania		Yes: Greece (2), Serbia (1);Montenegro (1 proposed); Croatia (4); Italy (1)	Greece (2): 2013, 2016; Serbia (1): 2016; Montenegro (1 proposal): 2017; Croatia (4): 1995, 2014, 2015, 2016; Italy (1): 2017		
*Australia		Yes: Indonesia (5); New Zealand (3)	Australia Does not share a border with any countries. Instead, I'll focus on those countries that are closest to Australia. Indonesia passed 5 restrictive CSO laws: 2004, 2008, 2013, 2013, and 2017; New Zealand passed 3: 2002, 2007, 2017.	X	6 (2013, 2014, 2015, 2016, 2018, 2018)
*Austria		Yes: Germany (1 adopted, 1 proposed); Hungary (3); Italy (1); Slovakia (2); Switzerland (2).	Germany (1): adopted 1 restrictive law in 2017 and proposed one in 2018; Hungary (3): 2011, 2017, 2018; Italy (1): 2017; Slovakia (2): 2013, 2016; Switzerland: 2012, 2016/	X	1 (2015)
*Belgium		Yes: France (5); Germany (1 adopted, 1 proposed)	France (5): 2010, 2015, 2016, 2017, 2017; Germany (1): 2017; 1 adopted in 2018.	X	1 (2002)
Bolivia		Yes: Peru (1)	Peru (1): 2002		4 (2007, 2008, 2013, 2013)

Bulgaria		Yes: Romania (1 proposed); Macedonia (1 passed, 1 adopted); Greece (2); Turkey (4)	Romania (1 proposed law): 2017; Macedonia (1 passed, 1 proposed): both in 2016; Greece (2): 2013, 2016; Turkey (4): 2013, 2015, 2016, 2017.		1 (2016)
*Canada		Yes: US (5)	US (5): 2001, 2003, 2009, 2015, 2017	X	2 (2013, 2015)
*Cape Verde		Yes: Guinea-Bissau (1); Mauritania (1 proposed)	Guinea-Bissau (1): 2015; Mauritania (1 proposed): 2016		
*Chile		Yes: Bolivia (4); Peru (1)	Bolivia (4): 2007, 2008, 2013, 2013; Peru (1): 2002	X	
Comoros		None			
*Costa Rica		Yes: Nicaragua (1), Panama (1)	Nicaragua (1): 2015; Panama (1): 2017		
Croatia		Yes: Hungary (3); Montengro (1 proposed); Serbia (1)	Hungary (3): 2011, 2017, 2018; Montenegro (1 proposed): 2017; Serbia (1): 2016		4 (1995, 2014, 2015, 2016)
*Cyprus		Yes: Greece (2); Turkey (4); Israel (9)	Greece (2): 2013, 2016; Turkey (4): 2013, 2015, 2016, 2017; Israel (9): 2011, 2011, 2011, 2015, 2016, 2017, 2017, 2018, 2018.		
*Czech Republic		Yes: Germany (1 adopted, 1 proposed); Austria (1); Slovakia (2); Poland (6)	Germany (1 adopted, 1 proposed): 2017, 2018; Austria (1): 2015; Slovakia (2): 2013, 2016; Poland (6): 2010, 2012, 2016, 2016, 2017, 2018.	X	
*Denmark		Yes: Germany (1 adopted, 1 proposed)	Germany (1 adopted, 1 proposed): 2017, 2018.	X	1 (2017)
Ecuador		Yes: Peru (1); Costa Rica	Peru (1): 2002; Costa Rica (1): 2017		
Estonia		Yes: Russia (3+)	Russia (3+): 2012, 2015, 2017	X	
*Finland		Yes: Norway (1); Russia (3+)	Norway (1): 2017; Russia (3+): 2012, 2015, 2017	X	1 (2015)
France		Yes: Belgium (1); Germany (1 adopted, 1 proposed); Italy (1);	France (1): 2002; Germany (1 adopted, 1 proposed: 2017, 2018); Italy (1): 2017;	X	5 (2010, 2015, 2016,

		Spain (3); Switzerland (2)	Spain (3): 2013, 2014, 2015; Switzerland (2): 2012, 2016.		2017, 2017)
*Germany		Yes: Denmark (1); Poland (6); Switzerland (2); Austria (1); France (5); Belgium (1)	Denmark (1): 2017; Poland (6): 2010, 2012, 2016, 2016, 2017, 2018; Switzerland (2): 2012, 2016; Austria (1): 2015; France (5): 2010, 2015, 2016, 2017, 2017; Belgium (1): 2002	X	1 (2017)
Greece		Yes: Bulgaria (1); Turkey (4); Macedonia (1 adopted, 1 proposed)	Bulgaria (1): 2016; Turkey (4): 2013, 2015, 2016, 2017; Macedonia (1 adopted, 1 proposed): 2016	X	2 (2013, 2016)
*Hungary		Yes: Austria (1); Slovakia (2); Ukraine (1 adopted, 1 proposed); Croatia (4); Serbia (1); Romania (1 proposed)	Austria (1): 2015; Slovakia (2): 2013, 2016; Ukraine (1 adopted, 1 proposed: 2017, 2017; Croatia (4):1995, 2014, 2015, 2016; Serbia (1): 2016; Romania (1 proposed): 2017	X	3 (2011, 2017, 2018)
*Iceland		None		X	
India		Yes: Nepal (1 proposed); Pakistan (2 adopted, 1 proposed); Bangladesh (6); China (2+); Bhutan (1)	Nepal (1 proposed): 2018; Bangladesh (6): 1860, 1961, 1978, 2014, 2015, 2016; China (2+): 2016, 2017; Pakistan (2 adopted, 1 proposed): 2012, 2015 & a 2018 proposal; Bhutan (1): 2007		4 (2010, 2015, 2016, 2017)
*Ireland		Yes: UK (3 passed, 1 proposed)	UK (3 passed, 1 proposed): 2010, 2014, 2016; 2017;	X	2 (2001, 2009)
*Israel		Yes: Egypt (2 adopted, 2 proposed); Jordan (3); Syria (1 proposed)	Egypt (2 adopted, 2 proposed): 2013, 2017, 2018, 2018; Jordan (3): 2008, 2009, 2018	X	9 (2011, 2011, 2011, 2015, 2016, 2017, 2017, 2018, 2018)

*Italy		Yes: France (5); Switzerland (2); Austria (1)	France (5): 5 (2010, 2015, 2016, 2017, 2017); Switzerland 2 (2012, 2016); Austria (1): 2015	X	1 (2017)
Jamaica		*Jamaica is an island			
*Japan		*Japan is an island		X	
Kenya		Ethiopia (2); South Sudan (2); Uganda (2)	Ethiopia (1): 2009, 2018; South Sudan (2): 2016, 2016; Uganda (2): 2013, 2016		2 (2014, 2016)
*Lithuania		Belarus (1); Poland (6 adopted, 1 proposed); Russia (8)	Belarus (1): 2011; Poland (6 adopted, 1 proposed): 2010, 2012, 2016, 2016, 2017, 2018, 2017; Russia (8): 2004, 2012, 2012, 2012, 2014, 2014, 2015, 2018.		1 (2014)
*Luxem-bourg		Belgium (1); Germany (1 adopted, 1 proposed); France (5)	Belgium (1): 2002; Germany (1 adopted, 1 proposed): 2017, 2018; France (5): 2010, 2015, 2016, 2017, 2017	X	
Macedonia		Kosovo (1); Serbia (1); Bulgaria (1 adopted, 1 proposed); Greece (2)	Kosovo (1): 2016; Serbia (1): 2016; Bulgaria (1 adopted, 1 proposed): 2016, 2013; Greece (2): 2013, 2016		1 (2016)
Madagascar		*Madagascar is an island			
*Mauritius		*Mauritius is an island			
Moldova		Romania (1 proposed); Ukraine (1 adopted, 1 proposed)	Romania (1 proposed): 2017; Ukraine (1 adopted, 1 proposed): 2017, 2017		
*Mongolia		Russia (8); China (2+); Khazakstan (2)	Russia (8): 2004, 2012, 2012, 2012, 2014, 2014, 2015, 2018; China (2+): 2016, 2017; Khazakhastan (2): 2015, 2016		
Montenegro		Croatia (4); Serbia (1); Kosovo (1)	Croatia (4):1995, 2014, 2015, 2016; Serbia (1): 2016; Kosovo (1): 2016;		

*Netherlands		Belgium (1); France (5); UK (3)	Belgium (1): 2002; France (5): 2010, 2015, 2016, 2017, 2017; UK (3): 2010, 2014, 2016	X	
*New Zealand		*New Zealand is an island		X	3 (2002, 2007, 2017)
Nicaragua		Honduras (1); Columbia (1)	Honduras (1): 2013; Columbia (1): 2016		1 (2015)
*Norway		Finland (1); Russia (3+)	Finland (1): 2015; Russia (3+): 2012, 2015, 2017	X	1 (2017)
Panama		Columbia (1)	Columbia (1): 2016		1 (2017)
Peru		Bolivia (4); Brazil (2); Columbia (1)	Bolivia (4): 2007, 2008, 2013, 2013; Brazil (2): 2014, 2016; Columbia (1): 2016		1 (2002)
*Poland		Germany (1 adopted, 1 proposed); Slovakia (2); Belarus (1); Lithuania (1); Russia (8)	Germany (1 adopted, 1 proposed): 2017, 2018; Slovakia (2):2013, 2016; Belarus (1): 2011; Lithuania (1): 2014; Russia (8): 2004, 2012, 2012, 2012, 2014, 2014, 2015, 2018		6 (2010, 2012, 2016, 2016, 2017, 2018)
*Portugal		Spain (3)	Spain (3): 2013, 2014, 2015	X	
Romania		Bulgaria (1); Hungary (3); Moldova (1 proposed); Serbia (1); Turkey (4); Ukraine (1 adopted, 1 proposed).	Bulgaria (1): 2016; Hungary (3): 2011, 2017, 2018; Moldova (1): 2017; Serbia (1): 2016; Turkey (4): 2013, 2015, 2016, 2017; Ukraine (1 adopted, 1 proposed): 2017, 2017.		
*Slovakia		Czech Republic (0); Austria (1); Hungary (3); Ukraine (1 adopted, 1 proposed); Poland (6 adopted, 1 proposed)	Austria (1): 2015; Hungary (3): 2011, 2017, 2018; Ukraine (1 adopted, 1 proposed): 2017, 2017; Poland (6, 1 proposed): 2010, 2012, 2016, 2016, 2017, 2018.	X	2 (2013, 2016)
*Slovenia		Yes: Austria (1); Italy (1); Croatia (4); Hungary (3)	Austria (1): 2015; Italy (1): 2017; Croatia (4):1995, 2014, 2015,	X	

			2016; Hungary (3): 2011, 2017, 2018		
South Africa		No: *Mozambique did, but in 1991, as did Zimbabwe, but both are too far outside my parameters of review, see note below.			2 (2012, 2017)
*Spain		Yes: France (5)	France (5): 2010, 2015, 2016, 2017, 2017	X	3 (2013, 2014, 2015)
*Sweden	2: Norway and Finland	Yes: Norway (1); Finland (1)	Norway (1): 2017; Finland (1): 2015	X	
*Switzerland	3: France, Germany, Austria	Yes: France (5); Germany (1 adopted, 1 proposed); Austria (1)	France (5): 2010, 2015, 2016, 2017, 2017; Germany (1 adopted, 2017; 1 proposed 2018); Austria (1): 2015	X	2 (2012, 2016)
*Taiwan	0: Island (but including Hong Kong/ China as a neighboring country)	China (1); the Philippines adopted 1 permissive law in 2015	China (1): 2017; the Philippines adopted 1 permissive law in 2015		
Thailand	4: Cambodia, Malaysia, Myanmar, Laos	Cambodia (1); Malaysia (3); Myanmar (1, but a positive one); Laos (1)	Cambodia (1): 2015; Malaysia (3): 2011, 2015, 2015; Myanmar (1, but positive): 2014; Laos (1): 2017		2 (1998, 2000)
*Trinidad & Tobago (Island)					
*United Kingdom	1: Ireland	Ireland (2)	Ireland (2): 2001, 2009	X	3 (2010, 2014, 2016)
*United States	2: Canada, Mexico	Canada (2); Mexico (3)	Canada (2): 1013, 2015; Mexico (3): 2013, 2014, 2019	X	5 (2001, 2003, 2009, 2015, 2017)
*Uruguay	2: Argentina & Brazil	Brazil (3)	Brazil (3): 2014, 2016, 2019		1 (2010)

APPENDIX 6: SOURCES FOR LOCATING RESTRICTIVE CSO LAWS

Locating civil society laws is not a simple and straightforward process as there is no single source that gathers all such laws in one location. Instead, it involves relying on a variety of sources, including the media, particularly for more recent cases.

Each of these sources listed below, in different ways and to varying degrees, collect data on CSO-related legislation, and some (like ICNL) provide commentary on each law as well. I used each of the sources below to locate restrictive CSO laws in the world's strongest democratic states.

The International Center for Not-for-Profit Law's Civic Freedom Monitor, available at http://www.icnl.org/research/monitor/. It contains detailed reports on 51 countries, which focus on their civil society legal and regulatory framework and, in many cases, includes brief commentary on whether such laws violate human rights norms. Reports are frequently updated.

The International Center for Not-for-Profit Law's Online Library, available at http://www.icnl.org/research/library/ol/. This extensive e-library contains access to the text of many CSO laws, as well as reports pertaining to civil society-related developments in individual countries. It contains 3884 resources from 206 countries and territories in 62 languages.

USAID's CSO Sustainability Index, available at https://www.usaid.gov/europe -eurasia-civil-society. The CSO Sustainability Index assesses progress in the development of nonprofit organizations and CSOs in 29 countries across Central and Eastern Europe and Eurasia. The index reports on the strength and overall viability of civil society organizations in each country it covers, and has a specific section focused on the country's civil society "legal environment." It includes a detailed discussion of any new or existing legislation impacting the civil society sector. For a detailed review of their methodology, go to https:// www.usaid.gov/what-we-do/democracy-human-rights-and-governance/cso-sustainability-index-methodology.

Annual country reports from the US State Department Bureau of Democracy, Human Rights and Labor, available at https://www.state.gov/j/drl/rls/hrrpt/ humanrightsreport/index.htm#wrapper. Includes reports on nearly 200 countries and territories worldwide, including all member states of the United Nations and any country receiving U.S. foreign assistance. Each report assesses whether the country under review has respected the freedom of association, and typically includes a discussion of the adoption of any legislation infringing on certain core human rights which underlie the existence and operations of CSOs, such as the freedom of association, assembly and expression. Reports are published annually.

The World Movement for Democracy's Defending Civil Society Project, available at https://www.movedemocracy.org/. Since 2007, the Defending Civil Society project has assisted activists and CSOs seeking to reform repressive laws targeting civil society. As such, they frequently report on the existence of such laws in their "News & Alerts" page located here: https://www.movedemocracy.org/news. They also provide useful resources in evaluating whether laws are restrictive or in violation of human rights norms in their "Defending Civil Society Toolkit", available here: http://prod.defendingcivilsociety.org/en/index.php/home.

CIVICUS: World Alliance for Citizen Participation, available here https://www.civicus.org/. CIVICUS, an organization dedicated to strengthening civil society around the globe, publishes a variety of reports, including their useful State of Civil Society annual report, which discusses the state of civil society around the globe, with many details from individual countries. They also produce a variety of other resources and publications that provide useful context on the legal and regulatory environments for civil society actors in many countries around the world. Annual reports began in 2010 and can be accessed here: http://www.civicus.org/index.php/media-center/reports-publications/annual-reports.

International Civil Society Centre, available here https://icscentre.org/. This Centre focused on international CSOS and maintains a "media library" with useful resources, reports and updates, some of which include discussions of newly adopted CSO laws.

Global Integrity, available here https://www.globalintegrity.org/. Global Integrity, which is focused on promoting open governance around the globe through citizen empowerment, conducts reports on nearly 140 countries, many of them democracies, which can be accessed here https://www.globalintegrity.org/research/countries/. Unfortunately, many of their reports are outdated; some ended in 2011, others cover through 2014, but few that I can locate go beyond this year.

Human Rights Watch's country reports (https://www.hrw.org/) and World Reports (https://www.hrw.org/world-report/2017), **Freedom House**'s Freedom in the World Reports (https://freedomhouse.org/report-types/freedom-world), and (while less helpful) reports by **Amnesty International** (https://www.amnesty.org/en/) all offer contextual and in some cases detailed information on the legal landscape for civil society in the countries they report on, which in the case of Freedom House includes all countries.

Google Alerts. By signing up for and using google alerts, I can ensure that I don't miss any legal developments – proposed amendments, rescissions of existing laws, judicial overturns of laws, new interpretations of old laws, etc. – pertaining to civil society laws around the world. It also keeps my information and knowledge updated, fresh and current. By signing up for google alerts, I receive a daily report on all existing articles appearing in any online source in which one of the following words or phrases appear: "civil society organization," "NGO Law," "closing space," and "civil society." Each day, I review all articles received through google alerts and, while many are not relevant to my research and can quickly be discarded, for the ones that are, I take detailed notes, which I categorize by country. I continue to gain extremely valuable data from doing this not found in other academic and policy reports.

APPENDIX 7: ADOPTED, PROPOSED & REJECTED RESTRICTIVE CSO LAWS IN THE WORLD'S STRONGEST DEMOCRATIC STATES

*Links to where I located most of the below-listed laws can be found here: https://docs.google.com/spreadsheets/d/13bK1DdCBZ0VntnV4Mej8ugg7PP0_PyZJAR4Vik7nIs4/edit#gid=0.

Albania: None

Australia: 6

2013–2014: Govt Funding Cuts to Environmental Defenders' Offices & Peak Environmental Offices [Domestic Funding]

2014: Amendment to Community Legal Centres Funding Agreements [Domestic Funding]

2015: Performance Bonds Required by The Department of Immigration and Border Protection of Organizations working in offshore immigration detention facilities [Domestic Funding]

2016: Indigenous Advancement Strategy (IAS) [Lifecycle]

2018: The National Security Legislation Amendment (Espionage and Foreign Interference) Bill of 2017 [Lifecycle] [Note, that on the eve of passage, this law was made less restrictive for CSOs, but the civil society sector remains concerned about their implications]

2018: Foreign Influence Transparency Scheme Bill 2017 [Foreign Funding] [Note, that on the eve of passage, this law was made less restrictive for CSOs, but the civil society sector remains concerned about their implications]

Austria: 1

2015: Amendment to the 1912 Law on Islam [Foreign Funding]

Belgium: 1

2002: Amendments to The Law on Non-Profit Associations [Lifecycle]

Bolivia: 4

2007: Law for the Negotiation and Execution of Foreign Donations (Supreme Decree No. 29308) [Foreign Funding]

2008: Regulations for the Mandatory Registry of Public and Private Donations at the VIPFE from January 2008 (Regulations of the Supreme Decree No. 29308) [Lifecycle]

2013: Legal Status Authorization Law no. 351 [Lifecycle]

2013: Supreme Decree no. 1597 (Regulating Law 351) [Lifecycle]

Bulgaria: 1

2016: Counter Terrorism Act [Lifecycle]

Canada: 2

2013: Bill C-309 [Assembly]

2015: Bill C-51 on Counter-Terrorism of 2015 [Lifecycle]

Cape Verde: None

Chile: None

Comoros: None

Costa Rica: None

Croatia: 4

1995: Law on Foundations and Funds [Lifecycle]

2014: Law on Associations [Lifecycle]

2015: Rules on financial management and control and the development and execution of financial plans of non-profit organizations [Lifecycle]

2016: Government Directive on Lottery Revenues to CSOs [Lifecycle]

Cyprus: None

Czech Republic: None

Denmark: 1

2017: Policy on withdrawing funding from NGOs that support BDS against Israel [Lifecycle]

Ecuador: None (while it was rated a democracy)

Estonia:

Finland: 1

2015: Government Policy to cut development aid by 43% [Lifecycle]

France: 5

2010: The Alliot-Marie Circular against BDS activism [Lifecycle]

2015: State of Emergency Law [Lifecycle]

2016: State of Emergency Extended [Lifecycle]

2017: State of Emergency Extended [Lifecycle]

2017: Security Law [Lifecycle]

Germany: 1

2017: Constitutional Amendment of Basic Law, Art. 21 [Lifecycle]

Greece: 2

2013: Law No. 4223/2013 Abolishing all tax privileges of public benefit foundations [Lifecycle]

2016: Ministerial Decision to Put all NGOs in Lesbos directly under state control [Lifecycle]

Hungary: 3

2011: Civil Code, Act (CLXXV of 2011) [Lifecycle]

2017: Transparency Bill Act (LXXVI of 2017) [Foreign Funding]

2018: The Anti-Soros Bill (Bill No. T/333 amending certain laws relating to measures to combat illegal immigration) [Lifecycle]

Iceland: None

India: 4

2010: Amendment to the Foreign Contribution (Regulation) Act [Foreign Funding]

2015: Amendments to Foreign Contribution (Regulation) Act [Foreign Funding]

2016: The Lokpal and Lokayuktas (anti-corruption) Bill 2016 [Lifecycle]

2017: Protest Ban in the historic Jantar Mantar area [Assembly]

Ireland: 1

2001: Amendment to the Electoral Act of 1997 [Lifecycle]

2009: Charities Act 2009 [Lifecycle]

Israel: 7

2011: The Law on Disclosure Requirements for Recipients of Support from a Foreign State Entity [Foreign Funding]

2011: Law preventing harm to the state of Israel by means of boycott [Lifecycle]

2011: The Nakba Law (Amendment No. 40 to the Budgets Foundations Law) [Lifecycle]

2015: Creation of new anti-BDS task Force [Lifecycle]

2016: Transparency Requirements for Parties Supported by Foreign State Entities Bill 5766-2016 [Foreign Funding]

2017: Amendment to Entry to Israel Law [Lifecycle]

2018: Creation of BDS Blacklist [Lifecycle]

Italy: 1

2017: NGO Code of Conduct on NGO Migrant Boats [Lifecycle]

Jamaica: None

Japan: None

Kenya: 2

2014: Security Laws (Amendments) Act [Lifecycle]

2016: Foreigner Work Permit Law [Lifecycle]

Lithuania: 1

2014: Amendment on Law on Meetings of 1993 [Assembly]

Luxembourg: None

Macedonia: 2

2016: Campaign Against Foreign Funded NGOs [Foreign Funding]

2016: Anti-Sorosization Policy [Foreign Funding]

Madagascar: None

Mauritius: None

Moldova: None

Mongolia: None

Montenegro: 1

2012: Law on Prevention of Money-Laundering and Prevention of Terrorism [Lifecycle]

Netherlands: None

New Zealand: 3

2002: Terrorism Suppression Act [Lifecycle]

2007: Amendment to the Terrorism Suppression Act of 2002 [Lifecycle]

2017: The Maritime Crimes Amendment Bill [Lifecycle]

Nicaragua: 1

2015: The Sovereign Security Law [Lifecycle]

Norway: 1

2017: Government Policy Announcement to Prohibit Funding to NGOs that support boycotts on Israel [Domestic Funding]

Panama: 1

2017: Executive Decree on CSO Registration and Oversight [Lifecycle]

Peru: 1

2002: Law on the Creation of the Peruvian Agency for International Cooperation [Lifecycle]

Poland: 5

2010: Amendments to the Public Benefit and Volunteerism Law [Lifecycle]

2012: Amendments to the Law on Assemblies [Assembly]

2016: Anti-Terrorism Law [Lifecycle]

2016: Amendment to the Act on Assemblies [Assembly]

2017: Bill on Funding for NGOs [Foreign Funding]

Portugal: None

Romania: None

Slovakia: 2

2014: Amendment to the Act on Public Procurement [Lifecycle]

2016: Religious Registration Law (Nov 2016) [Lifecycle]

South Africa: 2

2012: Policy Framework on Non-Profit Organizations [Lifecycle]

2017: Financial Intelligence Centre Amendment Act [Lifecycle]

Spain: 3

2013: Circular by the Ministry of Interior [Lifecycle]

2014: Royal Decree 304/2014 passing the Regulation of Act 1 on Counter-Terrorist Financing/2010 on Anti-Money Laundering [Assembly]

2015: Basic Law for the Protection of Public Security (Ley Orgánica para la Protección de la Seguridad Ciudadana) [Assembly]

Sweden: None

Switzerland: 1

2012: Referendum to amend the Law on Demonstrations [Assembly]

2016: Regulations on Foundations [Lifecycle]

Thailand: 2

1998: Regulations of the Ministry of Labor and Social Welfare on the Entry of Foreign Private Organizations to Operate in Thailand B.E.2541 (1998) [Foreign Funding]

2000: Regulation of the Committee on Consideration of the Entry of Foreign Private Organization Governing principles for consideration and instructions on the entry of foreign private organizations to operate in Thailand and the establishment of regional offices in Thailand B.E. 2543 [Foreign Funding]

Trinidad & Tobago: None

United Kingdom: 3

2010: Terrorist Asset Freezing Act [Lifecycle]

2014: Transparency of Lobbying, Non-party Campaigning and Trade Union Administration Act [Lifecycle]

2016: Charities (Protection and Social Investment) Act 2016 [Lifecycle]

United States: 6

2001: The US Patriot Act [Lifecycle]

2003: Mexico City Policy (Popularly called the "global gag rule", an Executive Order) [Foreign Funding]

2009: Revisions to the 990 Form [used by NGOs to report earnings and activities to the IRS] [Lifecycle]

2011: Amendment to Tax Code [Lifecycle]

2015: House Resolution 5 – Adopting rules for the One Hundred Fourteenth Congress [Lifecycle]

2017: Presidential Memorandum Regarding the Mexico City Policy (Popularly called the "global gag rule", an Executive Order) [Foreign Funding]

Uruguay: 2

2004: Reporting and Accounting Requirements [Lifecycle]

2017: Decree, modifying decree N°127/999 [Assembly]

Proposed Restrictive CSO Laws

Australia: 2

2016: Parliamentary Inquiry on whether to Strip environmental advocacy organisations of their deductible gift recipient status [Domestic Funding]

2017: Foreign Influence Transparency Scheme Bill 2017 [Foreign Funding]

Germany: 1

2018: Order to Ban State Funding for the National Democratic Party [Lifecycle]

Germany: 1

2018: Order to Ban State Funding for the National Democratic Party (awaiting constitutional review) [Lifecycle]

Hungary: 3

2018: Draft law on the social responsibility of organizations supporting illegal migration [Lifecycle]

2018: Draft Law on Immigration Financing Duty [Lifecycle]

2018: Draft Law on Immigration Restraints [Lifecycle]

Israel: 3

2016: Law Restricting Banning Groups that work to "damage the IDF" from speaking in education institutions [Lifecycle]

2017: Creation of a BDS Database to monitor all BDS supporters [Lifecycle]

2017: NGO Law [Lifecycle]

Moldova: 1

2017: Draft NGO Law [Lifecycle]

Montenegro: 1

2017: Amendments to Law on NGOs and Law on Games of chance [Lifecycle]

Poland: 2

2017: Law on Transparency in Public Life [Lifecycle]

2018: Law on Assemblies [Assembly]

Romania: 1

2017: Law 140/2017 on Associations and Foundations (amending Law 26/2000 on Associations and Foundations) [Lifecycle]

South Africa: 1

2016: Draft NPO Bill [Lifecycle]

Taiwan: 1

2017: New Law on Civil Associations (or maybe amendments to existing law – unclear, can't locate the draft law) [Lifecycle]

United Kingdom: 2

2017: Draft Charities Bill [Lifecycle]

Rejected/ Reversed/ Overturned/ Deemed Unconstitutional

Bulgaria: 1

2013: Amendments to the Law for Publicity of the Property of People in High Government Positions [Lifecycle]

Canada: 1

2012 [applied only to Quebec]: Bill 78, An Act to enable students to receive instruction from the postsecondary institutions they attend [Assembly]

Croatia: 1

2005: Amendment to Public Assembly Act [Assembly]

Ecuador: 1

Germany: 2

2003: Order Declaring the National Democratic Party Unconstitutional (deemed unconstitutional by the constitutional court) [Lifecycle]

2013: Order Declaring the National Democratic Party Unconstitutional (deemed unconstitutional by the constitutional court) [Lifecycle]

Hungary: 1

2013: Proposal to Regulate Foreign Funding of CSOs (withdrawn) [Foreign Funding]

Kenya: 2

2013: The Statute (Miscellaneous Amendments) Bill, 2013 (would have capped NGOs foreign funding at 15% of total budget) [Foreign funding]

2014: The Statute (Miscellaneous Amendments) Bill, 2013 (would have capped NGOs foreign funding at 15% of total budget) [Foreign funding]

Lithuania

2017: Law on Lobbying (negative provisions were rejected, rest of law adopted) [Lifecycle]

Peru: 1

2006: NGO Registration Law/ Law No. 28925 in 2006 (Key negative provisions repealed, a victory for CSOs) [Lifecycle]

Slovakia: 1

2016: Draft Bill amending the Law No. 217/1997 Coll. on non-profit organisations providing public community services as amended (proposed, then voted down) [Foreign Funding]

United Kingdom: 1

2016: Amendment to the Regulations on Government Funded CSOs (withdrawn) [Lifecycle]

APPENDIX 8: CIVICUS RATINGS FOR ENVIRONMENT FOR CIVIL SOCIETY FOR EACH OF THE 59 STRONG DEMOCRACIES

Democracy	CIVICUS Rating
Albania	Narrowed
*Australia	Open
*Austria	Narrowed
*Belgium	Open
Bolivia	Obstructed
Bulgaria	Narrowed
*Canada	Open
*Cape Verde	Open
*Chile	Narrowed
Comoros	Narrowed
*Costa Rica	Open
Croatia	Narrowed
*Cyprus	Open
*Czech Republic	Open
*Denmark	Open
Ecuador	Narrowed
Estonia	Open
*Finland	Open
France	Narrowed
*Germany	Open
Greece	Narrowed
*Hungary	Obstructed
*Iceland	Open
India	Obstructed
*Ireland	Open
*Israel	Obstructed
*Italy	Narrowed
Jamaica	Narrowed
*Japan	Narrowed
Kenya	Obstructed
*Lithuania	Open

*Luxembourg	Open
Macedonia	Narrowed
Madagascar	Obstructed
*Mauritius	Narrowed
Moldova	Obstructed
*Mongolia	Obstructed
Montenegro	Narrowed
*Netherlands	Open
*New Zealand	Open
Nicaragua	Repressed
*Norway	Open
Panama	Narrowed
Peru	Obstructed
*Poland	Narrowed
*Portugal	Open
Romania	Narrowed
*Slovakia	Narrowed
*Slovenia	Open
South Africa	Narrowed
*Spain	Narrowed
*Sweden	Open
*Switzerland	Open
*Taiwan	Open
Thailand	Repressed
*Trinidad & Tobago	Narrowed
*United Kingdom	Narrowed
*United States	Narrowed
*Uruguay	Open

INDEX

W

Waltz, Kenneth, 9, 38, 64, 65, 66,
    69, 133, 136, 137, 139, 146, 147
Washington Post, 28, 32, 40, 66, 86
Weinstein, Jeremy M., 30, 31, 36,
    37, 40, 105, 106, 117
Wendt, Alexander, 38
World Bank, 43, 46, 75, 149, 152
World War I, 12, 14, 69, 135
World War II, 12, 14, 69, 135

Y

Youngs, Richard, 21, 48, 49

www.ingramcontent.com/pod-product-compliance
Lightning Source LLC
Chambersburg PA
CBHW062028270326
41929CB00014B/2364